AMERICANS TODAY CHOOSE
from a dizzying array of schools,
loosely lumped into categories of "public"
and "private." In this timely study, Robert N.
Gross describes how, more than a century ago,
public policies fostered the rise of modern
school choice. In the late nineteenth century,
American Catholics began constructing rival,
urban parochial school systems, an enormous
and dramatic undertaking that challenged
public school systems' near-monopoly of
education. In a nation deeply committed
to public education, mass attendance in
Catholic schools produced immense conflict.
States quickly sought ways to regulate
this burgeoning private sector and the
competition it produced, even attempting to
abolish private education altogether in the
1920s. Ultimately, however, the public policies
that resulted produced a stable educational
marketplace, where choice flourished. The
creation of the educational marketplace that
we have inherited today—with systematic
alternatives to public schools—was as much
a product of public power as of private
initiative.

Gross also demonstrates that schools have
been key sites in the development of the
American legal conceptions of "public" and
"private." Landmark Supreme Court cases
about the state's role in regulating private
schools helped define and redefine the scope
of government power over private enterprise.
Judges and public officials gradually blurred
the meaning of "public" and "private,"
contributing to the broader shift in how
American governments have used private
entities to accomplish public aims. As ever
more policies today seek to unleash market
rces in education, Gross argues, Americans
uld do well to learn from the historical
ationship between government, markets,
d schools.

PUBLIC VS. PRIVATE

Public vs. Private

THE EARLY HISTORY OF SCHOOL CHOICE
IN AMERICA

Robert N. Gross

OXFORD
UNIVERSITY PRESS

OXFORD
UNIVERSITY PRESS

Oxford University Press is a department of the University of Oxford. It furthers
the University's objective of excellence in research, scholarship, and education
by publishing worldwide. Oxford is a registered trade mark of Oxford University
Press in the UK and certain other countries.

Published in the United States of America by Oxford University Press
198 Madison Avenue, New York, NY 10016, United States of America.

© Oxford University Press 2018

Library of Congress Cataloging-in-Publication Data
Names: Gross, Robert N., author.
Title: Public vs. private : the early history of school choice in America / Robert N. Gross.
Description: New York, NY : Oxford University Press, [2018] |
Includes bibliographical references and index.
Identifiers: LCCN 2017029075 (print) | LCCN 2017030417 (ebook) |
ISBN 9780190644581 (updf) | ISBN 9780190644598 (epub) |
ISBN 9780190644604 (online component) | ISBN 9780190644574 (hardback : alk. paper)
Subjects: LCSH: School choice—United States—History. | Public schools—United States—History. |
Private schools—United States—History. | Education—United States—History.
Classification: LCC LB1027.9 (ebook) | LCC LB1027.9 .G76 2018 (print) | DDC 379.1/11—dc23
LC record available at https://lccn.loc.gov/2017029075

9 8 7 6 5 4 3 2 1

Printed by Sheridan Books, Inc., United States of America

For Natalie

Contents

Acknowledgments

THIS BOOK WOULD not have been possible without the many teachers, students, colleagues, friends, and family members, who instilled in me a passion for the past. First and foremost is Bill Reese, who guided me through graduate school with generosity, trust, kindness, and rigor. I am immensely privileged to have worked with Bill, and since winding up in Washington, DC, am fortunate to be able to see him frequently during his many trips out east. I am also indebted to my undergraduate mentor, Mary Ann Dzuback, who introduced me to the history of education, and to the careful practice of historical scholarship.

Throughout the production of this manuscript I have received feedback from truly excellent historians and mentors. At the University of Wisconsin, Adam R. Nelson and Jennifer Ratner-Rosenhagen helped develop my abilities as a researcher and teacher since the beginning of graduate school, and were instrumental in helping me think through how to frame this book's questions and arguments. Colleen Dunlavy and Julie Mead generously lent their expertise in business history and education law to this project, and Jeremi Suri's guidance in the initial stages of the manuscript helped get me started. Comments at conferences on my presented work from Ruben Donato, Ruben Flores, Carl Kaestle, Kip Kosek, John Modern, Tracy Steffes, Maris Vinovskis, and Jonathan Zimmerman were also immensely helpful.

Colleagues throughout the country were equally instrumental in helping take this project to the finish line. Frank Honts, Campbell Scribner, and Christine Lamberson, in addition to being dear friends, are exemplary scholars and professionals, whose intellectual habits and precise feedback have deeply influenced me. Britt Tevis helped me clarify and strengthen the arguments in Chapter 6. Jon Shelton, through careful readings of several chapters, added a much-needed different perspective from my own, and—during the wonderfully interdisciplinary NAE/Spencer events—was a fellow historian who spoke my same disciplinary language. And Darren Speece provided terrific advice during the book's final stages. Other colleagues, friends, and students in Madison, Baltimore, New York City, Washington, DC, and elsewhere have provided much-needed cheerleading throughout—you are far too many to name, but you know who you are.

This book was the product of countless hours in archives and libraries near and far, and I am very grateful for all the physical, human, and financial resources that afforded me the opportunity to complete it. Most of the state documents on which this book relies are located in the Wisconsin Historical Society's library and archives—a national treasure. Without the expert guidance of librarians and archivists there, and elsewhere, I would have been lost. For all of their help I would also like to thank by name Burris E. Esplen at the Office for Archives and Record Center at the Catholic Diocese of Pittsburgh; Maria Mazzenga and William J. Shepherd at the American Catholic History Research Center; David Grinnell at the University of Pittsburgh's Archives Service Center; Scott Taylor at Georgetown University's Special Collections Research Center; and Shawn Weldon at the Philadelphia Archdiocesan Historical Research Center. A fellowship through the National Academy of Education/Spencer Foundation funded the final year of my dissertation, and I cannot speak highly enough of their unparalleled commitment to mentoring and developing young scholars. An additional fellowship from the University of Wisconsin's Department of History, along with travel grants from the UW-Madison Graduate School, enabled me to engage in a critical semester of research away from Madison, while a grant from the American Catholic History Research Center and University Archives at the Catholic University of America funded much of the research that contributes to Chapter 6.

Much of scholarship is the product of serendipity, and it was through good fortune that I was put in touch with Nancy Toff, who, together with her colleagues at Oxford University Press, guided this manuscript through production. Nancy chose two terrific anonymous reviewers, whose comments were invaluable in helping hone the book's arguments. Her own thoughtful suggestions helped make the manuscript considerably clearer.

I owe special gratitude to my family, old members as well as new ones. Aunts, uncles, cousins, and grandparents showed an interest in my work from the beginning. Greg and Liz Karas welcomed me into their family with incredible love and warmth, in addition to reading parts of the manuscript and lending their own expertise about the topic on many occasions. Ben and Allison provided love, encouragement, and, most importantly, friendship, throughout. No words can express how grateful I am to my mom and dad, Richard and Cathy, who, after all, chose the schools I attended as a child, and dedicated a lifetime to helping me sort through life's many paths. I could not have more loving and thoughtful parents. My newborn daughter, Miriam, lit up my life during the final year of this book's journey to production—she provided the best incentive ever to get the work done so that I could spend more time with her. Finally, I thank my lovely wife, Natalie, who so generously gave her own time and wisdom to improving this book, and whose unwavering and unconditional faith in me is apparent every single day.

Introduction

PRIVATE SCHOOLS AND PUBLIC REGULATION
IN AMERICAN HISTORY

AS UNION SOLDIERS returned to their Cayuga County, New York, homes in 1865, they walked one by one past the district's public schools. "God has signally blessed us as a nation," the school commissioner, Israel Wilkinson, reflected after watching the event. "Not only in giving us success to our arms in quelling the Slaveholders' Rebellion; rending the servile yoke from four millions of down-trodden Africans; . . . but also in inspiring in the minds of our people that the main pillar of Republican Institutions is our Common School System." One soldier, pointing to a public school, declared that "these are the safeguards of our Republic; we didn't find them down South." With the Civil War now over, public education could at long last spread throughout the United States, fully eliminating the traditions of private, market-based schooling that had once dominated the nation—or, in the South, of no schooling at all. That year, in Cayuga County itself, Wilkinson proudly announced that his district contained "no private schools . . . and we were congratulating ourselves upon the triumph of the common schools during the past year over every private enterprise of the kind."[1]

In the decades surrounding the Civil War Americans had observed, with pride and astonishment, the rapid spread of public school systems, first in the Northeast, then in the Midwest, and finally, as a consequence of Union victory, in the South. Their advocates, men like Israel Wilkinson, promoted public education as "common schooling," with the goal of educating the community's children together regardless of class, nationality, or creed. Despite the ecumenical rhetoric, public school systems were largely the project of American Protestants, who drew on the model of locally supported schooling established in Puritan New England and believed that effective education could never be severed from religious instruction. Wilkinson himself was a Baptist minister, but like other common school advocates believed it essential that schools put away sectarian differences to further communal unity. As the "pillar" of republican government, public systems could transform the nation only if they eliminated the socially and economically divisive private schools that otherwise dotted the American educational landscape.[2]

As public education dramatically advanced during the middle of the nineteenth century, private schooling receded. In American cities, especially, the provision of education in 1870 looked dramatically different than it had been a mere half-century earlier. Urban Americans living in 1800 scarcely would have recognized distinctions between public and private in education in the first place: privately governed schools often received various forms of public funds, while schools operated by elected or appointed boards frequently depended on parental tuition payments. By midcentury, however, clear differences between public and private schools had emerged, and a majority of American elementary school students throughout the nation were enrolled in schools that were financed, operated, and regulated by public agencies and officials, from local school boards to state superintendents.

Nineteenth-century public school systems were still quite different from our own today. School attendance was common though inconsistent, informal for young children, and rare among teenagers. Secular instruction, today a key component of public education, was largely anathema to schools both public and private. Despite these differences, Americans widely recognized the triumph of the public sector in education. Privately run or tuition-dependent schools, once the dominant form of educational provision in the eighteenth and early nineteenth century, had rapidly diminished. In many large urban areas, attendance in private schools declined by more than 50 percent from 1830 to 1850. Soon, many Americans hoped, private schooling would be eliminated altogether, replaced by public schools that resembled municipal utility systems—monopolies that operated on a noncompetitive basis.[3]

Yet, beginning in the 1870s and 1880s, public school supporters received shocking news: the decline of private schools not only appeared to have slowed but to have reversed. In 1889, especially, newspapers reported that newly constructed private schools were successfully competing with public education for students. One year earlier, the U.S. Commissioner of Education had issued a stunning report, suggesting that, for the first time in American history, public school enrollments in several Northern states appeared be declining. "There is going on a transfer of pupils from the public to private schools," the commissioner, Nathaniel H. R. Dawson, announced. "This circumstance," he continued, "is of the greatest significance" and "a matter of the highest gravity."[4] The report's readers agreed. One British writer, upon seeing the data, stated that the United States was undergoing a "social revolution [or] public school retrogression."[5] Private schools were jeopardizing the triumph of public education. "The School Question," as writers dubbed the emerging conflict between public and private education, gripped the nation.

What made the conflict over private education so pervasive, as well as explosive, was that the rise in private school attendance was spurred by American Catholics, many of whom were not native to the United States. In an age of rapid industrialization and urbanization, America's growing metropolises were increasingly populated by Catholic immigrants who elected to send their children to private, rather than public, schools. Catholic immigration swelled in the nineteenth century, first from Ireland and Germany and, later, from Southern and Eastern Europe. Between 1850 and 1890, the American Catholic population grew from roughly one million to seven million. By the late nineteenth century Catholics were the largest single Christian denomination in the United States.[6]

As Catholic immigration increased, so too did Catholic schooling. From 1875 to 1885 alone their schools increased from 1,400 to 2,500. Unlike older, expensive private schools serving the children of the elite, these schools, attached to local parish churches, served the Catholic masses. Parochial schools kept tuition low, or nonexistent, by drawing on priests and nuns for staff and on parishioners for donations. In urban areas, where in the late nineteenth century more than 85 percent of Catholics dwelled, it was especially difficult to ignore the constant noise of Catholic churches and schools being constructed. In cities such as Cleveland, Milwaukee, Cincinnati, Buffalo, Boston, and Pittsburgh, more than 40 percent of children enrolled in private, predominately Catholic, institutions.[7] In many smaller cities in New England and the Midwest, private schools enrolled local majorities. By the late nineteenth century Catholic schools educated nearly 900,000 children.[8] Out of their ethnic, religious, and educational commitments, they had created a popular alternative school system.

To the Protestants who had led the movement for "common," public schooling, the trend of rising attendance in these private institutions was deeply disturbing. In February 1889, a U.S. Senate committee heard testimony on a proposed constitutional amendment to prohibit public money from ever going toward private—namely, Catholic—schools. The Protestant public school advocates who testified frequently referred to parochial schools as a "menace" to public education, for siphoning off both students and, absent the proposed amendment, public funds.[9] Later that summer, at a conference of national school leaders, one prominent Catholic school critic asked his colleagues, "Has the parochial school proper place in America?" No, rang back the consensus.[10] At the same meeting Wisconsin's state superintendent of public instruction told a Catholic archbishop that parochial schools had become a threat to the public school system and that the Catholic Church "must not put itself or its parochial school across the legitimate pathway of the state, and obstruct its progress."[11] As these reactions in 1889 attested, the rise of private schools disrupted the steady progress of public school systems, one of the most notable developments of the middle of the nineteenth century. They threatened a vision of American education that went far beyond the instruction of reading, writing, and arithmetic. Most importantly, they challenged the common school's ability to be truly common.

Despite the threat posed by private education in the nineteenth century, Catholic schools would achieve astonishing growth from the 1870s to the 1960s. Catholic schools would become the largest private school system in the world, their attendance growing by 50 percent each decade, beginning in the 1880s. By the early twentieth century, American cities featured not one school system but two, public and private—a competitive marketplace of education that would have stunned public schooling's nineteenth-century proponents.[12]

How, in a nation seemingly committed to mass public education, did private, Catholic schooling expand? In the broader economic language popular both at the time and today, how did educational markets and competition emerge in the twentieth century given the strong support for a public school monopoly a century earlier? These are questions that inform current debates about private education, charter schools, voucher programs, and the dynamics of "school choice." Indeed, debates about "markets" and "competition" in education are not distinct to our current era. On the contrary, in ways that historians have yet to write about, the origins of modern school choice—the existence of systematic alternatives to public schooling—lay in nineteenth-century urban America. Much as parents do today, parents in the nineteenth century chose among schools, and the language of educational "monopoly" and "competition" pervaded formal discussions about the political economy of schooling.

The structures that enable school choice to flourish today owe their origins—more than a century ago—as much to public policy as to private initiative. As attendance in Catholic schools grew in the late nineteenth century, private school advocates, along with public officials, envisioned the many benefits of tethering private education to state goals. Together, Catholic and public school officials helped blur the sharp distinctions between public and private that had existed for much of the nineteenth century. Beginning in the 1870s, first in Rhode Island and then in Ohio, Catholics accepted, and indeed fought for, forms of public regulation in return for maintaining an important fiscal subsidy: the property tax exemption. Courts in these states, and elsewhere, generally obliged, and in doing so granted public bodies significantly greater authority to regulate private actors. Debates about education proved central to new conceptions of state regulation and the blending of public authority and private enterprise.

Public policy continued to expand private schooling in the decades that followed. A wave of compulsory attendance legislation, passed in the 1880s, transformed the relationship between schools and the state. Laws requiring school attendance introduced new dilemmas for school administrators and parochial school authorities. If states required children to attend school, how would public officials define adequate schooling? What kinds of regulations affecting school curriculum and pedagogy would be reasonable? Ultimately, public officials relied on private schools to achieve public ends, believing that their continued growth was key to limiting public expenditures and attracting Catholic votes. Local officials refused to enforce compulsory attendance laws that would close down Catholic schools and place undue burdens on already overcrowded public school classrooms. When politicians did venture to enact or enforce policies hostile to parochial schools, Catholics responded by mobilizing their political power against local and state incumbents, successfully defending private education. As a result of this mutually advantageous relationship between public officials and Catholic schools, private education continued to grow in the early twentieth century.

By the 1920s, public policies had forged a regulated educational marketplace in American cities. Catholic students frequently transferred between public and private schools. Effectively managing these shifts in school attendance required public officials to follow students as they moved between schools and systems, and to determine what grade they should enter. Urban school boards established the standards, rules, and procedures to facilitate parental choice between the two systems. Public regulations standardized the diffuse curricula and teaching practices of public and private schools. Parents transferred their children from public to private schools with the understanding that the latter fit within the state's minimal education standards and that their choice would not result in their child suffering academic or professional harm. From the perspective of school officials, meanwhile, more sophisticated pupil accounting mechanisms ensured that transfers between schools would occur efficiently, without students and their records getting lost in the system. New regulations tied public and parochial school governance together in ways unthinkable during the nineteenth century. Catholic school administrators and parents largely embraced these new laws, viewing them as essential for raising the status of Catholic education.

State and federal courts, too, joined legislatures and school boards in forging a robust and regulated educational marketplace. In the years following World War I, when conservative Protestant groups emerged to promote the abolition of private schooling, Catholic lawyers and federal judges protected private schools from wanton legislative discrimination. In doing so, they turned to the array of public regulations that already supervised and monitored private schools, arguing that because private education had been exacted to public standards, their abolition was unreasonable.

Public regulations thus not only helped expand private schooling in the nineteenth and twentieth century but also developed the rules, procedures, and standards to control a functioning marketplace. Laws defined which schools parents could choose from and structured how parents made those choices. They provided financial incentives for parochial schools to open their doors to inspectors and raised educational standards for parents and children anxious about Catholic education's reputation among high schools, colleges, and employers. Americans in the twenty-first century attend and choose schools within the context of this marketplace. Understanding how schools, markets, and public policy interact today requires turning to this past.

This history of public regulation's support for private schools also helps reveal how America's regulatory state, with its often blurred distinctions between public and private, developed over time. Scholars now recognize the ways in which American state and local governments routinely relied on the private sector to obtain public ends.[13] Historians have explored how nineteenth- and early twentieth-century state and local governments collaborated with private organizations—from railroads to charities—to expand their governing capacity, using techniques like subsidies, grants, and laws of incorporation. Of the earliest corporate charters granted by states in the Early Republic, for example, the vast majority fulfilled a special public function like constructing or operating canals, turnpikes, and bridges. In the absence of a large welfare state, public subsidies in the nineteenth century flowed toward private organizations dedicated to aiding veterans and needy children.[14] Yet, while education was one of the state's most significant functions, and frequently one of its largest investments, historians have yet to explore the creative ways that public officials used the private sector to advance public goals of universal instruction. Instead, they have largely written about private schools in the context of their ethnic and religious functions, leaving the immense similarities between education and other economic domains unexplored.

Much like canals and turnpikes, private schools were not only supervised by states but used strategically for their capacity to educate mass numbers of children. Private schools, in this quiet way, helped support the same public school systems against which they competed. Public officials understood that mass private school attendance provided immense fiscal relief to beleaguered municipal budgets and overcrowded public schools, since parents whose children were educated privately paid property taxes for (public) schools they did not use. Given the large percentages of children attending urban parochial schools, even anti-Catholic city school administrators acknowledged that private schools fulfilled an enormously public function. Elected officials, too, learned the benefits of appeasing constituencies with ties to Catholic schooling. Political competition over Catholic immigrant voters ensured that legislators would attack parochial schooling only at their peril. While state education administrators and national education leaders thus often spoke critically of private education, local officials frequently had a more nuanced view of private schooling. The resulting alliance between public officials and private education reflected the shape of the American regulatory state more broadly, marked by close, though often obscured, ties between public power and private enterprise. Just as the American state often has relied on private agencies to accomplish what might otherwise be accomplished by government, so too did public officials depend on private schooling to expand mass education.[15]

Indeed, schools were exemplary, if not determinative, sites of market regulation in the nineteenth and early twentieth centuries.[16] Public regulation at the state and local level was pervasive, deeply embedded in common law ideas of the "well-regulated society." States and localities managed markets in food, transportation, energy, finance, labor, and many other areas of private initiative long before Progressive Era reformers and Franklin Delano Roosevelt's New Deal.[17] In an age of growing attendance in public and private schools, however, it was frequently in education that Americans debated market regulation most vociferously. Should industries be governed by the state and run noncompetitively, or should they be privately operated, competitive, and governed by the demands of the marketplace? How should governments regulate private enterprises that compete with their own publicly operated institutions? How do private enterprises respond to state attempts at regulation?

Americans in the nineteenth and early twentieth centuries discussed these questions vigorously, believing that schools—like railroads and gas and electric companies—were key enterprises to debate the role of the state in managing private enterprise and public life. Economists routinely compared school competition and regulation to the forces affecting other segments in the American economy. Catholics, in turn, frequently discussed their own schools in the language of the marketplace, as "competitive" enterprises attempting to dislodge a "state monopoly." Finally, in the arena of American law, few, if any, distinctions separated religious, educational, and business corporations. The dioceses, churches, or religious teaching orders that sponsored parochial schools were private corporations, able to contract and to acquire, hold, and dispose of property with the same vigor as any business corporation.[18] Noting this fundamental similarity, the preeminent scholar of American church law, Carl Zollman, wrote in 1917 that a religious corporation is "a mere business agent," as "much a business corporation, within its limited powers, as the International Harvester Company is within its wider powers."[19] Private schools were in many ways quintessential private enterprises.[20]

Because scholars have not seen schools as sites of market regulation, histories of the American regulatory state remain incomplete. They have neglected to account for the key role that educational corporations played in the legal development of public regulation. Some of the most significant Supreme Court cases dealing with the relationship between the state and private enterprise centered on private religious and educational corporations. These cases, including *Dartmouth College v. Woodward* (1819), *Berea College v. Kentucky* (1908), and *Pierce v. Society of Sisters* (1925), had far-reaching consequences for corporate life that extended well beyond the confines of classrooms and schools. Education was crucial to the development of American law because disputes over the public regulation of private schooling touched on delicate questions of the police power—the state's authority to intervene in private affairs on behalf of the public good. What precisely constituted "public" and "private" ultimately became a question for judges to decide, and cases dealing with state regulation of private schools became a primary means to define and determine the proper scope of public authority. American conceptions of public and private, in short, are impossible to fully understand without placing education at the center of the regulatory state.

In the post–World War II era, private schools have taken on increasingly public roles. Legislators, policymakers, and intellectuals in the 1950s and 1960s proposed dissolving public school systems, replacing them with various schemes to support private education.

In the twenty-first century, voucher programs and charter schools became essential tools of urban educational policymaking. Even as distinctions between public and private in education shifted, attempts to privatize education have relied on older methods of public subsidies and state standards to accomplish their goals. The expansion of public school alternatives continues to be inextricably linked to the dense texture of laws and administrative procedures that envelop them.

1

Public Monopoly

IN THE 1850S and 1860s, advocates of public education foresaw a future with few, if any, private schools. Public systems had been growing rapidly in the North, and supporters eagerly noted that their rise had come at the expense of the nation's largely private provision of education. A "healthful competition has sprung up" observed H. H. Barney, the principal of a Cincinnati public high school, in 1851. Private schools "are discontinued for want of patronage" and parents everywhere, it seemed, preferred public education. Since the "public school is always better than the private," Barney wrote, "the schools which did not come up to the highest mark"—the private schools—"have gone down in public estimation."[1] Others agreed. In 1868 the Illinois superintendent of public instruction happily reported that "the public schools are steadily weakening and decimating private schools" before "ultimately crowd[ing] them almost wholly from the field."[2] In Akron, Ohio, a school superintendent recalled that as a result of the "best instruction [being] in the public free schools . . . the children from the private schools began to find their way to the public schools as fast as room could be provided for them, and before [long] the last private school had closed."[3] Public school reformers agreed that the public system would soon obliterate private alternatives.

These observations pointed to how the rise of free, public education transformed the market for formal education, particularly in cities. The competitive and quasi-private provision of schooling that existed in the first decades of the nineteenth century morphed into a largely public, uncompetitive one. These changes occurred relatively swiftly, except in the South, where public systems would not emerge fully until Reconstruction. Beginning in the first half of the nineteenth century, tuition-driven schools, along with free "charity" schools for the poor, gave way to tax-funded, publicly operated, and state-regulated urban public school systems.[4]

As public systems gradually replaced private institutions, ideas about the virtues of private schooling and educational competition shifted dramatically over the course of the nineteenth century. These shifts both reflected and encouraged broader developments in how American public officials and scholars thought about public ownership and government regulation. Writing in the early part of the nineteenth century, America's leading economists, influenced by Adam Smith, the eighteenth-century Scottish political economist and moral philosopher, argued that competition ought to be central to regulating the economy and education alike. Schools were similar to other market goods, they suggested, and educational competition was a virtue. Outside of a brief period following the American Revolution, when state-driven proposals for public school systems proliferated, these ideas dominated mainstream political economy.

By the century's end, however, a new generation of American scholars steeped in evangelical Protestantism no longer believed that competition should regulate all markets with equal efficiency. They argued that publicly operated, regulated, and noncompetitive schools could provide mass education with greater equity and efficiency than could competitive, private providers. These young economists pointed to areas of the economy where they believed the mechanisms of competition failed to operate, and asserted that many enterprises previously considered "private" and competitive were better suited for public, noncompetitive regulation or ownership. Schools, they held, fit into this latter category. Instead of likening schools to small, competitive firms, they frequently described public education as a "natural monopoly," akin to railroads and public utilities. Many public officials and scholars thus embraced schools as quintessential "public" goods, best when owned and operated by cities and states. When Catholics engaged in a wave of private school construction in the 1870s and 1880s they did so in an intellectual climate often hostile to their very enterprise.

Prior to the mass acceptance of free, state-supported schooling, American children enrolled in a diverse, market-driven array of schools. In urban areas such as Boston and New York, tuition-driven "venture" schools dominated formal education through the eighteenth century. These unincorporated schools, often operated by a single entrepreneurial instructor, sprang up to meet parental demand for instruction in subjects like writing and arithmetic that could be marketable in an increasingly commercial America. The masters who operated the schools vigorously competed for working- and middle-class students, placing advertisements in newspapers and adjusting tuition prices to maximize enrollment. In growing market towns, venture schools often competed with academies, another commercially oriented, tuition-dependent form of schooling. Serving more as secondary schools, academies sprang up by the hundreds in the decades after independence, offering a liberal education to ambitious children and a marker of prosperity for town boosters. Academies were incorporated by states and frequently received public funds. In contrast to their venture school competitors, therefore, these features gave them a greater degree of permanency and, in the eyes of many, more legitimacy. Nonetheless, academies, too, experienced the pressures of market demand. When a rival academy or venture school arose, students might flee, preceding an exodus of teachers seeking a more stable customer base.[5]

Even for the institutions most associated with the public, the "common" or "district" schools of rural America, market demand largely drove supply. These one-room, ungraded, multi-age, single-teacher institutions reflected the nation's still very rural settlement patterns, as well as the demand for rudimentary instruction that was cheaply provided and responsive to local demand. In the North, the overwhelming majority of schoolchildren, both girls and boys, attended one-room schoolhouses. They were referred to as "common" schools because they fell under the political control of the district or town, received funding from local taxes (along with occasional state disbursements), and were generally open to all the townspeople's children. Yet, despite their close ties to the community, common schools also operated according to demand. Public funds usually sufficed to operate the schools for only a few months a year. Parental contributions, whether in the form of tuition payments (termed "rate bills"), lodging of the schoolmaster, or fuel expenses to heat the schools, funded the rest. Indeed, throughout the North, these private payments likely constituted the majority of common school funding. Common schools were also not immune from the pressures of market competition. Even small, rural commercial towns like Lima, New York, supported a vibrant education market in the early nineteenth century, with an array of common schools, venture schools, and academies. In the countryside as well, local demand, rather than government regulation, structured educational provision.[6]

There were a few notable exceptions to this general rule of tuition-based, market schooling. Local and state governments, for one, were not absent from education. They provided the base funding for rural schools, aided academies, and regulated various aspects of educational quality through laws of incorporation. Only in New England, however, was there a tradition of colonial laws that required towns of a certain size to establish schools, and even these laws were widely ignored and rarely enforced.[7] Additionally, not all Americans, even excluding those enslaved, had access to a formal educational market. Educational opportunities for free African Americans were severely limited across America, especially in common schools, though some did have access to academies, venture schools, and, in Northern cities, church schools. Rural children faced barriers to education as well. Some lived in areas without any access to formal schooling. Others did not attend their common school at all, or attended only sporadically, obviating the need to pay tuition.[8] Finally, market-driven education did not fully characterize the education of the urban poor, who often had access to church-sponsored schools free of charge. These denominational "charity schools" provided education for destitute children, both white and black, with the financial support of urban elites. These schools were driven less by demand than by the desire among city leaders to nourish the spiritual and intellectual needs of other people's children and, in doing so, to prevent the entrenchment of a rebellious lower class. Charity schools were an important exception to otherwise clear patterns of market-based education in the early republic. Overall, however, the growth of education throughout the nation was spurred principally by private demand, not public supply and regulation.[9]

Reflecting the dominance of this market-based model, intellectual justifications for educational competition abounded in the eighteenth and nineteenth centuries. The prominent place American scholars gave to education markets reflected the immense influence of Adam Smith's *Wealth of Nations* (1776), which highlighted the centrality of competition to economic and educational welfare. In that work, Smith provocatively argued that market competition itself (namely, the rivalries between consumers and producers), not state control, would provide the economy with the most efficient regulatory mechanism. He applied these ideas about competition to schooling, even while recognizing that states had an important role to play in enabling an elementary education for all. He scorned proposals whereby states wholly financed a public system but acknowledged that governments must partially fund (and even compel attendance in) schools for the poor. Smith maintained that schools could operate efficiently only insofar as parents used their resources to make choices between competing educators, rendering teachers subject to the laws of supply and demand. State schemes that fully funded teachers and schools distorted the salutary effects of rivalry. Talented teachers who relied on private tuition payments would be reduced to penury, unable to compete with even the most ineffective public instructors who, by virtue of their subsidies, could charge parents less.[10] For Smith, efficient instruction required competition between teachers dependent at least in part on private parental payments. Though he was never a proponent of educational laissez faire, Smith nonetheless held that the logic of markets, generally, applied to schools, teachers, and parents.[11]

Smith's ideas about competitive education and limited government intervention permeated Northern colleges in the early nineteenth century, leaving few scholarly proponents of free public education. One of the most widely used college textbooks in political economy was the French economist Jean-Baptiste Say's *Treatise on Political Economy* (first published in English in 1824), which exposed elites to Smith's ideas about education. In Say, as in Smith, students read that excessive public subsidies would drive even the best private teachers out of the marketplace, and thus "talent may be superseded by mediocrity."[12] The New England economist Francis Wayland's *Elements of Political Economy* (1837), which soon surpassed Say's in popularity among college instructors, also contained Smith's core educational prescriptions. It joined South Carolina College professor Thomas Cooper's *Lectures on the Elements of Political Economy* (1826) in echoing the conviction that even poor parents should supply private tuition payments for schooling to spur an interest in their child's education and inspire teachers to instruct more effectively.[13] This deference to educational competition was pervasive. The Boston economist Willard Phillips, despite desiring a fairly robust state role in education, spoke for most American political economists when he praised Smith in 1828 for leaving "room enough ... for individual effort and the effect of competition in education."[14] These arguments, made in a time when America lacked state-supported systems of public instruction, reflected the widespread view that education was largely analogous to other market goods and would benefit similarly from healthy doses of competition.

Over the course of the nineteenth century, however, arguments on behalf of state-driven education gradually eclipsed this market-based system. Education markets had their American critics from the beginning of the republic, especially among the state-builders of the revolutionary generation. For many of the nationalists of the Early Republic, a greater state role in education was essential to maintaining a prosperous republic. American revolutionaries in the decades after independence tasked themselves with establishing a republican form of government whose rule depended on an "informed citizenry" of white men and women.[15] Schools would eliminate any vestiges of monarchy from American life. Whereas England weathered intense debates over educating the poor, Americans in the early nineteenth century rarely suggested that universal white male education would disturb a natural social order. Educating African Americans represented a threat to established social hierarchies, but, to many, schooling poor whites seemed a necessity.[16]

American elites also believed that mass, state-sponsored schooling would instill moral and religious values absent the strong educational influence of an established church. Although states did not uniformly end their tax support for churches until several decades into the nineteenth century, Americans nonetheless recognized that the nation lacked any equivalent to the Church of England. Without centralized religious authority, states would have to assume a larger role in providing education. Most Americans embraced this new responsibility. As Samuel Knox observed in his 1797 plan for a national system of education in the United States, "it is a happy circumstance peculiarly favorable to an uniform plan of public education that this country hath excluded ecclesiastical from civil policy and emancipated the human mind from the tyranny of church authority and church establishments."[17] In response, the systems of education contemplated in the early republic rarely conceived of a role for publicly financed, church-based education.[18] In the United States, civil governments gradually would have to fill the educational void left by disestablished churches.

Federalism, somewhat ironically, also promoted a strong rationale for state involvement in schooling. The same political economists who trumpeted the virtues of free trade and competition among nations agreed that individual towns or states possessed the duty to regulate education and impede competition. Thomas Cooper, for example, deemed all national trade barriers unnecessary. Yet he carved out large roles for state governments in furnishing and standardizing elementary instruction in his *Lectures*. For Cooper, states possessed vast regulatory powers, or "police laws," that included state promotion of education and regulation of competition. That the federal government did not share these same rights only reinforced their centrality at the state and local level. Cooper exemplified the belief among American political economists that state and local governments possessed substantial powers to intervene in public and private life, including in education.[19]

These interweaving traditions of republicanism, disestablishment, and federalism help explain why American elites supported a state role in education greater than what the market-based system seemed to enable. Thomas Jefferson's educational thought captured these influences well. Jefferson, a Virginia slaveholder and avid reader of political economy—he admired both Jean-Baptiste Say and Thomas Cooper—sought a more significant state provision of schooling than did most adherents of Adam Smith.[20] The preamble to his 1779 "Bill for the More General Diffusion of Knowledge" described the need for widespread education in order to stabilize republican governments, which were widely viewed as inherently unstable. That Jefferson had drafted his "Bill for Establishing Religious Freedom" two years earlier was no coincidence. Absent the authority of a nationally established church, the United States would need to be stitched together through the more subtle use of state policy—one that balanced local traditions with the demands of government. In theory, Jefferson's proposal—a tiered system of mass education for the young that gradually funneled selected male students into more advanced schooling—accomplished this aim. A state-driven plan by definition, Jefferson's proposal outlined the methods of local educational administration, curriculum, attendance, and finance. It mandated that the poor attend the lowest tier of schools free of charge, and that the best students be selected for subsequent tiers according to merit rather than ability to pay. Although Jefferson's plan involved a significant degree of decentralized educational decision-making, the role it gave to state authorities rankled other Virginia legislators concerned about local control, who declined to enact it. Nonetheless, its contents conveyed the American political elite's anxiety over a populace—slaves notably excluded—whose education would be left entirely to private enterprise.[21]

The distrust of private education extended to other elites as well. James Madison believed that the dependence on entrepreneurial venture schools was disastrous. "Nothing being more ruinous to education than the frequent interruptions & change of masters & methods incident to the private schools of this Country," he wrote.[22] Robert Coram, a Revolutionary War hero, wrote in his plan for education that "the first step to . . . reformation, will be, by turning private schools into public ones" throughout the countryside.[23] A 1795 essay competition sponsored by Philadelphia's American Philosophical Society provides additional insight into the desire for state-driven education plans. The society solicited essays on the best plan for "promot[ing] the general welfare of the United States" through a "plan for instituting and conducting public schools in this country." Though the society received only seven submissions—itself, perhaps, an indictment on state-oriented public school plans—those that did arrive attacked the market-based status quo. Academies and venture schools were operated based on the whims of private educational purveyors, one wrote, and "their permanence [is] unstable & precarious." Five of the seven essayists recommended a state-run school system that, though operated by local districts, would be coordinated at the county and state level, providing free education. The comprehensive education plans of the 1790s, promoted by Coram, Benjamin

Rush, and Noah Webster, also each called for free, tax-supported education systems that promoted universal attendance.[24]

Amid these public commitments for more publicly funded and administered education, federal and state provisions for standardized, articulated public school systems proliferated in the 1780s and 1790s, even if a lack of demand for them prevented their entrenchment. Congressional land ordinances in the Northwest during the 1780s encouraged common schooling by reserving sections of the federal government's public land survey system "for the maintenance of public schools" within new townships. By 1803, state lawmakers had included public aid to education in eight of fifteen state constitutions. In several of the states that did not include a constitutional commitment to public aid for education, such as in Kentucky and Virginia, statutes set aside public funds for schools.[25]

Despite the apparent support among elites for free, tax-supported schools, public laws failed to spur their widespread acceptance in the early nineteenth century. In New York, for example, rural constituencies maintained their support for one-room district schools controlled by local boards but substantially funded through private tuition payments. These rate bills allowed rural families to acquire the level of education they demanded, without paying substantial taxes for other family's children. Urban areas saw similar resistance to free, publicly supported education, especially in New York City. When, in 1795, New York City's Common Council began using state funds to finance the city's church-run charity schools, the result was not mass attendance in these free institutions but rather the opposite: middle-class families became even more convinced that schools receiving public funds were institutions for pauper children, rather than for the "commons," as was true in rural areas.[26] Ultimately, because these proposals envisioned such a dramatically different system of educational provision from what citizens demanded, they, like Jefferson's scheme, were dead on arrival. The resistance to a greater state role in education delayed the spread of free public education for another half-century.

By the 1840s and 1850s centralized public schools finally began to displace the market-based systems that had dominated formal education in the early nineteenth century. A new group of reformers in the North led the charge for schools to be fully controlled and financed by public agencies. The reformers were a relatively homogenous group of middle-class, Northeastern-born Protestants. Their shared desire for a more interventionist state role in social and economic affairs led them naturally to the Whig Party, the national political organization that had arisen to oppose Andrew Jackson and the Democrats in the 1830s. For Whigs, schools stood alongside "internal improvements" like turnpikes and canals that, because of their public benefits, merited state support. Whig reformers like Horace Mann of Massachusetts, Henry Barnard of Connecticut, William Seward of New York, and Calvin Stowe of Ohio supported public schools largely because of their potential for social reform. Amid the convulsions of immigration, urbanization, and industrialization, these men shared a variety of concerns about the American republic that they believed public school systems could address. Increasing disorder in America's cities, teeming with concentrated poverty and immigrants, drove some reformers to embrace public schooling as a social lever: to build character, promote order, facilitate unity, and encourage productivity with moral instruction and basic literacy and numeracy. They argued that the nation's polyglot religious and ethnic groups would benefit from the kind of "common" schooling available in rural areas, and set about replacing the nation's localized, tuition-dependent, and privately governed schools with centralized, state-administered, publicly funded systems.[27] Increased state supervision and tax support were among the central educational reforms they embraced. With these reforms in place, American schools could adopt a full range of innovative features: longer school terms and age-graded classrooms, staffed by trained teachers in new buildings.

To Whig public school advocates such as Horace Mann, market-based education threatened these ideals. Mann, the secretary of the Massachusetts State Board of Education, became the most renowned and influential proselytizer for public systems and common schooling. Absent universal public school attendance, Mann argued, the diversity of the nation's social classes, religions, and ethnicities would tear the fragile republic apart. Public schools needed to serve as instruments for reform, "the equalizers of the conditions of men—the balance wheel of the social machinery," he wrote. To Mann, traditions of privately operated schools and educational competition were obstacles. Mann did not shield his disdain for private education, especially the church-run private schools that existed across the United States. "The tendency of the private school system," Mann wrote critically in his first annual report, in 1837, "is to assimilate our modes of education to those of England, where . . . each sect according to its own creed [m]aintain separate schools, in which children are taught, from their tenderest years to wield the sword of polemics with fatal dexterity; and where the gospel instead of being a temple of peace, is converted into an armory of deadly weapons, for social, interminable warfare." The "hazards of private enterprise," as he put it in 1848, divided communities along religious lines, leading to dozens of sectarian institutions where one, larger "common" school could produce a superior education through age-graded classrooms. Mann proposed that state systems embrace the Protestant, though nonsectarian, legacies of New England. The public schools that resulted generally fit this description. They included a generically Protestant moral curriculum, frequently incorporating readings from the (Protestant) King James Bible but without commentary from a Congregational, Baptist, Presbyterian, or other denominational perspective. Only through this system of common schooling, Mann had asserted, could the American republic cope with the convulsive effects of immigration, industrialization, and urbanization.[28]

In cities, charity schools ironically became the primary vehicle for decreasing the private sector's influence in education. The example of New York City was illustrative, but not atypical. In 1825 the trustees of the Free School Society, which privately operated the city's charity school system, renamed the organization the "Public School Society," invited children from the middle classes to attend and successfully pressured the city council to cease distributing public funds to competing denominational schools. The

Public School Society soon monopolized public tax dollars. Within seven years it had ceased charging tuition for its wealthier students and had consolidated with other private school systems, including the Manumission Society's schools for African Americans. While the Public School Society would continue to be operated by a self-perpetuating board of trustees for another generation, its schools soon became more standardized, with common curriculum, grade promotion requirements, and teacher training.[29] The vast numbers of tuition schools, unable to compete with publicly funded institutions, like those in New York City, decreased considerably. In New York, the percentage of students enrolled in private institutions fell from 62 to 18 percent between 1829 and 1850, a trend reflected throughout urban areas in the North.[30]

Unsurprisingly, given the long history of market-based schooling, resistance to common school reform was often fierce. Many urban working-class families, along with rural farmers, opposed tax increases to pay for common schools and high schools to which they had no intention of sending their children. Because rate bills allowed families the choice of using their own private money to extend their child's schooling, their abolition proved controversial, especially for taxpayers who did not have children attending common schools. To extend free public schooling to all, without these tuition payments, would be to take money from some taxpayers and give it to others—an "unconstitutional, arbitrary, and unjust" policy, as one New York resident wrote in 1850.[31] Because of this fierce opposition, rate bills in the North were not fully abolished until the 1870s. Opposition to high schools functioned similarly. In a nation in which secondary school attendance rates did not break single digits until the twentieth century, some communities resented expensive new high schools—the pinnacle of the new public systems— as elite institutions for the middle class only. In one Massachusetts town, for example, working-class shoemakers and fishermen in overwhelming majorities voted to abolish their high school in 1860.[32]

Religious groups were more divided on common school reform, though those opposed offered manifold criticisms. To dedicate tax dollars exclusively to common schools meant that denominational charity schools and academies, which had previously received public funds, would be fully dependent on private sources for revenue. For denominationally-minded Protestants, furthermore, the common school curriculum undermined the religious sectarianism that they sought to propagate. Bible readings and school prayer without commentary from a denominational perspective necessarily meant that schools would ignore important religious distinctions between Protestant sects. For religious Catholics, a pan-Protestant common school curriculum itself was offensive, especially in the frequent choice of the Protestant King James Bible. In Philadelphia during the 1840s, major Catholic protests over Protestantism in public schools sparked city-wide clashes between Irish immigrants and nativists. Religious objections to common schooling from Catholics, in particular, would continue unabated through the century.[33]

These objections did not, however, dissuade the majority of Americans from supporting the expansion of free public schooling, much of which originated from decentralized demand. In rural areas, after all, common schools enticed near-universal attendance well before centralized state intervention. Indeed, communities in the North had gradually increased local tax support to fully fund six months of free schooling, in some cases eliminating the need for tuition "rate bills" before state legislatures had abolished them.[34] In cities, meanwhile, public schools gradually overcame the most significant obstacle to their widespread success: the association between free education and charity schools meant for the poor exclusively. This "pauper stigma" associated with free schooling gradually diminished as towering new public high schools, like the one that H. H. Barney oversaw in Cincinnati, helped attract the middle classes to the public system.[35] A new high school in Vermont, as one education committee observed in 1842, was enough to attract the "best educated and wealthiest families" to the public schools. "Nearly all the private schools have been given up," the committee's report noted.[36] Some upper- and middle-class families continued to send their children to elite private schools, but common school advocates assumed—or at least hoped—that the public system's superiority would ultimately attract them as well. As a result of this transformation the vast majority of private schools either closed their doors or transitioned into public hands. By the 1870s, public schools had become the dominant educational provider in the North. The same trend occurred in the South during Reconstruction, where states were required to adopt free public school systems in order to be readmitted into the Union.[37]

The rise of free public school systems accompanied a broader surge in public authority over the second half of the nineteenth century. While government had always played a prominent role in regulating American life, including at the municipal level, public ownership of education and other utilities increased. By 1870, public school systems were some of the most visible, if not leading, signs of the spread of public power. But in cities, especially, they were not alone. Where only 20 percent of American cities owned their own waterworks systems in 1830, for example, that number had increased to nearly 50 percent by 1870.[38] Sewer systems became even more overwhelmingly operated by municipalities. By the 1890s it was not uncommon for cities to municipalize garbage collection and, though less frequently, acquire gas works, municipal electricity generating plants, or street railway systems.[39]

"The cities provide for the individual citizens things which they might—and for a long time did—provide for themselves, or which might be provided by private enterprise," a professor specializing in public finance, Carl Plehn, wrote in 1915 about the preceding decades. "This is notably true of the schools," he continued.[40] And indeed it was. Public ownership of schooling expanded, and so too did the scope of public educational power. States, cities, and public school districts in the second half of the nineteenth century published lists of school regulations running to dozens of pages, detailing scores of rules affecting attendance, administration, finance, and discipline. Compulsory school attendance statutes proved the most theoretically invasive.[41] Between 1867 and 1883, the number of states with compulsory attendance statutes increased from a single one—Massachusetts—to fourteen. The "restraints and regulations affect almost everything imaginable," wrote the journalist Albert Shaw in 1887 in a wide-ranging essay on state regulation. Shaw, like Plehn, singled out public schools—free, tax-supported high schools, in particular—as among the most prominent areas where governments "emphatically repudiate" unrestricted competition.[42] School boards, departments of instruction, legislatures, and state courts were slowly shifting educational governance away from parents and local neighborhoods and toward centralized control, a process that continued well into the twentieth century.[43]

Alongside these developments, a rising generation of political economists rarely discussed the virtues of educational competition as they had in the half-century after the *Wealth of Nations*. As early as 1838, the University of Pennsylvania political economist Henry Vethake wrote that "very few educated men will be any where found to object" to the "propriety of a legislative appropriation of the public money to the support of common schools, in which every child in the community may have an opportunity of acquiring elements of an education."[44] College students who turned to the 1878 edition of Francis Wayland's textbook read that a "system of public education *must* provide free schools open to all classes," a far cry from the sentiments expressed in that volume's first edition from a half-century earlier.[45] Scholars no longer likened schools to other market goods. Instead, they compared schools to railroads and public utilities—areas of the economy that were increasingly characterized by heavy public regulation or outright public ownership.

The intellectual assault on market-based education found an organizational home with the formation of the American Economic Association (AEA) in 1885. Established by a rising generation of political economists, the group gave voice to scholars seeking stronger state intervention in the economy. Their platform condemned laissez faire and "the political economy of a past generation." In its place they highlighted the state's ability to regulate the economy successfully, positing that the state represented an "ethical agency whose positive aid is an indispensable condition of human progress." Leading the organization was a group of young economists steeped in evangelical Protestantism and German university training: Lester Frank Ward of the U.S. Geological Survey, Richard Ely of Johns Hopkins University, Henry Carter Adams of the University of Michigan and Cornell, Edmund James of the Wharton School, John Bates Clark of Smith College, and two former students of Ely's at Hopkins, Edward Bemis and Albert Shaw.[46]

The founders of the "new" political economy offered prescriptions that reflected a particular Protestant social and cultural milieu. Ward, Ely, Adams, and James grew up in pious, Protestant communities and households where, as Ely later wrote of his childhood in upstate New York, "the interests of the community were more often centered in its churches and schools than in economic problems."[47] Indeed, Protestant churches and common schools often merged seamlessly together in these small communities. In the nineteenth century, textbooks such as the *McGuffey Reader* weaved pan-Protestant messages into literacy instruction, which students then used to read the Protestant King James Bible—another staple of the common school classroom. As adults, these social scientists formed part of a broader movement that sought to combine the moral author-ity of evangelical Protestant teachings with the need for political, economic, and social reform. Though their cultural heritages were rarely on explicit display, the economists' similar backgrounds colored their collective work, producing a discrete intellectual com-munity. Their embrace of public education reflected a particular American identity and experience, one that others in the country did not share.[48]

Imbued with their benevolent and almost spiritual view of the state, the AEA econo-mists believed that governments under expert management could rationalize and human-ize the industrial order, including education. As Gilded Age America experienced rising wealth inequality, labor strikes, and agrarian populism, the AEA economists contended that the economy required greater coordination and bureaucratic order.[49] Together, they aimed to identify the areas of the economy where cooperation and state intervention, rather than competition, should organize social activity.

That competition ought not characterize all enterprises formed the crux of the AEA's disagreements with American champions of free competition—men such as the Yale sociologist William Graham Sumner. Where Sumner, for example, argued that social Darwinian ideas of competition should characterize nearly every sphere of American life, the younger insurgent economists insisted that social cooperation could be equally if not more operative in various arenas of public concern.[50] Richard Ely's seminal 1884 essay on the "Past and the Present of Political Economy," for example, discussed "the inadequate action of competition in regulating and controlling great corporations."[51] John Bates Clark dedicated an entire chapter of his 1894 textbook to what he termed "Non-Competitive Economics." Even Adam Smith's ideas, Clark wrote, had to be updated in an age in which "competition is no longer adequate to account for the phenomena of social industry."[52] This assault on free competition, together with promotion of state intervention, perme-ated the first four essays published by the AEA in 1887: Edmund James on municipal reg-ulation and ownership of gas supplies, Albert Shaw on "Cooperation in a Western City," Edward Bemis on "Cooperation in New England," and Henry Carter Adams on state intervention in industry.[53] In the America these scholars envisioned, many more private enterprises would become subject to government regulation or ownership, transition-ing, as Ely wrote, from a "private competitive condition, to a public non-competitive condition."[54] That vision increasingly reflected reality. Urban Americans had witnessed the process with the utility industry, where gas and electric companies along with water-works generally moved from private competition to public monopoly. In this context, more American political economists and legal scholars began questioning the virtue of unlimited competition, including in education.

The AEA scholars held that publicly sanctioned monopolies, schooling included, could be more beneficial than industries regulated solely by competition. As educa-tion itself became more public, scholars no longer treated it as a market good. Instead, with public school systems fully entrenched, political economists likened education to other industries characterized as "natural monopolies," or areas where technological and organizational innovations had rendered competitive principles obsolete. While the theory of natural monopoly failed to provide an explicit policy recommendation regarding educational competition, it forged an important link between public ownership and noncompetition. Richard Ely's dictum that "monopolies are the field for public activity" while "competitive pursuits are the field for private activity" exemplified this trend.[55]

The AEA economists increasingly argued that monopolies, when either publicly regulated or publicly owned, did not always function as the harmful entities that muckraking journalists later made them out to be. Consumers, after all, profited from the efficiencies that came with economies of scale in large industries, a dynamic that economists and regulators observed in the emerging structures of late-nineteenth-century railroads and municipal utilities.[56] Consumers would hardly benefit from two competing railroad tracks carrying long-haul goods between the same two points; ratepayers would have to absorb the cost of additional tracks, railway cars, terminal facilities, and so forth. Having two half-empty railway cars traveling to the same location in place of one full car was absurd.[57] Instead, as Henry Carter Adams asserted, it was exponentially cheaper for an existing railroad to expand its facilities to meet demand than "for a new industry to spring into competitive existence." For Adams, the "*possibility* of cheapness and efficiency" appeared "to lie in the very nature of a monopoly." That railroad corporations tended to merge with one another with incredible frequency reinforced this point. "If it is for the interest of men to combine no law can make them compete," he wrote. Railroad monopolies were not only "natural" but potentially preferable as well.[58]

The same anticompetitive logic that applied to railroads held for competing municipal waterworks and electric utilities. By virtue of their heavy capital costs, direct utility competition rarely occurred within a particular municipality for a sustained period of time. As with the railroads, the barriers to entry were substantial enough to keep a competing waterworks company from laying duplicate sets of pipes. Absent this competition, city residents complained that the utility monopolies had little incentive to fulfill the terms of their franchises. Rates were too high and services too constrained. By the late nineteenth century, cities either began to operate utilities themselves or regulate them by imposing rate ceilings. Even when privately operated, political economists and legal scholars argued, utilities deserved monopoly status because of their public nature and technological characteristics.[59] Where monopolies formed "naturally," states had a responsibility to channel their productivity and eliminate competition on behalf of the citizenry.

Schools entered into these conversations about natural monopoly despite the fact that comparisons between public education and public utilities were often strained. Schools and utilities were an odd match for at least three reasons. First, although public schools in the second half of the nineteenth century almost always enrolled the vast majority of schoolchildren, they did not monopolize local education in the same way that electric utilities, for example, monopolized lighting.[60] Private schools continued to operate in virtually every city in the country. Second, while schools absorbed a large share of tax dollars, they lacked the tremendous fixed costs of railroads, waterworks, or electric companies. Unlike those enterprises, schools did not seem to benefit as immensely from economies of scale. Educational reformers had long argued for larger schools to provide graded classrooms, always in short supply in rural areas with their ubiquitous one-room buildings, but as long as cities required dozens of elementary schools and, increasingly, multiple high schools, the analogies with public utilities seemed difficult to maintain. Finally, the fee structure of education differed substantially from the utilities. Public utilities charged rates and consumers paid according to the volume of their usage. By the 1870s, however, states and localities in the North prohibited public schools from raising funds through similar "rate," or tuition, bills, relying on property taxes and state aid instead.[61] Schools used various incentives to attract additional pupils, but scholars realized that pricing public education was hardly similar to financing public utilities.

Together, these distinctions struck some analysts as having significant policy implications. "The support of public education, police and fire protection and parks," the editors of the journal *Public Policy* wrote in 1904, hardly resembled the "gas and electricity supplied for light, heat and power, and transportation facilities." To equate the two represented an "illogical mixing up of non-commercial with commercial purposes."[62] Where the first group clearly deserved to be owned by the public, the latter needed only to be regulated. Similarly, the editors of the free-market journal *To-Day* believed that gas companies should receive monopolistic protection through state regulation but then argued that schools should be guided by laissez-faire principles, similar to bakeries or manufacturers.[63]

Despite objections to treating schools akin to public utilities, AEA members made frequent comparisons between public education and other natural monopolies characterized by noncompetition. John Bates Clark believed that railroads and education shared important "non-competitive" qualities given that "in both cases does a public agency intervene in order to secure the general diffusion of important utilities."[64] Richard Ely's 1894 textbook on political economy likened public schools to municipally owned gas works—all "natural monopolies" that are "best owned and operated by government, while competitive businesses flourish only in the atmosphere of private enterprise and free competition."[65] In his *Outlines of Economics*, published a year earlier, Ely similarly had applied the theory of natural monopoly to private institutions of higher education, arguing against the "uncohesive [*sic*] and wasteful character of private enterprise in education" in contrast to the "efficiently consolidated" and "unifying power . . . of the State."[66]

In 1901, the public ownership advocate Frank Parsons took the comparison still further, arguing that "public education rests upon the idea that learning is more likely to be well distributed among the whole people by means of public schools than by reliance upon private institutions." Private schools, like private utilities, lacked the incentive to deliver their services to outlying areas, for example. As Parsons put it, "private gas and water companies lay their mains only in streets that will yield a profit. Public works put their pipes into any street where there is a reasonable demand for the service. Private schools and turnpikes go only where they will 'pay'—can't go anywhere else except on the basis of charity; but public schools and roads go into every district where there are children to educate or people to travel." For Parsons, educational competition, like utility competition, had little business operating in cities.[67]

Lester Frank Ward conveyed the AEA economists' attacks against private education particularly succinctly. Schooling, Ward suggested, was not akin to other market goods to which early nineteenth-century economists had likened them. Instead, it was fundamentally similar to water provision, fire protection, sanitation, transportation, and the postal service—areas in which many municipalities and states in the late nineteenth century believed competition ought to be suppressed. Ward had long critiqued unrestrained competition, warning in 1894 that laissez-faire ideas would "involve the repeal of all the humane and industrial legislation." "It would turn over cities to private water companies and private fire companies," he wrote. "There would be a reversion to a system of strictly private, or 'wildcat' banking; public schools would be abolished, probably the last thing next to liberty that any enlightened nation would surrender; and all forms of sanitary regulation, including quarantine precautions against great epidemics, would be left to the wisdom of individual citizens."[68] In his 1883 *Dynamic Sociology*, Ward wrote that "education can not be successfully conducted on the competitive system" and that it must be "excepted from" the general laws of supply and demand. He attacked the "*laissez faire* principles" in English schooling, where "no system of public education can be said to exist," and praised America's preference for equitable, universal education instead of unequal, private schools.

Assailing the application of market-based arguments for education, Ward argued that demand for schooling differed from consumer demand for other goods. While Ward realized that the supply of private education might congeal to the demands of even negligent parents, he believed that a true market for education would produce privately operated schools perpetuating inequalities and diminishing learning. In private schools, "education [is] a business" and the "teacher, like the tailor, is obliged to suit his customers." Teachers dependent on tuition dollars had incentives to pass children regardless of merit—"in private education, there is truly 'no such word as fail'"—lest a rival school arise whose competitive advantage lay in granting even easier access to the credential. In order to attract and maintain pupils private teachers had to engage in advertising rather than instruction, the "tricks of diplomacy at the expense of educational progress." For Ward, this race to the bottom characterized the "self-regulating system" of private schooling, producing a result not only inferior to public education but "absolutely worse" than no formal schooling at all. He dismissed the critics of public schooling who insisted on a private, religious education for their children with a single line: "The few who object on the ground of conscientious religious scruples, considering the entirely secular character of state education, are not sufficiently numerous to command respect."[69] Ward's coolly economic reasoning, together with his swift rejection of denominational education, placed him squarely in the mainstream of the new political economy.

As one of the most visible, large-scale activities almost entirely converted into public ownership, schools provided a clear example to political economists of the benefits of public regulation and ownership. In his 1887 essay for the AEA's first journal publication, the Wharton professor Edmund James pointed specifically to public schools in a study on public ownership of gas utilities. He attacked opponents of public ownership as ignorant of "the history of government in ancient and modern times," a history that conveyed an abiding state role in economic life. "It is by such arguments as these [opposing public ownership]," he wrote, "that the government was kept for years from assisting in the establishment of free schools." Absent the persuasive arguments of public ownership advocates, James continued, Americans would have "to-day no free schools, no sanitary regulations, no safeguards of life and liberty such as we now have in many different fields; we should be in a sorry way indeed."[70] If governments could operate schools for the benefit of the people, then monopolistic public ownership in many other enterprises should necessarily follow, and competition reduced.

The language and metaphors that economists used to advocate for public ownership trickled into how public officials talked about schools. Like the AEA economists, these men were skeptical of educational competition and private schools. Nathaniel H. R. Dawson, the U.S. Commissioner of Education who had spent his later years in life fighting for the spread of public education in the South, believed that "universal education" reflected "new developments in political economy." Education, he wrote, "should be afforded without price, and should be as free as the water we drink . . .. Private agencies may supplement but can never supersede the necessity for their support from the public revenues."[71] Other officials similarly drew from the language of public utilities. Just as "light and water should be furnished at public expense," a Savannah, Georgia, school official wrote in 1873, so should all elementary instruction "be provided" without charge.[72] Six years later, Wisconsin's state superintendent of public instruction, O. B. Wyman, observed that "as to the efficiency of private enterprise in promoting the education of the masses, it is too irregular in its action, too costly in its methods, and too inadequate in its means. Private enterprise never has—we believe it never will—educate the whole people."[73] The AEA economists' emphasis on noncompetitive economics both mirrored and likely influenced how public education officials thought about schooling in the United States.

The marketplace of education that characterized both the theory and the practice of American schooling in 1800 was quickly in retreat by 1870. Public schools not only dominated urban attendance but also changed how many Americans conceived of education—from a competitive market good to a noncompetitive public service. Scholars in the nineteenth century gradually severed the intellectual links, forged by British and American classical economists, between schooling and other marketable commodities. By the late nineteenth century, they argued that schooling represented an uncompetitive good, better left to government regulation or outright ownership. The stated educational benefits of competition that had been a staple of antebellum political economy textbooks were, a half-century later, absent from discussion. Growing public school systems not only disrupted actual practices of competition among schools but also produced a new generation of scholars—individuals with deep ties to Protestantism and public schooling—who suggested that publicly governed, tax-supported schools could educate all of the members of the community in the same neutral manner that a publicly owned utility provided electricity.

The remaining defenders of educational competition in the late nineteenth century were predominately advocates of Catholic parochial schools, a set of institutions that were growing rapidly throughout urban America. That ideas about educational competition were shifting just as Catholic schools exploded in numbers contributed to the clash between public officials and Catholic school sponsors in the late nineteenth century. The new Catholic schools of the 1870s and 1880s entered into a very different educational marketplace than had the private schools of 1800—one that would be vastly more regulated and managed by public authorities.

2

Competing Schools

IN 1905, ROBERT FITZSIMMONS traveled from Cincinnati to Pittsburgh to attend
a gathering of alumni celebrating their beloved Duquesne School. By all accounts the
reunion was a grand affair, a time to relive fond memories. The Duquesne alums cheerfully sang "Ye Olden Times" and ate Slade's Taffy, a candy from their youth. "It was a day
to meet old friends, to recall the ties of youth, to talk about things that had happened
when the world was very young," a booklet commemorating the event noted. On this
one lovely June afternoon in Pittsburgh the Duquesne alums were "children again for a
day." More than six hundred of the school's former pupils, teachers, administrators, and
their family members gathered for the reunion. In a city with larger-than-life personali-
ties—names like Carnegie, Mellon, and Frick—the Pittsburgh celebrities on hand were
decidedly local, if not equally as popular. Mary Eaton, the school's longtime principal,
traveled from Illinois to see her former students. Pittsburgh's public school superintendent, Samuel Andrews, also attended.[1]

As the school's oldest alumnus, Fitzsimmons was a particularly notable presence. The
Duquesne School claimed the honor of being Pittsburgh's first public school, established
in 1835, one year after Pennsylvania's "Common School Law" had set in motion a system of universal, free, state-supported public schooling.[2] Fitzsimmons had attended the
school, then called the First Ward School, when it was in its infancy. He was the sole
alumnus present who remembered its initial location in the basement of a Methodist
church. Fitzsimmons was now in his eighties, and those days seemed distant. When he
was born, Pittsburgh, like most other American cities in the early nineteenth century, had
no free public schools at all, but rather a mixture of tuition-based schools and church-run
institutions.[3] That its first school met in a church basement was no accident. Thousands
of urban public schools in the first half of the nineteenth century had emerged out of privately governed religious schools. Within a couple of decades of the Duquesne School's

opening, the vast majority of Pittsburgh's children attended free, tax-supported, publicly administered, nonsectarian schools. The Duquesne School moved to a new building shortly after opening.[4]

The triumphant expansion of public education in Pittsburgh and throughout early industrial America—a story symbolized by the Duquesne School, its reunion, and Fitzsimmons's presence—seemed to come to a halt when Catholics embarked on an ambitious program to build an alternative system of schools. As millions of Catholic immigrants entered into industrial cities they constructed parochial schools at a rapid pace, producing educational competition and religious conflict. At the very same time that public schools became associated with "natural monopolies," in other words, immigrants were reshaping American educational history in ways their fellow Americans did not foresee. Reformers had sought to expand public schooling as "common" institutions, places where children from all classes would learn together under a curriculum guided by the moral teachings of Protestant Christianity.[5] They intended those schools to be governed by the people and their elected leaders at the state and local level. Catholic schools represented a challenge to that vision: schools run by parishes, not state-drawn districts, for the secular and religious instruction of Catholic children.

The explosion of Roman Catholic parochial schools in urban areas in the 1870s and 1880s introduced competitive, alternative school systems for parents and their children, fundamentally altering the landscape of urban education. From the construction of a single parochial school in Pittsburgh's First Ward, to dozens of schools in cities such as Chicago and Cleveland, Catholic school competition had a profound impact on attendance, employment, and public school governance. Protestants and lawmakers generally abhorred these new schools, resenting the competition parochial schools introduced with public schools for Catholic students, and fearing the consequences of large numbers of students attending private institutions. Some local school boards responded by accommodating certain Catholic educational demands, such as foreign language instruction, hoping that these reforms would attract Catholic immigrants to public schools. Other school boards attempted more dramatic compromises and provided direct public money to Catholic schools so long as they relegated denominational instruction until after hours. The sharp division between public and private schools that buttressed educational competition did not uniformly occur across the United States. Where it did not—the countryside, the South, and the Southwest, in particular—efforts at accommodation were strongest. In America's urban areas, however, school competition was pervasive. The more pervasive response among public officials was to pass laws regulating parochial schools.

While nineteenth-century cities differed substantially from one another in character and history, they all experienced the broader forces of industrialization and immigration. Urban education was transformed in the process. The Duquesne School, like the urban environment around it, had changed dramatically since the middle of the nineteenth century, when Fitzsimmons had attended. These changes were the product of deeper shifts in Pittsburgh's economic and social life. At the school's reunion, the proud alumni could not help but note that their beloved institution, nestled in the city's oldest neighborhood, the First Ward, had declined considerably in the past forty years. At its height in 1869 the school had enrolled 424 children. In 1893, only twenty-nine attended.[6] Industrial development produced dramatic changes to the First Ward, known colloquially as "The Point," denoting the area where the Allegheny and Monongahela rivers fed into the Ohio. That convenient geographic location made the area the city's center for manufacturing and commercial activity. In 1850, the downtown core of the city's oldest four wards featured a mixed economy, where banks and bankers lived among manufacturers, professionals, and workers. More than three-quarters of the city's professionals lived in these four downtown wards.[7]

By the 1880s, however, a transportation revolution had drastically shifted the demographics of the First Ward. As commuter railroads and streetcars facilitated geographic mobility, the downtown central business district steadily lost population to the city's suburbs and new manufacturing centers on the South Side and further along the rivers to the east. The more established Protestant families of these downtown wards had the resources to benefit from early suburbanization. As these families departed, increasing numbers of skilled and unskilled immigrant workers, largely Irish Catholics, took their place.[8] From 1868 to 1900, the city grew from roughly 55,000 inhabitants to over 300,000, while territorial annexation increased its size from 1.77 to more than 28 square miles. By 1880, the largely Catholic foreign-born population totaled over one-quarter of Pittsburgh's population. In thirty years, the children of these immigrants would make the city majority Catholic.[9] As early as 1890 one-third of the First Ward's population was foreign-born, giving rise to its reputation as a seedy slum area. When the Census reported on the neighborhood's vital statistics in 1894, it noted only that one "section . . . was occupied by prostitutes" and that in the "remainder of the ward the residents were largely Irish and Italians."[10] Four years earlier, the Pittsburgh Bureau of Health referred to the cramped working-class dwellings there as the "hovel of the Irish laborer."[11]

These trends of Catholic in-migration and Protestant out-migration resulted in the dramatic decline in attendance at the Duquesne School. For the alumni, these demographic changes were intensely personal and local. Robert Fitzsimmons had witnessed them over his long lifetime. The Duquesne School reunion's directors noted their beloved institution's decline briefly in their booklet. They referred to "the pressure of business" forcing people to "seek homes outside the ward" and spoke of the neighborhood's newcomers as "of foreign birth and tongue . . . with no knowledge of the English language or American history."[12] The neighborhood had changed, and so had its school.

Nowhere, however, did the booklet mention what the school's alumni surely remembered as another principal reason for its decline: the erection of a parochial school in 1890. The public Duquesne School, once housed in a Methodist basement, did not attract all of the ward's immigrant Catholic parents, many of whom instead sought a Catholic education for their children. The school that Catholics attached to their nearby St. Mary of Mercy Parish represented a challenge to the Duquesne School. Catholic parents who had sent their children to the local public school now faced a choice over their children's schooling.

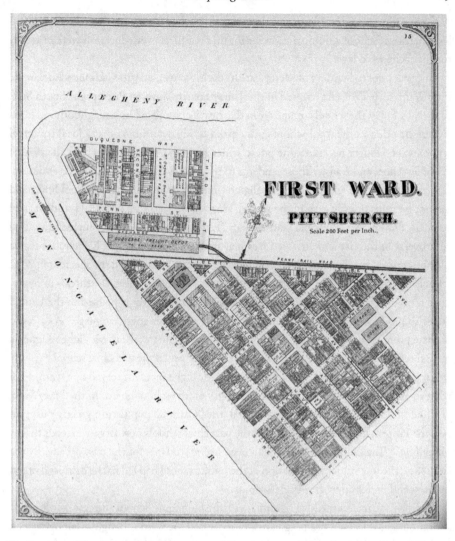

The Duquesne School, on the northeast corner of First Avenue and Short Street, was in a quickly industrializing neighborhood of Pittsburgh known as "The Point." The school faced dramatic competition from a nearby Catholic parochial school.
Atlas of the cities of Pittsburgh, Allegheny, and the adjoining boroughs: from actual surveys & official records (1872), Plate 15, courtesy of Historic Pittsburgh Maps Collection

In growing numbers, those parents elected the parochial school. As the Duquesne School hemorrhaged students to its new competitor, the city's public school promoters feared that the ground was shifting under their feet. Catholic parishes were building schools throughout the city. The Protestant ideal of the "common" school was under dire threat.

The brewing conflict over schooling in the First Ward reflected Pittsburgh's decentralized public and private school administration. Neighborhoods run by local sub-district committees, not district, municipal, or state governments, were chiefly responsible for governing Pittsburgh's thirty-six ward public schools.[13] Likewise, individual Catholic parishes, rather than dioceses or archdioceses, established most educational policies. This local nature of school administration meant that conflicts over education were intensely fought at the ward level.

One year prior to St. Mary of Mercy Parish's decision to enlarge its Catholic school in the First Ward, such a conflict erupted in the Thirty-Fourth Ward on Pittsburgh's South Side. In the fall of 1887, the school committee in that heavily populated Irish neighborhood hired a Catholic priest as the ward school's principal. Having determined that a local parochial school was no longer necessary, the priest, James McTighe, proceeded to close the parish's Catholic school and transfer those students to the local public school. Cautious about setting off a storm, McTighe prohibited religious instruction during public school hours and did not wear his priestly garb in the school. He even insisted that the ward's students and parents call him "Mr. Principal" rather than "Father." Nonetheless, the incident aroused controversy in the city and attracted national attention. McTighe and his school became the object of several threats from local Protestant groups, who viewed the specter of public schools dominated by a Catholic priest with alarm. McTighe viewed the threats in hyperbolic terms, declaring that "since the fall of Sumter nothing ever happened in the United States to produce such intense excitement, to provoke such angry language." As a result of these protests, as well as from pressure from his own congregation, McTighe resigned a mere three months into his tenure as principal and reopened the parochial school.[14]

An article in the *Chicago Tribune* about the McTighe incident served as a warning of what to expect if Catholics composed a majority on the school board. In the First Ward, just like McTighe's, the *Tribune* announced, the "Catholic population greatly outnumbers the Protestants" and "attendance at the parochial schools now largely exceeds that at the public."[15] The Duquesne School had been losing students for the past decade. By the late 1880s, the low student population at the public school had led to the dismissal of ten teachers and increasingly empty classrooms.

Less than a year after the McTighe incident, the Duquesne School's directors concocted a solution that they believed pragmatically addressed the ward's changing demographics. In the summer of 1888, they designed a plan to rent out the school's unused classrooms to Morgan M. Sheedy, an Irish-born Catholic priest whose parish school needed room to expand. Here was a way to raise additional funds for the public school while efficiently using the building's previously empty classrooms.[16] As one admirer of the plan observed in the *Commercial Gazette*, Sheedy "scrubs the floor and takes the cobwebs from the windows of the unused rooms in the First ward building and gathers in a few children from the alleys of the Point."[17] There appeared to be little downside.

But the Duquesne School directors' plan quickly backfired when news of the scheme leaked out to the city's Protestant leaders in August 1888. The directors knew that Pittsburgh's Protestants might not look fondly upon a Catholic priest again "occupying" public school property. They had tried but failed to keep their solution to declining enrollments a secret until Sheedy opened his school in September. Now made public, the plan by the school directors produced a firestorm. A nativist organization, the Junior Order of the

American Mechanics, was the first to denounce the deal in late August, saying that the plan would allow "the enemy within the lines" of the public schools.[18] In early September, the Presbyterian Ministerial Association announced its own opposition to the rental agreement.[19] When local newspapers reported that the plan had forced two "efficient teachers" from the public school—the result, in part, of even greater numbers of pupils abandoning the public school side of the building for the Catholic side—those opposed to the school grew more strident. The First Ward's alderman remarked that Sheedy "was as much mistaken in taking the step as was Father McTighe" and that "the feeling against the action of the board in renting the rooms for a parochial school, as well as dispensing of two efficient teachers, is very high, and it will certainly react upon those who were parties."[20] The Methodist *Pittsburgh Christian Advocate*, in one of several vituperative columns, called it "an effort on the part of Romanists not only to show their disapproval of the public schools, but to supplant them with their own system."[21] By the end of September, newspapers reported that Protestant leaders were prepared to bring suit against the contract and that both the city and state superintendent of schools had declared the rental agreement illegal.[22] In October, angry Protestants even brought their case to the city's impotent central board of education, reading aloud portions of the Pennsylvania state constitution in hopes of persuading the city's elites that the sale violated the law of the land.[23]

Father Sheedy reveled in the controversy. He, like scores of other parochial school promoters, believed that American public education generally consisted of nothing less than a collection of de facto Protestant schools. For generations, Pittsburgh's public schools, including the Duquesne School in its early years, had been used by Protestants for Sunday school and other religious purposes. Public schools with large Protestant majorities, after all, had long featured readings from the (Protestant) King James Bible as a standard part of the school day. Catholics imagined the typical public school teacher being a young, female, evangelical Protestant—and no doubt they were frequently correct. Given his perception that public education was implicitly Protestant, Sheedy believed there could be no objection to explicitly Catholic taxpayer-funded schools. Only then could Catholics be given the very same benefits accrued to Protestants: free, publicly financed, religious schools. Sheedy thus found the outrage directed at him to be hypocritical. "Does this mean that [public schools] may be used for a variety of purposes so long as those using them are not Catholics and their use denied when application is made to the directors of Catholic citizens?" he asked in an interview with the *Pittsburgh Press* one month after his school had opened. As he later put it, "the whole point seems to be that a prejudiced class of narrow and illiberal views would deny to Catholic citizens the rights and privileges claimed and used by themselves."[24] The opportunity to open a Catholic school directly adjacent to a public one represented a unique opportunity. It would reveal the equality, if not superiority, of the parochial school, and it would demonstrate the continued demand among Catholic parents for parish over public education.

Sheedy gained a national platform in August 1889 when he published an essay entitled "The School Question: A Plea for Justice" in *The Catholic World*. There, he highlighted the surging need for parochial schools in Pittsburgh, citing the Catholics' "constant demand for additional school room." On several occasions he remarked upon the suprem-acy of the Catholic schools and concluded by suggesting ways "of testing the superiority of one system over the other" through "an honest competition between the pupils in equal grades of the two systems." The parochial school Sheedy directed, housed in the same building as a public school, represented a laboratory for these ideas about Catholic education and educational competition.[25] When the editors of New England's *Journal of Education* read Sheedy's essay they remarked that "the church of Rome is making war upon the American school system."[26]

The rental arrangement, as intended, did not last. While Protestants failed to chal-lenge it successfully in court, Sheedy fulfilled the terms of his contract and left the Duquesne School after one year. By all accounts, he had achieved his goals. As one news-paper observed, the Catholic side of the Duquesne School enrolled more than two hun-dred pupils, whereas the adjacent public side had a "much smaller" attendance.[27] Sheedy acknowledged that school quality should not be measured exclusively by attendance, since "most parents are influenced by other considerations in selecting a choice of schools for their children" other than "comparing the efficiency of one system with the other." Nonetheless, in the popular imagination, and likely for Sheedy as well, numbers mat-tered. Speaking in the language of competition, Sheedy knew that the ultimate arbiter would be the consumer, "the choice of the parents."[28]

It came as little surprise to Pittsburgh residents, then, when Sheedy announced in 1889 that a large new parochial school attached to St. Mary of Mercy Church, in the First Ward, would open within a year's time. Parochial school attendance, according to Catholic sources, had continued to keep pace with the city's growing population, rising from 7,152 students in 1880 to 12,426 (compared with 31,000 in public schools) a decade later.[29] In April 1889, Father Corcoran of St. Agnes Church, in the city's Fourteenth Ward, told parishioners that their Catholic school would be expanding within the year and that, as the *Pittsburgh Dispatch* recounted, "parents who had been sending their children to public schools should take them away."[30] Each August and September, the local news-papers reported on the Catholic schools that had opened, as well as on the sermons of Catholic priests urging their parishioners to attend them. In 1888 the *Pittsburgh Catholic* remonstrated its readers to appreciate "their duty in reference to the selection of school in which they are intending to entrust their little ones for training and educational pur-poses."[31] Father Corcoran reportedly announced in a sermon that he would refuse absolu-tion to parents who sent their children to the public, "unchristian" school.[32]

Public school officials and Protestant clergymen issued their own laments each August and September as hundreds of Catholic students transferred from public to parochial schools. On the opposite page from the story on Corcoran's exhortation, the *Dispatch* featured a sermon from the Methodist preacher Charles E. Locke, who called Catholic parochial schools "non-American" and a "menace" that will "destroy the most splen-did system of public education that the world has seen."[33] In early September 1889, the

Dispatch reported that Father Corcoran's efforts had in fact moved around two hundred students in the Fourteenth Ward to transfer to the parochial school. "The [public school] teachers . . . are viewing with alarm the exodus of Catholic pupils from their school," the article read. "If the attendance drops off it may become necessary to discharge several teachers." Such an event, the newspaper continued, was not unusual. "About one year ago teachers were dropped in the Mount Albion schools for the same reason. When St. Kyrnan's school was opened the Catholic parents withdrew their children from the public school and sent them to Father Briley."[34] "Catholics Want More Room," a *Dispatch* headline declared in early November. The city's Catholics, it appeared, could not expand their parochial schools fast enough.[35]

In the First Ward, the *Pittsburgh Press* warned that the majority of the 127 children of the Duquesne School "will be taken away . . . in November when Father Sheedy's parochial school opens." While the Duquesne School's principal guessed that the opening would cause fifty public school students to depart, the school's former principal and now city superintendent—George J. Luckey—was more pessimistic. "Nearly all of the Protestant families moved out of the ward" to the city's East End, he remarked. "In a year or so from now there will scarcely be a Protestant family in the district." While the majority of the estimated 350 Catholic children in the ward currently attended the public school, the *Dispatch* wrote, "when the new school opens these children will be drawn off, and the public school will be almost depleted." At that point, the school directors would be saddled with an empty edifice that might potentially be a worthless asset, a "school building on their hands with no way of getting rid of it," as the *Dispatch* put it. Special legislation would be needed to dispose of the school. The First Ward's traditional assets, along with the Protestant families that had first contributed to them, were deteriorating. While the new parochial school did not spur these trends, it certainly accelerated them.[36]

The new St. Mary of Mercy Parish school in the First Ward opened in early 1890 to much fanfare. Three hundred children marched around the parish as Catholic priests sang hymns and sprinkled holy water in the classrooms. One week before George Washington's birthday, Sheedy sermonized on the first president's Christian values. Later in the ceremony, officials read letters from the archbishop of Baltimore, who regretted his absence. Leading the children in song were a group of nuns from the Sisters of Mercy. The Sisters would work as the school's teaching force, and they were essential to its survival. Like the thousands of nuns staffing parochial schools throughout the country, the Sisters required barely any remuneration. Low teacher wages allowed parochial schools like St. Mary of Mercy's to keep tuition at $1 or less per month. It allowed Catholic elementary schools to offer a form of private, mass education that rivaled that offered by the public schools.[37]

Shortly after the parish school's opening, the principal of the Duquesne School resigned. The *Dispatch* reported that "while there was no danger of his being dropped for the present, the directors felt assured that it would be only a matter of time until there would be no need of the services of a principal." With only three teachers remaining, "it will not be necessary to elect any person to his place."[38] A dwindling one hundred

children remained in the public school, around a third of the parochial school's attendance. In 1892 the school closed, reopening a year later with a mere twenty-nine students.[39]
In the 1860s, when the Duquesne School was at its height, it was inconceivable that a
public school could face this type of competition. By 1890, such competition among
schools for Catholic pupils was impossible to ignore.

The events in Pittsburgh were emblematic of broader national trends in American
Catholicism and national politics. The timing of the controversy surrounding St. Mary
of Mercy's parish school was no accident, coming in the midst of a longer, broader, and
transnational nineteenth-century revival of Catholic religious fervor. The nineteenth-
century revival, like earlier incarnations since the Protestant Reformation, was a Jesuit-
initiated, Vatican-centered movement encompassing a variety of methods and goals, each
one intended to beat back the assault on Catholic power by Protestants, secularists, and
liberals in Europe and elsewhere. In the United States, Roman-trained American bishops found common cause with a large group of Jesuits fleeing Europe from the political, and often anticlerical, upheavals of 1848. Together, these groups emphasized respect
for church hierarchy and a commitment to "ultramontanism": looking to the unifying
authority of the pope in Rome rather than to the unique expressions of Catholicism
within and outside of the borders of the nation-state. The nineteenth-century Catholic
revival was responsible for new organizations, institutions, and professions—youth
groups and schools, teachers and writers—but had less tangible effects as well. American
Catholics brought to their churches and their lives a renewed and more intensive piety,
one filled with beliefs in miracles, apparitions, and the suffering Jesus of the Passion.[40]

Parochial schools stood centrally within this vision of a revitalized Catholicism.
Beginning in the 1840s and continuing through the decades following the Civil War, the
Catholic bishops of New York (John Hughes), Cincinnati (John Purcell), and Rochester
(Bernard J. McQuaid) dedicated immense resources to building Catholic schools within
their dioceses.[41] In the wake of several dramatic confrontations between Catholics and
Protestants over prayer and Bible reading in public schools—including, most notably,
riots in Philadelphia—Catholic bishops assumed increasingly hostile stances toward
state education. They urged parishes to construct parochial schools and sought to persuade state legislatures that those schools should be funded with public tax dollars. This
emphasis on Catholic education reached a climax with the 1884 Third Plenary Council
of Baltimore. While the bishops at the Third Plenary Council addressed a whole range of
issues facing American Catholicism, a full quarter of the Council's legislation dealt with
matters of Catholic education.[42] The bishops linked parochial schools to the future of
American Catholicism. They decreed that every Catholic Church must organize a school
and, with several noted exceptions, that every parent send their child to it.[43] Within a decade of the Third Plenary Council, Catholics had expanded parish school buildings and
attendance numbers by over 50 percent, with nearly 800,000 children—the majority of
them the sons and daughters of working-class first- and second-generation immigrants—
enrolled in close to 4,000 parochial schools.[44]

These decrees from above combined with Catholic immigrants' demand from below to invest in Catholic education. Catholic attendance in parochial schools increased exponentially even while, to the hierarchy's chagrin, it was never universal. Particular Catholic parents chose to enroll their children in parochial rather than public schools (or vice versa) for complex reasons. Many parents believed their children's attendance in Catholic schools aligned them with God, the Catholic hierarchy, or their religious and cultural heritage. Still others compromised, sending their children to Catholic school until they received First Communion, before transferring them to public schools or into the labor market. Spatial considerations also mattered. Some parents lacked easy access to a parish school because of where they lived; better to enroll their children in proximate public schools than risk their health by sending them over railroad tracks and rivers. A range of other, more personal and idiosyncratic considerations also influenced these decisions.

Generally, however, the most significant barriers to attendance in private schools were cost and geography. Cities with large working-class Catholic populations in the late nineteenth century were also sites of low wages and economic depressions. Unemployment skyrocketed to roughly 25 percent in the years after the panics of 1873 and 1893. In response to these economic realities, parishes like St. Mary's in Pittsburgh kept tuition down to remarkably low levels. In larger, more established parishes, general church coffers could remove the need for any tuition at all, or provide grants to parents who could not afford it. These policies helped parochial schools grow in hard times, but competing with public schools on cost would always be nearly impossible. For working-class parents making $400 or less annually—particularly those with many children—tuition charges could amount to a significant percentage of the family's annual income. Many parents chose to send their children to public schools or to the workplace and to save their money for expenditures on other goods.[45]

The range of spiritual, ethnic, linguistic, and geographic identities that composed American Catholicism made any simple characterization of Catholic attitudes toward schools impossible, particularly as Poles, Mexican Americans, Italians, Czechs, Slovaks, and other Catholics entered cities in large numbers beginning in the 1890s. Catholics had a diverse and shifting relationship to parochial schools. Italians tended to enroll their children in Catholic schools at low rates, a result in part of their alienation from centralized, Irish-led dioceses. The demand for Polish Catholic schools, meanwhile, was typically quite high, as the Polish diaspora (the "*Polonia*") strove hard to replicate the language and piety of the old country.[46]

School attendance patterns also varied by locale. Different cities, despite relatively similar demographics, could build parochial schools at highly divergent rates. In New York, Brooklyn, Newark, Philadelphia, and Pittsburgh anywhere between 35 and 60 percent of parishes had parochial schools. Chicago's Catholics educated 50 percent of their children in the parish. In Boston, in contrast, only 12 percent of parishes had a Catholic school in 1880, enrolling 25 percent of Catholic children.[47] Several factors accounted for Boston's divergent Catholic school attendance in the nineteenth century. In a city that was arguably the birthplace of public education in America, Boston's public schools possessed a unique aura that had benefited the city's rising Catholic middle class. Having attended Boston's elite public high schools themselves, they did not share other Catholics' faith or desire that parochial schools compete for Catholic students. The city's bishops, meanwhile, were more reluctant supporters of school-building campaigns than their peers elsewhere. With money perpetually tight, Boston's Catholic leadership preferred to expand Catholic churches. By the latter decades of the nineteenth century, the economic and political ascendance of Boston's Irish Catholics produced further support for public education. Catholics were now graduates, teachers, elected school board members, and even administrators of the city's schools. The city's public institutions thus proved more responsive to Catholic demands, and when they failed to do so, elections would eject offenders from office.[48] While attendance in Boston parochial schools grew more steadily in the twentieth century, evidence of old attitudes remained. As late as the 1940s Catholic public school teachers expressed disdain for how "the increase of parochial schools put them out of jobs" and how enrolling their own children in parochial schools would represent "bit[ing] the hand that feeds me."[49] The Boston case exemplified how a particular urban context could produce a vastly different set of educational preferences.

Native-born public school advocates ignored these ethnic and regional variations in Catholic school attendance, seeing instead only a uniform threat to the dominant Protestant culture. In this context, the battles over single parochial schools in a given city or ward, as witnessed in Pittsburgh, formed part of a broader narrative of public school decline. Throughout the urban North in the late 1880s public officials noted a drop in public school attendance as a result of parochial school construction. The U.S. Commissioner of Education, Nathaniel H. R. Dawson, dedicated a year to determining why public school attendance and the proportion of enrollments had dropped over the previous decade.[50] With parochial schools threatening enrollments, public school authorities often reacted bitterly to Catholic education. At an 1889 conference of national school superintendents, one prominent Catholic school critic asked his colleagues, "Has the parochial school proper place in America?" The response from several prominent conference speakers was a definitive "no."[51] At the same meeting Wisconsin's state superintendent of public instruction told a Catholic archbishop that parochial schools had become threats to the public school system and that the Catholic Church "must not put itself or its parochial school across the legitimate pathway of the state, and obstruct its progress."[52]

This perceived threat to public education had broader political reverberations. Within national politics, public schools by the 1870s had become inextricably tethered to the Republican Party, which since its founding had been composed almost exclusively of Protestants. The party responsible for Union victory, slave abolition, and national Reconstruction, Republicans were politically dominant in the early 1870s, especially in federal politics. Public schools stood near the center of their ideology. Republicans believed that public schools could unite a nation reeling from conflicts produced by the Civil War, Western expansion, and mass immigration. In the South, schools would instill whites' loyalty to the Union and ensure African Americans' ascent from slavery. Out West they would assimilate Native Americans into European-American values and practices. And in the North they would transform impoverished European immigrants, most of whom were Catholic, into productive American citizens.[53]

By constructing parochial schools, immigrant Catholics threatened the Republican Party's program. The *Harper's Magazine* cartoonist (and German-American Republican) Thomas Nast captured these perceived threats well, illustrating the frequently anti-Catholic timbre behind Republican, common school advocates' rhetoric throughout the decade. In an 1870 cartoon, he depicted a group of foreign and sinister-looking Catholics firing on an island with a common school on it. "Fort Sumter," Nast titled his cartoon, connecting in his readers' imaginations the battle for national unity, common schooling, and anti-Catholicism.[54]

The product of these recriminations was a divisive cyclical process. More Catholic parochial schools produced more anxiety among Protestants, fueling greater anti-Catholic sentiment and, in turn, louder calls among Catholics for their own schools. Catholic leaders also kept a close eye on liberal European governments seeking to separate church and state and cripple the traditional power of the Catholic Church. The 1871 Paris Commune, the 1879 Ferry Laws under the French Third Republic, and the

Thomas Nast's anti-Catholic cartoon, satirically titled "Fort Sumter," depicting an assault on a public school captured both Republican commitments to union and their fears of private schooling.
Harper's Weekly, March 19, 1870

1879 Humbeeck School Laws of Belgium each sought to remove the church's influence from schools in unprecedented ways. Thus, Catholic educational authorities wondered whether American Catholic schools would soon also be under siege.[55]

On this national stage, battles between Catholics and Protestants over school politics represented a true culture war. Readers of Catholic and Protestant periodicals in the 1870s and 1880s encountered long, passionate diatribes on public and Catholic schooling. To Catholic writers, public schools were "anti-Catholic," "Protestant," or worse, "godless." To Protestants, Catholic schools were "Romish" and "foreign." In this volatile climate, nearly every major issue of the 1870s became grafted onto battles between Catholics and Protestants over schools. Protestants, for example, associated Gilded Age corruption and urban bossism with New York City mayor William M. Tweed's support of public funding for parochial schools. The politics of Reconstruction, too, entered into these debates. Several prominent Northern Protestant Republicans evoked the horrors of Southern legal racial segregation in their attempts to promote common over "sectarian" schooling. Only through public schools could the North avoid the kind of caste system featured in the South, they asserted. Behind every area of American public life, it seemed, lay a symbol of Catholic–Protestant enmity.[56]

Religious conflicts over schools migrated seamlessly into federal politics. Beginning in 1875 and 1876, the Republican Party rallied around a proposal from Ulysses S. Grant and Maine Senator James G. Blaine to add an amendment to the federal constitution that would bar public funds for religious schools. The amendment was widely perceived in the press to be aimed at Catholics, who ran the largest system of religious schools in the nation. The public school advocates who would go on to testify at Senate committee hearings over the subsequent decades in favor of the amendment did little to alleviate this suspicion, referring to parochial schools as a "menace" to public education, for siphoning off both students and, absent the proposed amendment, public funds.[57] While Catholic schools rarely received direct taxpayer dollars, Protestant Republicans viewed the Blaine amendment as a way to permanently foreclose any potential political and financial ties between urban Democratic political machines and Catholic voters. When the amendment consistently failed to pass the Senate, Republican-controlled state legislatures took up the call instead. By 1876, fourteen states had enacted legislation or had amended their state constitutions to prohibit public funding of religious institutions; by 1890, those measures stretched to twenty-nine states. Preventing Catholics from having access to public funds, Republicans believed, would severely curtail efforts to build up robust parochial school systems.[58]

To Catholic hierarchs, the Blaine amendments represented an anti-Catholic attack on their schools. Several claimed that the United States was on its way to establishing a dangerous, secular "state monopoly" of education that paralleled European governments' attempts to constrain the influence of Catholic schools. For these Catholic officials, state control of education summoned the same set of fears that drove Protestant

Republicans' mistrust of Catholic schools: each was an expression of antidemocratic sentiment and a corruption of American values. To one Jesuit commentator, writing in the *American Catholic Quarterly Review*, the battle between the state and parochial schools was nothing less than a "struggle . . . between individual, domestic, and religious liberty on the one hand, and State monopoly of education on the other."[59] These types of remarks drawing stark ideological contrasts between Catholic and public schools were common in American periodicals during the 1870s and 1880s. Amid this backdrop of Catholic–Protestant enmity, Catholic school construction proceeded apace, transforming American urban education in the process.

Stories of parochial school construction and competition similar to Pittsburgh's appeared throughout the United States in the 1870s and 1880s. In school reports, evidence of their effects typically would yield a sentence or two. In Cincinnati, the superintendent noted the Third Plenary Council's effects in 1889, writing that "there has been an increasing pressure upon parents to induce them to send their children to parochial and other church schools," resulting in a "falling off in the number of pupils attending the [public] schools." The Cincinnati data suggested the movement from public to private schools was most dramatic "in the districts where . . . new parochial schools have been established."[60]

In the industrial cities surrounding Boston, reports of Catholic school building in the wake of the Third Plenary Council created significant conflict along religious lines. The Catholic leadership of Waltham, Massachusetts, finally realized its goal when a large parochial school opened in 1888. The sudden rush of 800 Catholic students from the public schools into the new parochial school attracted national attention. Newspapers reported that public school attendance had been reduced by more than one-third, closing two schools in the process. "Children then had to be transferred, and teachers discharged," announced the *New York Times*. Such events produced noticeable tensions in the town: "The Waltham school system is in a demoralized condition, and the Protestants are not inclined to look with favor upon the parochial school which has caused the trouble."[61] As school committee elections approached in late 1888, newspapers elsewhere reported scores of new Protestant voters—women, in particular—fighting off what they deemed "priestly encroachment on the public school domain." As the *Boston Evening Transcript* reported, "the beginning of the movement of the sudden waking up of the women of Waltham to the value of the school committee franchise . . . dates from the opening of the great parochial school."[62] Catholics no doubt responded that parochial school building represented the very opposite of encroachment on public schools, but the broader context mattered: the events in Waltham mirrored patterns occurring throughout the cities that ringed Boston. The specter of emptying public schools occasioned impassioned feelings and exacerbated longstanding tensions between American Catholics and Protestants.

In these smaller urban areas, the erection of a single school could have dramatic effects on town-wide public school enrollments and jobs. In the industrial city of Malden,

Massachusetts, the opening of a large parochial school in 1881 attracted close to 500 students, requiring several public schools to be closed and teachers dismissed. When the public schools opened in September 1888 to continued diminished attendance, their proponents charged the parish priest with coercing Catholic students. "Intimidation of Public School Children," a headline in the *Boston Evening Transcript* read.[63] The *Chicago Tribune* even covered the story, adding that "when the public schools opened this morning . . . many of them showed scanty attendance." As was the case seven years earlier, the parochial school's opening had repercussions for the public schools. "This action of the Catholic parents will necessitate the closing of some of the schools there probably, as at Waltham," the *Tribune* commented. Newly opened parochial schools were becoming a news sensation.[64]

The fallout from parochial school construction even tore apart a school committee in one city. In Woburn, ten miles north of Boston, the construction of a new parochial school in 1884 resulted in 300 students leaving the public schools. The school board splintered over whether to consolidate the public schools, given the diminished attendance. A majority of the board felt such a course, while necessary, should only be practiced minimally so as not to "disturb the efficient running of our schools." A vocal minority disagreed. With fewer students attending the same number of schools, the minority—pushing for consolidation—alleged that the board was left exposed "to the charge of extravagance." When the board's majority discovered that the minority planned to publish their comments in a dissenting report, they approached the local publisher and forbade him from printing it. Parochial schools had torn a school board apart. The political fallout of new parochial school construction could be enormous.[65]

Far from New England, conflicts over ethnic identity dominated the politics of parochial school construction. Catholic immigrants from non–English-speaking nations placed an enormous value on preserving their cultural and linguistic traditions from the presumed assimilationist emphasis of American public schools. European Catholic immigrants from Germany, Poland, Italy, Slovakia, and elsewhere also refused to assimilate into the predominately Irish-led and English-speaking American Catholic church. Instead, they constructed their own parishes, with their own priests conducting church services in their own languages. For centuries in Europe, Catholic parishes had been defined by geographic boundaries, but the diversity of American cities belied attempts to impose such territorial designations. Catholic immigrants sought and largely succeeded in superimposing their own ethnic parishes onto preexisting Catholic parish boundaries.

In Chicago, the nation's most diverse Catholic archdiocese, a patchwork of ethnic "national" churches coexisted alongside the traditional English-speaking (and increasingly Irish-led) "territorial" parishes. Within these national churches, the language of the old country filled priestly sermons, devotional practices, and dozens of parish societies. Foreign-language schools, meanwhile, served as central ethnic institutions, capable of meeting immigrant groups' distinctive ethnic demands more effectively than the local public schools. Ethnic Catholic schools offered instruction in foreign languages, in addition to teaching about the history, culture, and devotional practices of the mother country. Half of Chicago's Catholic school students attended national parochial schools: German, Polish, Bohemian, Lithuanian, Slovak, and others.[66] In 1886, the *Chicago Tribune* noted that only 10 percent of the city's Polish-American schoolchildren attended public schools.[67] In the 1870s it was estimated that 80 percent of German Americans in St. Louis attended German-language private schools.[68]

Public schools struggled to attract immigrant parents away from the allure of ethnic parochial schools. When the Chicago school board refused to adopt German-language instruction in 1879, the result was a mass exodus to parochial schools. As the German-language *Illinois Staats Zeitung* reported, one local public school "has practically no attendance, while the neighboring parochial and private schools, which teach German, are crowded—and in these institutions there is no free tuition!"[69] Many immigrant community leaders resisted public school attendance even when those schools did offer foreign-language instruction. When Milwaukee Poles attempted to introduce Polish-language instruction in the public schools, they faced opposition by their own parish priests, who advised the school board that "[we] know that the above measure will be of no advantage to us, as we now have all necessary facilities for learning our language."[70] Luring immigrants away from their national parishes and schools proved exceedingly difficult.

Public officials tried nonetheless to attract immigrants to public schools, frequently by adopting several of the distinctive features of ethnic schools. In Washington, DC one member of the board of trustees recommended in 1873 introducing German into the public schools in order to "mak[e] German schools superfluous" and "make [public schools] attractive for the whole population, so that they will predominate over all private schools."[71] Likewise, in Cleveland, the public schools attempted to reform their own curricula in order to remain competitive. "Were the people dissatisfied with their [public] school, they would send their children to private schools, which is always the first remedy to suggest itself," Cleveland's public school superintendent, Andrew Rickoff, affirmed in 1876.[72] Thousands of German immigrants living in Cleveland in the 1850s and 1860s had done just that and enrolled their children in German-language private and parochial schools. By 1870, the city's school board began promoting German instruction in the public schools, in large part to siphon German-American children away from private alternatives.

In the decades that followed, officials in Cleveland frequently boasted about the competitive advantages that accrued to the public schools once German was introduced. In a city where one in three children attended church schools throughout the 1870s and 1880s, adopting the very methods that made private schools attractive in the first place promised vast dividends. As Rickoff explained in 1874, Germans "think they can do better for the preservation of their peculiarities by founding and maintaining private Schools." Why not, then, coopt some of these peculiarities? "That the Public Schools are free is not sufficient to draw the German children into them," said Rickoff's successor in 1886; only the addition of German-language instruction in the public schools could induce large transfers from private schools. By 1887, the president of the school board triumphantly attested that "many parochial and private schools have been largely abandoned, and the German-American now shares in common with the Anglo-American ... the privileges of a common popular education."[73]

But the reality was more complicated. The extent of a massive German migration to public schools in Cleveland was difficult to quantify precisely; based on their own statistics, the public school officials appeared to exaggerate. Eight years after German-language instruction had been adopted in the public schools, the percentage of children enrolled in church schools had fallen only 1 percent. To the consternation of many Protestant public officials, parochial schools consistently proved attractive to immigrant families.[74]

These conflicts over private schools were neither universal nor inevitable. Many places outside of the major Northern industrial cities featured various attempts at public–private cooperation, precisely the kind of reform that Pittsburgh's First Ward school board members had implemented in renting out their public school space for Catholic use. The most heralded local cooperative arrangement began in Poughkeepsie, New York, in 1873, soon publicized nationally as the "Poughkeepsie Plan." There, the city's school board arranged a deal with the local priest to lease the Catholic school building. Public tax dollars would pay for Catholic teachers and, in return, these new Catholic "public" schools would be required to follow public school rules and regulations, which included limiting religious instruction to after-school hours. Catholic officials agreed to similar plans in nearly two dozen small cities throughout the North in the 1870s and 1880s. For school boards, consolidating parochial schools within the public system had the benefit of attracting Catholics to public schools, eliminating the expenses for new buildings, and diminishing the disruptions imposed by educational competition.[75]

In a period in which distinctions between public and private education were hardening, and competition between public and private schools was increasing, the Poughkeepsie Plan represented an alternative path motivated by cooperation. Yet, it was precisely the plan's attempt to blur conceptions of public and private that led to its defeat. As in Pittsburgh, Protestant periodicals abhorred the use of public funds for Catholic schools. Even though these arrangements precluded religious instruction during school hours, public money would still go toward paying for Catholic teachers—nuns in religious garb—in schools attached to Catholic churches. Furthermore, critics of Catholic education reasoned, these arrangements incentivized attendance in Catholic "public" schools by guaranteeing free tuition. State school officials, meanwhile, often felt that these local arrangements undermined the goals of public systems. Many Republican state superintendents of public instruction, such as New York's, viewed their mission as fulfilling Horace Mann's vision of common schools. Public education simply could not be "common" if it employed teachers in religious garb. "Public" schooling entailed a degree of uniformity—and, increasingly, secularization—in education that the Poughkeepsie Plan made impossible.[76]

The Poughkeepsie Plan proved even more controversial within the American Catholic Church. German Catholics declared that, by agreeing to public school rules and regulations, these reforms would imperil their ethnic curriculum and independence. Conservative Catholic archbishops, meanwhile, refused to compromise the religious nature of their schools by marginalizing Catholic education to after-school hours. When John Ireland, the liberal archbishop of Saint Paul, Minnesota, proposed the Poughkeepsie Plan in two small Minnesota towns, conservative Catholic hierarchs reacted furiously. The ensuing "School Controversy" over Ireland's plan, lasting between 1890 and 1893, featured intense national debates and, ultimately, the pope's intervention. When the dust had settled, America's conservative bishops appeared victorious. Ireland's school plan in Minnesota, like the Poughkeepsie Plan, failed when state officials squashed the local arrangements.[77]

As the Poughkeepsie Plan suggested, the divide between public and private in education was never inexorable, nor universal. While clear distinctions had hardened in America's coastal and Midwestern cities, elsewhere the divide was blurred. In poor, rural areas many late-nineteenth-century schools maintained market-based elements of the early nineteenth century: "public" schools that received various forms of private parental investment. In Louisiana, for example, the public school term lasted for five months. Parents who wanted their children to be enrolled for longer periods relied on private contributions to do so, turning a "public" school into a temporary "private" one overnight.[78] In other rural areas the divide between public and private barely existed at all. In farming communities with homogeneous Catholic populations, "Catholic-public" schools, funded with tax dollars, with nuns as teachers and crucifixes on walls, remained well into the twentieth century.[79]

Vague boundaries between public and private education were especially common in the South and Southwest, products of new public systems, racial oppression, and Hispano-Catholicism. In the years immediately following the Civil War several Southern cities established enduring financial relationships between the public treasury and Catholic schools that were similar, albeit less heralded, than the Poughkeepsie Plan. From the 1870s and 1880s to the first decade of the twentieth century elementary school students in three cities in Georgia—Savannah, Macon, and Augusta—had the option of attending tax-funded Catholic schools. While these arrangements reflected the power of particular local Catholic communities, along with the political skills of Savannah's bishop, Augustin Verot, they also spoke to the revolutionary impulses of Reconstruction, where school systems were created anew under Republican-led state constitutional conventions.[80] Savannah's public officials, for example, believed that public funding and oversight over private schools were essential to avoiding a "retrograde" move back to when schools were "conducted as private enterprises" before the war.[81]

The line between public and private was similarly blurred for African Americans in the South in the decades following the Civil War. Black Catholics fought for access to parish schooling in Catholic population centers like Baltimore, Louisville, and New Orleans.

Outside of New Orleans, however, Catholic parishes in the 1870s and 1880s were formally segregated and black Catholic communities often lacked the resources and religious teaching orders to establish their own parochial schools, especially as resources for public schools and Catholic Church buildings became greater priorities.[82] Estimates from the 1880s suggest that only around 2,500 African Americans attended Catholic schools throughout Southern dioceses. Catholic commentators acknowledged that Protestant missionary organizations far more zealously provided private religious education for African Americans.[83] Unlike European immigrant groups, black attendance in traditional Catholic parochial schools was limited.

The vast majority of African-American schoolchildren, instead, attended institutions that frequently bridged the divide between public and private. Among the earliest schools that sprang up to educate emancipated African Americans in the 1860s were privately operated and financed, initiated either by local African-American communities or entrepreneurs.[84] Even after Northern philanthropic and Southern tax dollars began flowing toward "public" segregated black schools, the amounts were never adequate. African-American families frequently had to contribute their own time and donated money to maintain their schools. Because Southern white officials frequently diverted public money legally entitled to African-American schools toward white schools, blacks rightfully complained of being subjected to "double taxation": once directly by public officials, and then again indirectly by blacks themselves in order to fund their schools sufficiently.[85] While Southern whites could boast of attending fully tax-funded schools, African Americans, therefore, rarely could. The public–private hybrid schools African Americans created marked a sharp contrast with the more defined boundaries between public and private that characterized the North.

In the Southwest, finally, nonsectarian public schools took nearly a century to emerge. The Catholic, Spanish-speaking character of New Mexico's population produced close associations between church and schooling. When U.S. officials first entered the recently acquired territory in the middle of the nineteenth century they encountered schools that long had been influenced by Catholic priests from Spain and Mexico. In response, as early as the 1850s territorial officials began cooperating with the Archdiocese of Santa Fe to provide formal schooling. The territorial legislature included the bishop of Santa Fe as an ex officio member of the first board of education, and in addition provided public funds for Catholic schools. Statehood and revised state constitutions gradually chipped away at most, but not all, of these close connections between public education and the New Mexican Catholic Church. As late as the 1940s, for example, public schools in several areas of New Mexico still employed dozens of Catholic sisters.[86]

While the divide between public and private was never uniform, the trends were nonetheless clear. The fluid boundaries between public and private that characterized many areas of the country had little chance of surviving in a nation whose politics and demographics were pulling it toward two competing school systems, one public and one Catholic. The rise of Catholic schools, one of the most unexpected and dramatic developments of the late nineteenth century, imperiled the very mission of common schooling. In 1890, no one knew how this competition would shape the future of American schooling. "Has the public school system reached and passed its maximum phase in the North and West?" the U.S. Education Commissioner, Nathanial Dawson, asked in a report.[87] Advocates of public schooling feared that the explosion in parochial school attendance represented a future where the common school ideal would disintegrate, pulled apart by the conflicting demands of differing ethnic and religious identities. Catholic authorities, meanwhile, envisioned that in a country dominated by Protestantism and public education, parochial schooling would become harassed by the state and its so-called monopoly over children's upbringing. In response to these conflicts, states sought ways to regulate this new educational competition.

3

Educational Regulation

WHEN CATHOLIC IMMIGRANTS engaged in a wave of parochial school construction in the 1870s and 1880s, parish authorities anticipated a devastating backlash. Would states attempt to prevent attendance at private schools, or try to abolish Catholic education altogether? Such questions were not products of paranoia: scholars and school leaders frequently discussed public schooling as a "natural monopoly," most effectively governed when operated without competition. Anti-Catholicism, meanwhile, remained a latent strain in American politics and society, migrating into both Republican Party policies and popular beliefs that Catholic schools were a threat to American government. As Catholics embarked on their school-building campaign of the late nineteenth century, they faced the possibility of public laws that could restrict their growth.

Although these regulations occasionally materialized, more often than not the opposite occurred: public policy in these decades helped expand Catholic school attendance. States did increase their oversight of parochial schools, yet, far from opposing these new public policies, Catholics welcomed them. The very same regulations that restricted private schools' religious and institutional autonomy also enabled their access to valuable public funds. Beginning in the 1870s, parochial school advocates first in Rhode Island and then Ohio accepted, and indeed fought for, forms of public regulation in return for maintaining an important fiscal subsidy: the property tax exemption. Catholic educators elsewhere echoed these sentiments, arguing that their private schools served a public purpose and so were deserving of the public subsidies—and public regulation—that came with that legal designation. While many Catholic school authorities feared state oversight, they invited it nonetheless, knowing that such regulation was essential to financial solvency.

These attempts by Catholics to secure public subsidies in return for public regulation reflected a broader effort to blur legal distinctions between public and private over the course of the nineteenth century. What were the boundaries of state regulation? Could an institution run by a private religious corporation be eligible for public funds? Schools were frequently central to the legal debates over these questions. The Supreme Court's infamous early nineteenth-century ruling, *Dartmouth v. Woodward* (1819), was one such case that focused on a school but had far-reaching consequences for state regulation of private corporations, generally. *Dartmouth* pointed to a future where public institutions would be regulated by states in exchange for public money, while private institutions would be substantially free from state regulation, in return for forgoing access to public subsidies.

While this arrangement functioned well for the minority of wealthy private schools that did not depend on public money, it threatened the vast majority of poorer religious institutions for whom public subsidies were essential to survival, including Catholic parochial schools. Catholics in the second half of the nineteenth century thus fought to receive public financial support in return for public regulation. As a result, they desired to be treated as "public" institutions under the law. Courts generally obliged, gradually shifting from the starker contrast between public and private established in *Dartmouth*, and in doing so granted public bodies significantly greater authority to regulate private actors. Legal disputes over public and private schools did not always cause these broader changes, but debates about education were nonetheless central to new conceptions of public regulation.

The sharp division between public and private schools that emerged in the nineteenth century was a legal innovation. Legally, states and localities assumed vast powers to shape schooling at the beginning of the century, regardless of its provider. Their authority stemmed from the ancient basis of common law regulation, the state's "police power," derived from the idea that the sovereign can intervene in the polity on behalf of the safety, health, morals, and general welfare of the people. The police power gave states broad license to regulate children's upbringing and prevent them from encountering harmful influences, including in schools. It also extended well beyond education, suffusing the economy at large. Laws of incorporation in the first half of the nineteenth century transformed private entities into corporate "creatures of the state," created by public acts of state legislatures. Courts treated corporations largely as private or quasi-public enterprises carrying out public functions such as transportation, finance, lighting, and water provision. Corporations, therefore, had few claims to autonomy from state control. Corporate charters enabled state governments to attach numerous regulations to how enterprises operated, limiting their actions to those specified in their charter and reserving state rights of supervision. Under this wide-ranging conception of what constituted "public" activity, states could regulate much of American life on behalf of the "people's welfare."[1]

The Supreme Court's ruling in *Dartmouth* narrowed that broad understanding of public power. *Dartmouth* carved out new legal distinctions between public and private schools, in addition to establishing new rights for private corporations.

The Court's decision, which protected the private Dartmouth College from substantial state regulation, reasoned that Dartmouth's "private" governance outweighed its "public" function; only publicly funded and administered schools merited regulation by the state. In the years preceding the rise of public schooling, the *Dartmouth* ruling helped provide a legal justification for the emerging line between public and private.[2]

The question the court faced in *Dartmouth* was whether the New Hampshire legislature could amend the college's original colonial corporate charter (by installing new trustees) without infringing on the college's constitutional rights under the contract clause. Few legal scholars at the time doubted that education was a clear "public" undertaking. The court's challenge in *Dartmouth* was to reconcile the college's public function with its private operation. In short, the court needed to determine whether a corporate charter had the same binding power as a private contract.

While states chartered all corporations, the appeals courts hearing the case distinguished between the regulation of "private" and "public" corporations. The New Hampshire Supreme Court and the U.S. Supreme Court agreed that private corporations served individuals while public corporations benefited the "common privileges" and "common interest." This bifurcation signified that while states could perpetually amend the charters of such evidently "public" corporations as their municipalities and counties, they had significantly fewer constitutional means to interfere with the property rights of "private" corporations such as banks, insurance companies, and manufacturing firms. As the New Hampshire Supreme Court put it, pithily, "all publick interests are proper objects of legislation." Private interests, on the other hand, had greater autonomy from state regulation.[3]

Whether New Hampshire could amend Dartmouth College's charter thus depended on whether or not the college was a "public" or "private" corporation. Here the New Hampshire Supreme Court and the U.S. Supreme Court differed. Giving two reasons, the New Hampshire court ruled that the college was public and susceptible to such forms of state regulation. First, the justices asserted that Dartmouth's original charter implied that its educational services would benefit all of the state's inhabitants. The charter spoke of the college's purpose as "spreading christian knowledge among the savages of our American wilderness," as well as providing that "the best means of education be established in our province of New-Hampshire, for the benefit of said province." To the justices, these words implied a public purpose. Second, the judges argued that insofar as education was inherently public, "sound policy" would dictate that it should be subject to some form of state regulation. Education "is a matter of too great moment, too intimately connected with the public welfare and prosperity, to be thus entrusted in the hands of a few," the decision read. "The education of the rising generation is a matter of the highest public concern, and is worthy of the best attention of every legislature." Given the public nature of the college's charter and educational purpose, the state had every right to amend its corporate character; indeed, no educational institution, the court implied, could claim immunity from such regulation.[4]

On appeal, the U.S. Supreme Court, in a majority opinion written by John Marshall, agreed that education represented a central public concern but denied that such an interpretation gave states license to perpetually interfere with schools and colleges. Indeed, Marshall contended that treating all forms of education as "public functions" was itself absurd: "Does every teacher of youth become a public officer, and do donations for the purpose of education necessarily become public property, so far that the will of the legislature, not the will of the donor, becomes the law of the donation?" he asked. Marshall held that regardless of how many of New Hampshire's citizens benefited from the college, its charter intended it to serve the charitable interests of its private benefactors. As a private institution, Dartmouth College's incorporating charter represented a contract that could not be unilaterally altered. Its charter was similar to any contract between two private parties.[5] States therefore had substantially less plenary authority to regulate private corporations, whether private schools or private businesses, once they incorporated.

By establishing clear distinctions between private and public corporations, the *Dartmouth* ruling had consequences that extended well beyond schools and charities. Most significantly, it gave private corporations substantial autonomy from government regulation. The ruling had enormous benefits for large corporations that exercised virtual local monopolies, like Dartmouth College, and whose charters were now constitutionally protected. For smaller private entities, however, the implications of *Dartmouth* were more disturbing. A central assumption in John Marshall's opinion in *Dartmouth* was that governmental bodies would exercise public regulation at the peril of private corporations. But if states had no ability to alter the frequently monopolistic charters they had long ago established with particular private corporations—whether for education, transportation, infrastructure, and so forth—private enterprise and competition would never flourish.[6] For Catholic schools, successful competition often required blurring the boundaries between public and private established in *Dartmouth*. Thus did parochial schools in the second half of the nineteenth century seek public regulation as a way to obtain various benefits from the state.

In the wake of *Dartmouth*, it seemed that private schools would receive substantial autonomy from state regulation. When policymakers in the period considered educational regulations, after all, they thought principally of state and local governments' struggle to regulate public schooling. Understanding the eventual attempts to regulate private schools needs to be placed in that context. State oversight of public schools rose dramatically over the second half of the century, though American traditions of voluntary attendance and local control thwarted most efforts by state reformers to impose their will on local educational decision-making. In contrast to European nations, mass schooling in the United States had never been associated with centralized government policy. In rural areas especially, antebellum Northerners generally achieved high rates of school attendance *prior* to any legislation that provided school subsidies and compelled attendance.[7] By 1871, Northern states had abolished the parental tuition payments ("rate bills") upon which public schools long depended, replacing them with local property taxes and small amounts of state aid.[8] This triumph of public financing of schools, however, did not produce dominant, top-down state control over local districts. Local traditions of self-reliance in education were a powerful force in community resistance to centralization.[9]

Nonetheless, state legislatures subjected public schools to hundreds of laws and regulations. Rhode Island's 1882 *School Manual*, prepared by the state school commissioner in accordance with a Rhode Island General Assembly resolution, ran to well over 300 pages. The list of laws passed by the legislature pertaining to schools was enormous, touching on virtually every area of public education. Regulations addressed a broad range of topics: where the permanent school fund could be invested; the amount of money the city of Providence could raise for its schools via property taxes; the methods of tax collection; the composition, elections, terms, meeting schedules, and authorities of the State Board of Education and of local school committees; the maximum annual salary of the State Commissioner's clerk; the duties of the State Commissioner; the permissible amount of state funds to purchase "dictionaries, encyclopedias and other works of reference, maps, [and] globes"; the correct methods of local bookkeeping; the corporate privileges of school districts; the conditions for joining districts; the maximum teacher–student ratios permitted; and the requirements for student expulsions, teacher licensure, and teacher dismissal. The *School Manual* mandated the minimum distance that swine must be kept from school property and prevented school authorities from profiting from their own textbooks. State authority had obviously yielded a surfeit of rules and regulations over public schools.[10]

Individual cities and school districts passed hundreds of additional regulations not listed in these state manuals. State law charged local school boards (called "committees" in Rhode Island) to make "rules and regulations for attendance and classification of the pupils, for the introduction and use of text-books and works of reference, and for the instruction, government and discipline of the public schools, and [to] prescribe the studies to be pursued therein."[11] Local school committees thus set policies ranging from teacher discipline and student misconduct to examination schedules and janitorial guidelines.[12]

Occasionally, local regulations conflicted with state prerogatives, in which case state authorities exercised their legal supremacy. In North Kingstown, Rhode Island, Regulation No. 26 was one such example. The regulation, which the school committee passed in 1852, gave teachers the right to order students to make the daily fires that heated the schoolroom. When parents in the town challenged the law that same year—presumably because it imposed an excessive, if not dangerous, burden on young students—the state school commissioner, Elisha Potter, upheld the "power of the committee to make regulations" but found this particular one too onerous. The state's authorizing statute read that school committees had the power "to make and cause to be put in each school-house, or furnished to each teacher, a general system of rules and regulations for the admission and attendance of pupils, the classification, studies, books, discipline, and method of instruction in the public schools." Potter believed that forcing children to make the daily fires exceeded this authority. If this particular regulation was permissible, Potter wrote in 1853, "we might as well infer a right to require the scholars to cut and saw the wood," which he considered ridiculous. Enforcing this ruling would have been challenging for state departments of instruction, given their small number of employees, but Potter's words were symbolically significant: even such a relatively minor issue as school heating allowed state commissioners like Potter to exercise their authority in regulating schools.[13]

Public regulations over private schools in the 1850s were a different matter, over which Commissioner Potter, like the Supreme Court justices in the *Dartmouth* decision, did not believe public administrators had much, if any, authority. School manuals outlining state education laws in the 1850s and 1860s generally said little about private schools. Potter explained the reasons behind this silence in his 1853 opinion. He argued that public schools were by definition state institutions, not only established by statute but also written into state constitutions. As such, they were institutions where each parent had a "legal right to send his children." While the state could pass laws circumscribing the conditions through which parents exercised this right, local school committees and authorities could not legally abrogate it through their own regulations.[14]

Parents, however, did not possess a similar right to attend those schools operated by private actors. In the private school, therefore, the nature of the contract between parent and schoolmaster differed substantially. "In a private school the teacher has a right to prescribe his own terms," Potter wrote. "The parent who sends children to the school delegates to the teacher the right to govern them according to his own rules, and to punish to a reasonable extent for the violation of them." When public schools violated parental liberties, the parents could rely on their statutory and constitutional rights. However, the options for parents with children in private schools were different: "The remedy of the [private school parent], if he does not like the school or its regulations, is in not sending [her child] to it." The binary applied in *Dartmouth* was apparent in Potter's analysis: private schools would be governed not by states and localities, but by parents acting as consumers.[15]

Potter's generally laissez-faire attitude toward private schools gradually retreated in Rhode Island and throughout the North. This decline represented a response to rising parochial school enrollments. Rhode Island, with its growing Catholic population, became one of the first states to pass laws regulating private schools. The state experienced the effects of parochial school building and educational competition well before its neighbors. Catholic parochial schools there began increasing rapidly as early as the 1850s. In 1851, the Providence school committee lamented that "a considerable diminution of the numbers attending several of the schools has recently taken place by the removal of children of Roman Catholic parents; schools having been provided for them under the immediate supervision of the clergy of their order." Four years later, it again noted that "this apparent decrease in the number of children attending our public schools, notwithstanding the large increase in population," was accounted for "by the fact that several hundred children have been withdrawn to attend upon the Roman Catholic schools."[16] In response to such dramatic developments, anxious legislators sought to curb parochial school expansion and restrict the private sector.

Just as Potter became state commissioner, legislators in the state house debated ways of restricting parish education. In 1853, the same year as Potter's opinion on state regulation, the General Assembly considered a set of compulsory school attendance bills that would have effectively treated all students not enrolled in public schools as truants. In the context of a strong nativist Know-Nothing movement in the state—which also sought to impose the King James Bible on Catholics enrolled in public schools—the bills would have virtually outlawed parochial school attendance. Potter, however, remained committed to his belief that states had little regulatory authority over parochial schools, and he spoke out against these attempts until the bills ultimately died in the state Senate.[17]

With the abolition of parochial schools defeated in the legislature, Rhode Island spent the next thirty years debating how to regulate parochial schools and the educational competition they introduced. Lawmakers ultimately determined that parochial schools performed too important a function to operate autonomously from state oversight. As a result, they attempted to regulate their operations through the existing legal mechanisms. States tended to recognize private schools, and their church sponsors more generally, through two legal channels. The first was through state incorporation laws that, in Rhode Island, gave private entities the ability to take, hold, transmit, and convey specified amounts of property; to elect their own officers; to make "by-laws and regulations" for their governance; and to partake in various other privileges.[18]

The second legal relationship between private school and state was through statutes delineating church property liable to taxation. Various churches had been exempt from taxation throughout American history, dating back to the earliest colonies. In New England, where states had tax-supported, "established" churches well into the early nineteenth century, tax exemption was so commonplace that legislatures felt no need to codify it through written statutes. Only when states began severing the direct fiscal ties between church and government (Massachusetts and its Congregational Church was the last to disestablish in 1833) did legislatures enact laws exempting church property, along with property belonging to governments, educational and charitable institutions, and a smattering of other legal bodies.[19] Rhode Island, like most other states, retained the right to exempt property specified by charter through acts of incorporation.[20]

In the two years following the Rhode Island legislature's failure to pass an act criminalizing private school attendance, lawmakers there succeeded in regulating privately operated schools by amending their tax and school laws. In early 1854 the General Assembly passed a law allowing for inspection of all tax-exempt private educational institutions.[21] Schools that refused such visits would be fined $100 and their tax exemption immediately removed. This "Act to enlarge the powers of the School Committee" was motivated by an attempt to inspect a newly proposed Catholic orphan asylum, and while it, like tax exemption statutes generally, applied to schools run by Protestants and Catholics alike, the nativist context suggested that Catholic parochial schools were the intended targets. The bill's opponents in the House recognized its bigoted, "sectarian" nature. Henry A. Potter, a relative of the State Commissioner, argued that it was "exceedingly unjust to empower [school committee members] to visit Catholic schools" when several of those members were Protestant clergymen.[22] For its aim at Catholic institutions the act soon acquired the name "the Nunnery Bill."[23] If Rhode Island's Catholics wanted the state legislature to charter their religious corporations and receive tax-exempt status, lawmakers insisted that they open their doors to state inspection. The Rhode Island law gave Catholic schools a distinct choice: maintain their fiscal subsidy and a "public" status at the cost of regulation, or refuse this exemption and become legally "private."

Rhode Island's 1854 act tying regulation to tax exemption became a model for other states during the 1870s, when a nationwide financial panic forced legislatures throughout the country to reassess their revenue streams. In this environment, private schools became an easy target to tax. Taxes on urban Northern property owners had already been skyrocketing since the end of the Civil War. Cities built new public schools, constructed sewer and transportation systems, and began to light the streets. As taxes, property valuations, and municipal debts soared, cities faced a growing revolt from their middle classes, who complained of bearing a vastly disproportionate share of the burden. From 1865 to 1875 the number of property owners in the North's thirteen largest cities rose by 70 percent, while taxable valuations increased by 157 percent and taxes by 363 percent. So long as cities relied on taxes on tangible property for revenues, urban property holders felt squeezed, bearing the cost of low taxes on corporations and the wealthy—railroads and corporate leaders were notorious for tax evasion—and absorbing the cost of caring for the non–property-owning poor. As a result, urban tax policy emerged as a central arena of conflict following the 1873 Panic, and tax commissions formed in its wake searched for new revenue sources and reformed fiscal policies.[24]

In state after state, these commissions turned to what they considered low-hanging fruit: the property tax exemptions held by churches, charities, and private educational institutions. Religious exemptions came under particular scrutiny for several different, often overlapping, reasons. Many Republican legislators and Protestant ministers feared the growing ecclesiastical properties held by the Catholic Church, and said as much publicly. Protestant periodicals detailed the ways in which tax exemptions on Catholic property were "starving the treasury of the state," with "disastrous results to state interests."[25] This mixture of fiscal trouble and anti-Catholicism proved a potent force. Regarding efforts in New Jersey, a Presbyterian commentator wrote that "the prime moving cause [of movements to remove church exemptions] is undoubtedly the tendency to enormous accumulations of property by the Romish hierarchy, and the immense advantage which they gain by its exemption from taxation."[26] Secular considerations also contributed to the attack on church exemptions. Legislators in Northern states pointed to proud disestablishment traditions and of state constitutions proclaiming religious freedom. Tax exemption, they argued, was simply tax support by another name. To a number of

Republican legislators, taxing the growing property of the North's increasingly expansive Catholic parochial schools helped accomplish each of these objectives. It could help raise additional revenues, arrest the growth of public school competitors, and sever the privileged financial ties between the state and the parochial school.

Battles over tax exemption demonstrated the fiscal and symbolic significance of parochial schools on municipal government. In the minds of many Protestants, parochial schools competed with public schools for students and for funds. If their tax exemptions continued, each additional Catholic school represented a new building whose land could not be taxed to support the public schools. In his annual message to Congress in 1875, President Ulysses S. Grant implicitly highlighted the connection between public education and religious tax exemptions. He proposed that states be required to maintain public school systems and that "no sectarian tenets shall ever be taught" in any public school. "In connection with this important question," he continued, states ought to make "all church property . . . bear its own proportion of taxation." For Grant, spreading public education went hand in hand with limiting the fiscal privileges given to religious communities.[27]

Others far from federal offices in Washington called for increased taxes on parochial schools to support public education. Public officials commonly complained about public schools' lack of funds to expand, in contrast with growing parochial schools. An alderman from Boston attending a hearing on the city's dire fiscal state complained that public schools did not have "much money"; they "have drifted behind for the last five years" while the "number of parochial schools has increased." "We have got to have new schools, primary and grammar schools, without driving the children out into other schools," the alderman concluded.[28] The *Pittsburgh Dispatch* explained the desire to tax private institutions for public benefit by noting that "as there are a large number of schools in this city of the [Catholic] class alluded to, the tax would make quite an item in the city's tax list." Lawmakers concluded that the fiscal health of cities depended on taxing these schools, which meant removing whatever "public" vestiges they might have, including state rights to supervision.[29]

Rhode Island's experience in the 1870s typified this volatile mix of tax policy and parochial school politics. By 1870, it had the highest percentage of Catholics of any state, roughly one-third of its inhabitants. Irish, German, and French-Canadian Catholic immigrants filled cities like Providence and smaller mill towns like Woonsocket and Warren.[30] To the dismay of local public school officials, many Catholics did not assimilate or send their children into existing public school systems but rather swelled parochial school rosters. Between 1873 and 1886, the number of parochial schools in the diocese nearly doubled to seventeen. By 1880, 63 percent of Providence's Catholic parishes had a school—a number that dwarfed neighboring Boston's 37 percent.[31] The 1875 census enumerated Catholic school attendance at 12 percent of the state's total school population. In Rhode Island's cities, the census reported far higher rates of Catholic school attendance. Over one in five Providence school pupils attended a Catholic school. In Newport, it was one in three. In the Francophone-dominated mill town of Woonsocket, an astounding 44 percent of pupils attended the Catholic schools.[32] Rhode Island's governor, Henry Howard, highlighted the competition spurred by these new schools, noting in 1873 that the "existence of a large number of private . . . schools have [*sic*] done much to draw from the attendance upon our public day schools."[33] In response, city and state officials demanded legislation to restrict parochial school growth.

Whereas the Rhode Island legislature in the 1850s attempted to attach inspections to parochial school tax exemptions, the Assembly in the 1870s sought to eliminate the tax privileges of church institutions. Parochial schools had long been exempt from taxation in the state, falling under the broad designation of "houses for schools, academies and colleges . . . owned by any town, company or corporation."[34] In an 1870 act the Assembly placed a $20,000 limit on the amount of church property exempt from taxation.[35] Four years later, the legislature formed a joint committee to amend the state's tax exemption statute in the wake of the financial panic. In public hearings, the Catholic bishop of Providence argued that the city's parochial schools saved the municipality large sums of money by educating children at no expense to the taxpayer. Other Catholic authorities, as well as several Protestant religious and educational leaders, echoed the bishop's call to maintain the property tax exemptions of churches and their schools.[36]

The joint committee, however, regarded these as minority voices in the state and concluded that the exemptions "should either cease entirely, or at least be checked." Feeling that complete revocation of exemption for churches was too drastic, the committee held that "a due consideration for the wishes of perhaps a majority of the citizens of the State should lead [church leaders] to surrender a *portion*, at least of those privileges and immunities which rest on so precarious a foundation." The committee then proceeded to suggest a compromise, exempting church and private educational buildings but not the land underneath them.[37]

The final bill that emerged from the legislature in spring 1876 differed dramatically from the joint committee's proposal. It maintained exemptions on church land and instead taxed church schools. In mid-March, several legislators—newspaper accounts did not reveal their names—had worked to add the language of "free public" before schoolhouse exemptions, distinguishing state schools from private schools in ways the statute had not done earlier. By the end of the month, private schools ("academies and colleges," as the original statute read) had been removed entirely from the list of exempted institutions in the amended bill. While one state senator, in the words of the *Providence Evening Press*, found it a "reproach to the State to tax educational institutions, whether public or private," the amendment removing private schools from property tax exemption passed.[38] The law applied to all private schools, but parochial schools, by virtue of their large and growing numbers, were the chief targets.

Not surprisingly, Catholic authorities defended their institutions against the new tax. The value of untaxed parochial school property, while difficult to measure precisely, was not trivial. Providence's tax books aggregated church property by parish, meaning that city officials did not list the assessed real estate value of particular parochial schools. In

1875, the city valued St. Joseph's church's property at $29,100, which resulted in a tax of $421.95.[39] Assuming its school was valued similarly (as a percentage of the total church property) as other parochial schools in the state, it would have been taxed at roughly $50, enough to cover the annual educational costs of at least ten children. Such a tax would have diminished, if not eliminated entirely, attendance in some private schools.[40]

When in the late 1870s Providence city officials attempted to enforce the new tax code against the parochial school attached to St. Joseph's parish, the church sued Providence's tax assessors. The church's lawyer, Charles E. Gorman, declared that parochial schools, by virtue of their mass attendance, were functionally public and, subsequently, deserving of both tax exemption *and* state regulation. Gorman was one of the leading Roman Catholic political figures in the state—the first Irish-Catholic to join the Rhode Island bar, the state legislature, and the Providence City Council. In the 1870s he led a movement to amend the Rhode Island constitution, which placed property requirements exclusively on foreign-born voters, most of whom were Catholic.[41] The fight to maintain parochial school tax exemptions formed part of this broader struggle of the state's Catholics to assert their religious, political, and educational rights. Gorman claimed in court that the statute's exemption of "free public schools" included parochial schools, since they were open to all and frequently tuition free. He hoped, in short, to overturn the logic of *Dartmouth* and retain gray areas between public and private where parochial schools could reside.

The Rhode Island Supreme Court, however, was not persuaded. In the 1878 ruling in *Saint Joseph's Church v. The Assessors of Taxes of Providence*, Chief Justice Thomas Durfee retained *Dartmouth's* fundamental distinction between public and private. Later an outspoken opponent of easing access for foreign-born residents to the franchise, Durfee asserted that because parochial schools were not operated by the state and, therefore, not subject to state regulation, they could not be construed as public in the meaning of the statute. "Free public schools," Durfee wrote, "signify the schools which are established, maintained, and regulated under the statute laws of the State." Parochial schools did not qualify and thus were not exempt from taxation.[42] Durfee's opinion abided by the logic of Rhode Island's 1853 parochial school inspection act. Where that law gave public school authorities the right to inspect parochial schools in return for tax exemption, the ruling in *Saint Joseph's* implied that when the legislature removed tax exemption from parochial schools, those schools could no longer be subject to public oversight and became legally "private." To be "public" was to be regulated. The court, ultimately, denied the state regulation sought by the private schools themselves. Ultimately, in response to continued pressure, the state legislature revisited the issue and restored the parochial school tax exemption in 1894.[43]

Similar stories played out in other states, where courts placed Catholic school authorities in the position of defending state regulation of parochial schools in order to maintain tax exemption. In Ohio, as in Rhode Island, Catholic school lawyers fought on behalf

of a regulated, "public" designation. When the 1873 Panic hit Ohio, Republican legislators attempted to place church property generally, and parochial schools specifically,
onto the tax rolls. Again, these efforts, like others aimed at parochial schools, were driven
by a mixture of narrow anti-Catholicism and a broader concern for the commonweal.
Separation of church and state advocates argued, as one Cleveland Republican put it
during the state's 1873–34 constitutional convention, that these exemptions "compe[l]
people—though indirectly—to support places of worship."[44]

While any church or school exemption would affect both Catholic and Protestant
schools, fears of vast "Romish" untaxed property nevertheless inundated public discussions of church exemption in Ohio. By the early 1870s, Ohio was no stranger to controversy between Catholics and public school officials. In 1869 a so-called (bloodless) war
broke out in Cincinnati over the public school committee's resolution to remove Bible
reading from the city's public schools. While the resolution likely originated out of secular
rather than Catholic motivations, the practice of reading the Protestant King James Bible
in public schools had long discomfited Catholics and drawn the ire of the city's powerful
archbishop, John Purcell. And while many pious Catholics agreed with Protestants that
a school without religious instruction was "godless" and dangerous, the city's diocesan
newspaper nonetheless came to embrace the committee's actions. The result was local,
and then national, outrage by Protestants, who claimed that Catholics—not sufficiently
satisfied with their attempts to gain access to public funds for their church schools—now
sought to remove all Protestant influence from the public schools.[45] Given this tense relationship between Catholics and Protestants, attempts to tax Catholic churches produced
legal conflict in Ohio.

The language of Ohio's constitution made taxation of Catholic school buildings legally
feasible. While other state constitutions authorized the exemption of "educational institutions" and "schools," Ohio exempted only "public school-houses." Nonetheless, when
the Hamilton County treasurer began to tax the property of church schools in Cincinnati
in 1874, Archbishop Purcell challenged it in court. The county's lawyers believed they
had a straightforward case and relied on the same kind of division between public and
private articulated in *Dartmouth*. They insisted that the Catholic church and its schools
constituted a private corporation. Unlike the "public" or "common" schools, the government did not administer Catholic education. Equally important, the county's lawyers
argued, "state authorities [lack] any right of visitation or criticisms; so to all intents and
purposes they are private, not public schools." Ohio's parochial schools, in other words,
were private precisely because they were unregulated by the state. As the Rhode Island
lawmakers similarly had insisted, to be "public" was to be subject to regulation.[46]

To preserve their tax-exempt status, Purcell's lawyers, like the Catholic Church's in
Rhode Island, had to contend that, to the contrary, Catholic schools were indeed public. They argued that "public" referred not to the "nature of the title to the property,
but to the character of its uses." Public, they held, signified "open for public use" and

not "owned by the state, city, county, or school-district." The Supreme Court of Ohio's ruling in *Gerke v. Purcell* in 1874 rejected the diocese's claim that parochial schools were "public school-houses" in the meaning of the constitution but decided that they did fall under the exemption for "public charity." The court found that regardless of its private Catholic administration, the parochial schools were open to a broader public, including Protestant students. Under the statute and the state constitution, they asserted, parochial schools qualified as "public" institutions, no different than the private academies and colleges explicitly exempted by statute. Thus, while the court did not go as far as Purcell's lawyers in arguing for the legal equivalency of public and Catholic schools, they clearly placed private parochial schools in a "public" category, chipping away at *Dartmouth*.[47]

Desperate to tax private schools in the state, Ohio Republicans continued to assert the logic of the *Dartmouth* ruling and retain a legal distinction between public and private. Two years after *Gerke v. Purcell*, Cleveland public officials attempted to tax the parochial schools in the city, generating a new lawsuit. The lawyers for the named defendant, the Cuyahoga county treasurer Frederick Pelton, went beyond the arguments made in *Gerke*. They held that parochial schools qualified as neither free, nor public, nor charitable. Moreover, they argued, parochial schools by definition were hostile to the public, "so opposed to the public policy of the state that they are not and ought not to be exempt from taxation." In other words, tax incentives to schools that competed with the public schools contradicted the very idea of state education.[48]

Unconvinced, in *Gilmour v. Pelton* (1887) the Ohio Supreme Court upheld an 1883 ruling by the Ohio Court of Common Pleas of Cuyahoga County that definitively preserved Catholic schools' exemptions. Insofar as the schools were religious in nature, the Court of Common Pleas judge had argued, they could not be against the religious policy of the state—in a religiously neutral nation, there was no such religious policy. Neither could the schools be construed as contrary to public policy insofar as they were private, for "it certainly can not be claimed that it is the public policy of the state that the children of the state shall not receive any education in any other school than in one of the public schools established by itself," the opinion read. "Neither do we think that it can be truthfully claimed that it is the public policy of the state that children shall not be taught religious faith and morals in addition to secular instruction, either in the public or private schools in the state."[49] Parochial schools may be private, but the Ohio judges again sided with the Catholic school authorities in asserting that private institutions fulfilled a "public" function. As the lawyers for the state in *Gerke* asserted, "public" entailed state regulated. The "public" designation kept from Catholic schools by the spirit of *Dartmouth* had been granted.

The same terms of debate recurred throughout the country: *tax-exempt* implied being public and regulated, while *taxed* implied being private and unregulated. In an 1874 Massachusetts legislative hearing on tax exemption, the president of Harvard College, Charles Eliot, contended that church buildings and private schools deserved the same tax exemption as a sewer or public highway. He argued that both performed public services that translated into a net savings to taxpayers. As tax-exempt public institutions, however, Eliot insisted that private schools and church buildings merited some form of regulation. These institutions, as he put it, "must admit the ultimate right of the State to inquire into the administration of their affairs." Once these institutions were taxed like a "private person," they could claim immunity from such "state inquiry." The arguments that private school advocates made on behalf of tax exemption, Eliot surmised, were equivalent to those in favor of state regulation.[50]

Lawmakers seeking to place parochial schools onto the tax rolls insisted, similarly to the lawyers in *Gilmour*, that such schools were rivals with public schools, undeserving of any public recognition or subsidy. In an 1881 Pennsylvania case in which tax assessors challenged Catholic schools' exemption, the state's lawyers argued that the schools were against the "public utility" and "in competition with the public schools."[51] In 1894 a Rhode Island lawmaker argued that "no aid should be given to any school which in any way comes in direct competition with the free public schools."[52] Anti-Catholic legislators believed parochial schools could be limited by starving them of funds. Until the 1890s, legislatures largely wanted to *remove* state oversight of these schools. In the 1870s and early 1880s, parochial school advocates defended the "public" status of their institutions, since it would preserve exemption, even at the expense of regulation.

Catholic arguments on behalf of tax exemption highlighted the extent to which the legal distinctions between "public" and "private," codified in *Dartmouth*, became blurred in the late nineteenth century. State court judges in several states had ruled that private schools were "public" in nature. In that regard, private schools joined a host of other industries that underwent a legal revolution in the late nineteenth century. As part of a broader movement to place large industries under public regulation, federal judges in the 1870s and 1880s held that private railroad and grain elevator corporations similarly were "affected with a public interest" and thus deserving of special tax and regulatory treatment. Some legal scholars and Supreme Court justices lamented this Gilded Age judicial trend, fighting to clarify and maintain distinctions between public and private corporations in order to delineate more assiduously the limits of government regulation. The "public purpose" doctrine, however, lasted well into the twentieth century, defeating any attempt to sustain *Dartmouth*'s divisions between public and private.[53]

A 1908 Supreme Court ruling concerning educational regulation, *Berea College v. Kentucky* (1908), exemplified the extent to which private schools had become vastly more "public," and thus subject to state regulation, since *Dartmouth*. Since the Civil War, Berea, a private, incorporated college, spurned broader educational trends in the South by offering racially integrated instruction on its Kentucky campus. In 1905 the Kentucky legislature passed a law, aimed at Berea, preventing such educational integration. Berea sued, claiming that the state law deprived the school, its teachers, and its students of property without due process of law, a violation of the Fourteenth Amendment. Unlike

Catholic school lawyers in the 1870s, Berea's counsel sought to preserve the spirit of private corporate autonomy articulated in *Dartmouth*. Berea's lawyers argued that "a private school stands upon exactly the same footing as any other private business" and that, therefore, the "right to maintain a private school is no more subject to legislative control than the right to conduct a store, or a farm, or any other one of the various occupations in which the people are engaged." While the Supreme Court in *Dartmouth* had relied on the Contract Clause to protect corporate autonomy, here Berea's lawyers argued that the Fourteenth Amendment placed defined limits around the state's police power.[54]

Yet, in making this case nearly a century after *Dartmouth*, Berea College had entered a very different legal environment, one that, in the previous decades, had benefited Catholic schools by granting them public regulation. In *Berea*, the majority of Supreme Court justices, affirming the Court of Appeals ruling, determined that the college could expect very little autonomy from public oversight. "As a corporation created by this state," the majority's opinion read, "[the College] has no natural right to teach at all. Its right to teach is such as the state sees fit to give to it. The state may withhold it altogether, or qualify it." Ruling on the narrower grounds of the state's right to amend Berea's charter, the Court upheld the law. The deeper meaning of the decision was clear: in the context of state-imposed racial apartheid in Southern public schools and public facilities, privately run institutions that contradicted "public" norms would be forced to reform or shutter their doors.[55]

The response to the majority's opinion in *Berea* looked past racial segregation to focus on the consequences of the decision for state regulation more generally. Here, again, a case about a private school had far-reaching ramifications for the scope of public power. Justice John Marshall Harlan's dissent declared that while states had every right to impose segregation in their own schools, the Fourteenth Amendment protected privately governed institutions from such regulations.[56] While Harlan did not mention *Dartmouth*, the relationship between the two was unmistakable. The *Virginia Law Register* explicitly praised the *Berea* decision for its repudiation of *Dartmouth*. Recalling the race- and class-based populism of Southern intellectual life, the *Register* insisted that their support for the decision was not so much for the "set back it gives the Negrophile, but for the salutary doctrine laid down as to the right of a State to control its creations, the corporations." To the *Register*'s editorialists, no longer would public policy tolerate private "corporate aggression." While the legal autonomy of privately incorporated schools remained murky, state and federal court rulings suggested that they could no longer expect the same autonomy from state oversight that they could following *Dartmouth*.[57]

For Catholic school authorities, however, this increase in state regulation had distinct advantages. The 1870s and 1880s witnessed the initial tradeoffs of regulation for tax exemption, but Catholics continued to cite its benefits in the decades that followed. "All private institutions are, in a sense, public beneficiaries," a Catholic University of America professor wrote in 1916. "By reason of the public service which they discharge, the State exempts them from taxation. It has, therefore, a right to see that they discharge their social function in a proper and reasonable manner."[58] Catholic school authorities feared the effects of state oversight, but those fears did not translate into a refusal to be regulated. So long as property tax exemptions served as an essential state subsidy to parochial school growth, Catholic school leaders were willing to accept state regulation in return. As the growing regulatory state steadily blurred public and private realms, Catholic authorities recognized that public policy could aid, rather than hinder, parochial school growth.

4

Public Policy and Private Schools

ON A COLD January day in 1898, Philadelphia's public school superintendent, Edward Brooks, sent a private letter to John W. Shanahan, the Archdiocese of Philadelphia's Catholic school superintendent. Brooks wanted to discuss Pennsylvania's compulsory school attendance law. Passed three years earlier, it mandated that all children between eight and thirteen years of age attend "day school" for at least thirteen weeks. For public school officials throughout the state, the law was a long-awaited triumph. Brooks was particularly pleased: he had dedicated much of his long career to seeing compulsory attendance laws adopted and now was charged with administering the law in Philadelphia. When he died, the influential New England *Journal of Education* properly called him a "pioneer in compulsory education."[1]

Catholic officials like Shanahan, on the other hand, had good reason to fear compulsory attendance laws as tools to regulate their schools. Although Catholics had welcomed public regulation in the 1870s and 1880s, they feared that compulsory attendance laws represented a different, if not mortal, threat. Republican legislators and school officials frequently admitted their disdain for parish education and its success in luring thousands of students from public schools. Through their annual reports, public officials implored state legislatures to pass stricter laws that would close or dramatically reform the Catholic system. Compulsory attendance statutes enabled these regulations. For the next century, every major law affecting private schools would be layered, like a collage, onto compulsory attendance statutes that dated to the late nineteenth century. Lawmakers who introduced these bills argued that private schools operating with "substandard" buildings and teachers, or instructing in a foreign language, might not fulfill the statutory meaning of a "school." Children attending parochial schools, then, could be considered truants and their parents prosecuted. Pennsylvania's new compulsory attendance law thus placed the Archdiocese of Philadelphia's 115 parish schools and 40,000 students—roughly 40 percent of the city's public primary school population—in legal jeopardy.[2] If truant Catholic children avoided attendance in their parish schools, would public attendance officers place them in the local public school? Would public officials fine Catholic parents? Would they close down Catholic schools that did not meet some unwritten standard?

Brooks's letter to Shanahan, perhaps surprisingly, contained none of these threats. Instead, his message to the Catholic superintendent was simple: Pennsylvania's compulsory attendance laws would not be enforced on students attending Catholic schools in Philadelphia. As Brooks wrote in his letter, the "relation of . . . all Private Schools to the administration of the law is one of considerable delicacy":

> I have instructed the Attendance Officers not to demand anything from these Private Institutions. The law is new and it requires care and tact in its execution, and I have taken great pains in cautioning the Attendance Officers not to give any annoyance to the Private Schools. Of course they will cordially co-operate with the authorities of the public and parochial schools as soon as the law is fully understood.[3]

Lacking the will, let alone the mechanisms, to enforce the law, Brooks privately assured Shanahan that the relationship between parochial schools and public administrators would remain respectful. Attendance laws may have barked at Catholic schools, but in Philadelphia, as elsewhere, they did not bite.

Indeed, despite new attendance laws and heightened anti-Catholic rhetoric, Catholic school enrollments in the United States more than doubled between 1880 and 1900. By the turn of the century, the number of children attending parish schools approached one million students.[4] What explains this discrepancy between Catholic fears of legislative strangulation and the reality of Catholic school growth? Catholic determination to construct schools in spite of threats by public officials was an important reason. Brooks's letter, however, suggests an additional, if not more significant, cause. Even when legislatures passed laws that ostensibly introduced strict regulations affecting private education, those laws did not have a significant impact on the state's relationship with parochial schools. Nor did they negatively affect attendance in these schools. Behind the threats of public laws, in other words, lay the compromises embedded in private letters and tacit agreements between public and private school officials.

Despite all the controversies surrounding state regulations of parochial schools in the 1880s, in practice regulation was loose and enforcement rare. Local school committees rarely attempted to use compulsory attendance laws to shut down parochial schools. The strategy's impotency resulted from both political and economic forces. In the late 1880s and early 1890s, Republican politicians throughout the North staked their campaigns on state regulation of private school curricula and teaching. But legislatures that tried to enforce stricter compulsory attendance statutes encountered opposition sufficiently

fierce to merit either reconsideration or repeal. Politicians who favored such legislation found themselves facing dire reelection prospects. Given the growing numbers of
Catholic voters, together with the fear that hostile laws would produce a single-issue
(Catholic) voting bloc, few lawmakers dared pass or enforce statutes that would result
in a swift backlash.[5] Likewise, in towns where Catholics composed the majority of the
school board, laws that placed an undue burden on Catholic schools simply went ignored
out of respect for communal stability. Legislatures passed laws that elicited ethnic and
religious conflict and aimed to reduce parochial school attendance, but their actions
did not restrict educational competition. Brooks's attention to the political "delicacy" of
compulsory attendance laws was a case in point.

In addition to these political reasons, many public school officials failed to enforce regulations that would lessen the economic benefits of parochial schools. Parochial schools
resembled a release valve, limiting the pressures exerted by compulsory attendance laws
on public systems. As school administrators attested on numerous occasions, parochial
schools relieved overcrowding, lowered property taxes, and lessened the need for new
public school construction. In short, they provided municipalities and states with virtually cost-free classrooms, desks, and teachers. Though public school advocates may have
resented the ethnic or religious values that parochial schools propagated, they recognized
that without them, the quality of public school education might deteriorate, while taxes
would surely rise. Public officials thus self-consciously relied on private institutions,
believing that parochial schools served a crucial, though often obscured, public function.
Once again, arguments about the public nature of private education were persuasive.

Contrary to lawmakers' desires, and Catholics' fears, compulsory attendance laws
did not diminish the numbers of Catholic schools. In Rhode Island and Massachusetts,
Republican politicians' attempts to constrict parochial school growth faced significant
legislative hurdles and implementation obstacles. In Wisconsin and Illinois, Catholics
and Lutherans made swift work of the state Republican leaders responsible for new compulsory attendance laws: they voted them out of office at the first available opportunity.
So long as states compelled school-going without the will to pay for universal public
school attendance, parochial schools would not only be permitted to exist, but would
flourish. As a result, the first major attempts to regulate private schools in the 1880s actually contributed to their expansion.

Compulsory school attendance laws originated in Northern states during the 1870s as
a wedge issue for Republican politicians. Prior to 1867, only Massachusetts had such a law,
but by 1883 legislatures in Vermont, New Hampshire, California, Michigan, Connecticut,
Kansas, New Jersey, New York, Maine, Ohio, Wisconsin, Illinois, and Rhode Island had
passed statutes compelling school attendance. These laws typically mandated that every
child in a given age range—usually seven to fifteen years old—attend school for a period of around three or four months per year. While individual motivations differed,
Republicans generally found that compulsory attendance legislation accorded with their
broader ideas about the role of the state in promoting national growth and unity.[6]

In particular, following the Civil War, the promotion of compulsory school attendance tied the Republican Party's goals in the South with those in the North. In both regions Republicans saw their central governing task as assimilating populations into the greater body politic. In the South it was former rebels and newly freed African Americans; in the North, immigrants. Republicans believed that each of these groups needed to endorse and support public schools as the central vehicle to mold them into effective American citizens and help reunite a fractured nation. Republicans insisted that former Confederate states adopt public school systems for readmission to the Union. In the North, they pushed for laws that criminalized parental efforts to avoid school attendance. Partisan calculations mattered immensely to Republican support of these measures. Republicans believed they could forge a long-lasting national electoral strategy by gaining the votes of all Protestant voters—a proposition that was historically difficult given Southern opposition to the party. A compulsory public school system, Republican leaders believed, could help build a unified Protestant American culture centered on the public school, which would help to peel Protestants away from the Democratic Party in the South and unite them with their coreligionists in the North.[7]

Massachusetts Republican senator and future vice president Henry Wilson articulated the role education should play in the party's aims in a widely read 1871 essay for the *Atlantic Monthly*. With slavery defeated, he wrote, "the Republican Party should accept as one of the living issues of the hour the proper education of the people." Spreading public schools in particular, Wilson argued, was central to peeling away votes from a Democratic Party that preyed on the ignorant, the foreign-born, and the American Catholic. Wilson urged his Republican colleagues in statehouses throughout the country to pass compulsory attendance laws and support a stronger federal role in education. These policies would not only unify and strengthen the nation, but they would work "to the advantage and the permanence of the party itself!" Wilson ended the essay by praising Prussia, a nation that had a long tradition of compulsory school attendance, for its recent victory over the "ignorant, priest-ridden" French in the Franco-Prussian War. Anti-Catholicism was never far from the surface in Wilson's writing, or the Republican Party's rhetoric. Wilson wanted voters across the country to associate public schools and compulsory attendance laws with Protestant virtues and the Republican Party. By the 1880s, the close connection was impossible to miss.[8]

Given their partisan, quasi-Protestant origins, it was no surprise that compulsory school attendance laws would be controversial. But the substance of the laws mattered as well: in no other area of the law did states so powerfully intrude on local educational practices and values. The legislation found its legal basis in the common law doctrines of the police power and the related concept of *parens patriae*, the sovereign's right to act as "the parent of the nation." It was precisely this theoretical replacement of children's guardians by the state that many parents and religious groups found offensive. Traditionally in the nineteenth century parents dictated children's school attendance according to labor opportunities, family economic needs, and individual decisions surrounding the value of formal education. If a father or mother needed or desired a child to work, in other words, that decision was widely perceived as the parent's prerogative. States generally did not grant local school boards the authority to interfere in those family choices, or to punish employers for hiring young children. Compulsory attendance laws drastically changed that relationship. While few people questioned the state's authority to regulate large areas of children's experience within the public schools, compelling attendance therein was a different matter.[9]

Compulsory school attendance, according to critics, broke a longstanding tacit, voluntary social contract between parent and school. It represented a substantial intervention into family life and parental authority. As the *Catholic World* put it in 1891, "here is State interference and State control in matters which had hitherto been considered as within the exclusive right and jurisdiction of the parents," an attempt "to dictate to the family how much and what sort of schooling it must give the child, and where and at what time."[10]

In terms of meaningful public policy, these laws were only moderately effective. They did not produce a revolution in school attendance during the nineteenth century. Northern communities already had achieved extraordinarily high rates of school attendance and literacy, and communities lacked the capabilities, as well as incentives, to pry more children away from the farm, factory, or street. Nonetheless, compulsory school attendance laws ushered in widespread parental protest and evasion. Equally fierce opposition followed when these laws began to regulate private schools as well.[11]

Rhode Island exemplified the controversy introduced by compulsory attendance laws. It was a heavily urban, industrial, and Catholic state, and its patterns of school attendance reflected those educational, ethnic, and religious practices. Debates over compulsory attendance laws in Rhode Island thus often pitted Protestant Republicans against immigrant Catholic parents whose children did not attend school, as well as factory owners who employed child labor. Large enrollments in Rhode Island's Catholic schools also shaped battles over compulsory attendance. Lawmakers debated whether attendance in Catholic private schools could satisfy these new laws, and how compulsory attendance would affect the state's coffers. Ultimately, politicians grew convinced that the key to successfully administered attendance laws lay in regulating parochial schools in new ways.

Rhode Island's compulsory attendance law originated in the 1870s and early 1880s, when state Republicans believed they were losing ground to rivals who had such legislation. That every other Northern state with the exception of Pennsylvania already had such laws made its absence in Rhode Island an embarrassment. Leading opinion makers in Rhode Island joined the crusading state school commissioner Thomas B. Stockwell in calling for compulsory attendance legislation. In previous decades, the state's manufacturing elite had made persuasive arguments that such legislation, by reducing child labor, would harm factory productivity, drive up prices, and harm exports. But as other states proved that successful local economies and attendance laws could go hand in hand, those arguments disappeared. As the Republican *Providence Evening Press* editorialized in early

1883, "if . . . a compulsory education law has been successful in Massachusetts, there is no reason why it should not be so in this state." Indeed, the editorial continued, the state's economic competitiveness demanded it: "We cannot afford to maintain our bad preeminences of having a larger percentage of illiterates than any other northern state," it read. "It will place in jeopardy our industrial standing, since in the fierce competition which has to be met in every kind of business, intelligent workmanship alone will enable us to hold our own."[12]

Other commentators feared that high rates of illiteracy would lead to economic degradation. A late-nineteenth-century commentator familiar with Rhode Island's education laws also found a direct link between the state's lack of a compulsory attendance legislation and its economy. The state, he said, "became an inviting field to parents who opposed these restrictions" since "the want of restrictions in the employment of children in factories brought to the state a large foreign and illiterate population." Rhode Island's original settlers famously had sought religious liberty, but immigrants now, according to this opinion, viewed the state as a safe haven for their ignorance.[13]

Census statistics in Rhode Island confirmed that increasing numbers of children were not attending school, particularly in the state's largest city, Providence. Between 1879 and 1882, the number of unschooled children rose faster—both in relative and in absolute terms—than those in either the public or parochial schools of the city.[14] In 1883, attendance statistics revealed that 14,700 boys and girls in the state, or one in three children between five and fifteen years old, were not in school.[15] As Rhode Island's industries required increasing numbers of workers who could read manuals, engage in mechanical drawing, and do basic arithmetic, the numbers of the unschooled became a significant concern. Much to Rhode Islanders' horror, the 1880 federal census showed that relative to its population Rhode Island was the North's most illiterate state.[16]

When state assemblymen took up a compulsory attendance bill in 1883, Rhode Island's illiteracy rates among Irish and French Catholic immigrants stood foremost in their minds. In 1878, Commissioner Stockwell had successfully urged the Assembly to enact a law mandating an annual census of attendance. Armed with those statistics, Stockwell and other public school officials now pleaded with the Assembly to stem the rising tide of illiteracy among immigrants and to Americanize the foreign-born. "Few people are aware that in some of our largest towns and villages the number of foreign born persons and their immediate descendants far exceeds those of strictly American parentage," Stockwell wrote in 1880. "The key to this whole matter," he continued, is that "this illiteracy is almost entirely confined to the foreign element," the Francophone in particular.[17] Without new laws, he feared, it was only a matter of time until "this State will come into the power of an illiterate majority."[18] With these threats looming, the General Assembly in the spring of 1883 considered Stockwell's law compelling school attendance.

The existence of large numbers of Catholic laboring children raised uncomfortable questions for state lawmakers and local school officials. After all, if compulsory attendance legislation pushed immigrant, Catholic children into schools, would not Catholic parents choose parochial schools? Might not these laws spur further parochial school construction? Cities like Woonsocket suggested that such a reality would be immediate. By 1882, the city's 7,000 Francophone millworkers maintained five French-language parish schools. With roughly 40 percent of the student population already enrolled in parochial schools, few doubted that such a number would increase if laws forced laboring French children out of the factories.[19]

The framers of the compulsory attendance bill knew that parochial school attendance was exploding throughout the state. In Providence, attendance in parochial schools had quadrupled in the quarter-century between 1855 and 1879, rising to 2,676 students. Public school attendance also rose, but at less than half that rate. In particular neighborhoods, attendance data suggested that private schools were siphoning off students from public schools. In Providence's Third Ward the number of children attending Catholic schools increased from 11 to 295, while the public schools' population dropped from 1,040 to 807. Long-term trends in some wards showed even sharper patterns. In the First Ward, public school attendance diminished from a high of 1,647 students in 1855, not to regain that level of attendance again until 1887. Over the same period, the parochial school attendance in the First Ward rose from 181 pupils to more than 700.[20]

Rhode Island state officials resented these growing parochial schools. Many of them harbored anti-Catholic and nativist views that spilled over into beliefs about immigrant children and their parishes. Politically, Rhode Island's dominant Republican Party had largely kept the franchise away from immigrants until an 1888 amendment to the state constitution removed property qualifications for foreign-born voters. Apportionment rules favoring rural districts, meanwhile, further skewed representation in the state away from urban areas where the vast majority of Catholic immigrants lived. Because each Rhode Island town was allotted one senator, voters in small towns could have over 200 times the per capita representation as voters in Providence.[21] One indication of Republican power was the governor's office, which the Republicans held for all but two years between 1857 and 1903.[22]

The Republican drafters of the 1883 attendance bill feared a compulsory education law that neglected private schools. Deeply mistrustful of Catholic schools and the parents who sent their children to them, the assemblymen envisioned numerous scenarios whereby immigrants would use private schools to skirt public attendance laws. They might establish parish "schools" that in practice amounted to merely a superficial education: educational facades that might fulfill the letter but not the spirit of the law. Or, even if immigrants actually attended schools, they might receive instruction exclusively in foreign languages and cultures, undermining the Republican Party's assimilationist goals.

To prevent these problems, the committee in charge of drafting the compulsory attendance bill inserted language that placed parochial and other private schools under the supervision of public authorities. The bill mirrored almost every other compulsory education law in the country in mandating that every child between ages seven and fifteen attend a public school for at least twelve weeks (six consecutive). And, like other state laws, its first section listed various ways that a child could fulfill the law without attending a public institution, including if a child attended a "private day school approved by the school committee of such town." Here the Rhode Island law borrowed from neighboring Massachusetts. As early as the 1830s Massachusetts had child labor statutes that required children seeking employment to have attended public schools or private day schools with a "qualified" teacher. In the 1850s they again amended the child labor law to include private day schools "approved by the school committee," and in 1873 similar language of private school "approval" was included in the state's compulsory attendance law.[23] In 1878, Massachusetts attempted to clarify what constituted "approval": private school instruction had to mirror the quality in local public schools and had to be conducted in English.[24]

Rhode Island's law reflected Massachusetts's provisions. It defined "approval" as "thorough and efficient" instruction "in the English language." To quell any fears that the colony founded on religious liberty now persecuted Catholic schools, the lawmakers, also borrowing from Massachusetts, inserted a clause prohibiting school committees from "refus[ing] to approve a private school on account of the religious teaching therein." It was *foreign* parochial schools, not Catholic education per se, that represented the true menace, the bill's framers insisted. In April 1883, the legislature passed the bill into law.[25]

In the ensuing decades, state officials justified the law by referencing precisely the rationale for state regulation that Catholic schools had embraced in the 1870s as they fought for property tax exemptions: that private schools were sufficiently "public" to warrant it. As the State Board of Education wrote in 1897, the "state has assumed the responsibility of deciding who shall practice law, or medicine, or dentistry, within its borders, thus aiming to protect its citizens from being imposed upon. Has not the State an equal responsibility to protect its citizens and itself from being imposed upon in the character and extent of the education which it is proposed to give to the children who attend schools not under direct public control?"[26] A year later, the State Board continued to defend its increased supervision of private schools, claiming that "unless some connection is established between the State and these private enterprises, what means has the State of securing that uniform attendance at school which should be required of every normal child?"[27] According to these officials, states had the same authority to regulate private schools as they did a host of professions and private enterprises. Insofar as they performed a public service affecting the citizenry, parochial schools merited some form of public supervision. As soon as the state began compelling attendance on behalf of the public good, then, every school by virtue of its public nature fell under its regulatory orbit.

The Rhode Island law ushered in muted, though by no means insignificant, protests. Within the assembly, only Elisha Dyer, a Providence Republican and future governor of the state, voiced any opposition to the "approval" language found in the bill. Dyer's move to strike out the language, the *Providence Evening Press* noted, "was defeated by a very large majority." Opposition to the bill was neutered by the leadership of William

P. Sheffield, an imposing presence on the House Judiciary Committee. A Republican from Newport, Sheffield spearheaded the bill through the assembly and made no secret of his particular disdain for Catholics, foreigners, and parochial schools—nor of his belief that the state should regulate them. When the House in 1884 debated a bill that would regulate liquor sales near public schools, Sheffield moved to insert language that included parochial schools as well. Children in those schools will become "peculiarly susceptible to the baneful influence of the grogshops," he commented. When a Catholic assembly-man chastised him for the remark, Sheffield responded (inaccurately, as it turned out) that "the reason the gentlemen cannot see it is because he was brought up in one of those schools."[28] Catholics who viewed attendance laws as attacks on their schools needed only to cite Sheffield's contempt for Catholic education. Many Rhode Island Catholics resented the legislation. According to the Providence superintendent, Catholics feared that the law would provide a backdoor avenue for truant officers to force Catholic children into public schools, exclusively—an interpretation he denied.[29]

Many public school officials, however, did hope to use regulations to close down parochial schools. They believed that immigrant children belonged in public schools, and that state law was one tool to achieve this outcome. The new legal role of the state in eliminating illiteracy among the immigrant population suggested that the bar for an approved parochial school ought to be quite high. As a result, public officials frequently expressed their belief, rooted in a combination of hearsay and inspections, that parochial schools were inferior to the public schools, and that the competition they introduced depressed overall educational quality.

Frank McFee, Woonsocket's superintendent, frequently lambasted the extent of non-public education in Woonsocket, where anywhere between 25 and 40 percent of pupils attended private schools. "Only of five out of eight [children] can we predicate with certainty the quality and quantity of their education, or what they are doing to become good American citizens," he wrote. "We desire … to make the un-American, American; to send out from our schools, not Irish, or French, but Americans." McFee held four "French schools" in particular contempt, claiming they were "crowded all the time," a point he determined "need[ed] re-emphasizing this year and every year until they are provided with better accommodations." "What can parents be thinking of," he demanded, "to allow their children to breathe the foul air of such rooms for six hours a day and eleven months in the year, to have the light, which should strike from the left or the rear, strike directly on the eye, producing near-sightedness or other defects of vision?" For McFee, it was precisely the existence of such substandard private schools that necessitated the sort of legal intervention that the 1883 law permitted. He urged the school committee "to place under the full control of the [school] Committee for four hours a day the French parochial school," under a scheme similar to the famous Poughkeepsie plan. "The Public School for All," McFee titled his report on the subject.[30]

In Warren, another industrial mill town, the superintendent, Benjamin Bosworth, wrote in 1892 that parents sending their children to parochial schools "do not understand the object of the public schools." Fearing that Catholic schools left the state with a mass of unassimilated adults, he lamented that "if these children attending private schools are to remain among us and become, as citizens, interested in our community . . . it is to be regretted that they are not receiving the education and culture the public school affords." The private schools, Bosworth grumbled, were conducted "in a language foreign to our own," particularly troubling since they served a quarter of the town's children. Alluding to the 1883 compulsory attendance law, he urged parents to pay attention "to the laws of the State" that "approve of a private school only when the teaching is in the *English* language." Once the parents became convinced of the public schools' superiority, despite currently "acting in violation of the law, they would at once recognize the duty they owe their children and the community at large." Bosworth, like McFee, saw regulation as a means to shift attendance from parochial to public schools.[31]

These Rhode Island school officials abhorred the competition that parochial schools introduced in large part because they believed it fundamentally antithetical to the meaning of public education. If one of the central goals of schooling was assimilation, a variety of competing schools mocked that ideal. Insofar as ethnic parochial schools gained their popularity from resisting the public school curriculum and clientele, they would continue to breed a dangerous class of people. In 1894, Frank Draper, the school superintendent in Lincoln—a town halfway between Providence and Woonsocket—articulated public fears that the competition unleashed by parochial schools inflicted permanent damage on public education. "The Public schools of our country," he wrote,

if they are to continue, must do so because they are manifestly superior to the many religious and secular private schools which are entering the field and are to prove by no means trifling adversaries to our common schools. For these private institutions represent organized effort towards ends which are widely at variance with, if not directly antagonistic to, the aims of the public schools. The latter seek to unite and assimilate the diverse elements of our school population, and are distinctively levellers of un-American class distinctions, the children of rich and poor, native and foreign-born, meeting upon terms of equal rights and common duties. The former are for sects and classes, and are openly and honestly maintained to perpetuate distinctions of race, creed, or social conditions which their patrons refuse to expose to the atmosphere of the common schools.[32]

To Draper, public education thrived in the absence of educational competition. Draper's ideal of the truly "common school," much like the visions of Horace Mann and the proponents of natural monopoly, precluded alternatives.

Trends in Rhode Island, however, continued to point to more competition, not less. The official Rhode Island school census measured enormous gains in parochial school attendance throughout the 1880s and 1890s. The 1889 report of the Commissioner of Industrial Statistics reflected these fears. More attuned to labor than to educational matters, the commissioner, Josiah Bowditch, was nonetheless charged with keeping track of school attendance, recorded in tandem with the statistics on child labor. In the conclusion of his report Bowditch told the Rhode Island General Assembly that "the rapid spread of parochial schools in our towns is a serious menace to the success and efficiency of our public school system." He admitted that "the Catholics have an undoubted right to establish these schools—as much right as Protestant denominations have to establish religious schools," but believed that Catholic school building would be dire for the state. Like so many other public school proponents in the 1880s, Bowditch feared that unless public schools reformed in some way, they would continue to hemorrhage students to their Catholic competitors. "The numerous changes of Catholic children from the public to the parochial schools is to be regretted," he wrote. "It is incumbent upon us to make every effort to increase the efficiency of our schools, and, as a natural sequence, reduce the grounds of dissatisfaction with them." Bowditch wanted to enhance demand for public schools by making them more attractive to parents. Other lawmakers in the state clearly disagreed, believing that laws should limit the supply of parochial schools.[33]

Given the venomous rhetoric expressed toward parochial education in the state, what accounted for the continued growth of Catholic school attendance? Catholic persistence, along with property tax exemptions, explains some of the story. The subtle role of municipal finances accounts for the rest. One significant reason that local school committees did not ruthlessly prosecute private schools and their parents—despite laws that authorized them to do so—was that the public schools had much to gain from their existence. As Catholic groups ceaselessly pointed out, laws producing parochial school closures inevitably placed additional tax burdens on the public. Each student educated in the parish school represented one fewer the state had to finance, and taxes paid by Catholics also helped the public system. Parochial schools thus provided states and municipalities with an enormous, often unrecognized, subsidy. While estimates of these savings varied enormously and were nowhere near precise, to Catholic parents they showed up every year in the form of their property tax bills and tuition costs. The *Catholic World* estimated that American taxpayers in 1876 collectively saved more than $5 million on the backs of Catholic parents.[34]

To many urban school officials, the specter of Catholic children flooding into already overcrowded public school classrooms posed a graver threat than that of Catholic children attending parochial schools. Tales of drastic public school overcrowding permeated Rhode Island superintendents' reports throughout the 1880s. Localities could not build schools fast enough to accommodate the influxes of children who arrived from the countryside or from across the Atlantic. While public officials were generally delighted by compulsory attendance legislation, they simultaneously expressed concerns about the burdens that new students could impose on the schools.[35] In Providence, the superintendent referred to the prospect of overcrowding as the "dark side of the picture" of compulsory attendance.[36] Numerous pages in his annual reports implored the city to build "enough good schools to supply the demand."[37] When children complied with the laws and attended parochial schools instead of public ones, as many did, local officials realized immediate savings. In Warren, 140 children illegally employed in factories began attending a French-language parochial school after truant officers began enforcing the child labor and compulsory attendance laws in 1893. The town's superintendent lamented the school's operating in "palpable violation of [the] law" against schools conducted in foreign languages, but officials never closed it.[38]

School administrators understood that parochial schools relieved overcrowding and reduced the need for additional buildings. Providence's superintendent remarked in 1887 that "the only thing that should cause delay [in further school construction] is the question as to what the Catholics will do about their proposed parochial schools," adding that "if these are built as has been proposed by them, in every parish, the public schools will be greatly relieved."[39] The city's parochial schools consistently educated between 15 and 20 percent of the school-going population. To have the Catholic truants and child laborers—whose numbers in many wards dwarfed the parochial school population—attend Catholic rather than public schools would save the city tens of thousands of dollars. Not surprisingly, few public officials risked raiding the public treasury by shutting down parochial schools. Over the decade following passage of the compulsory attendance law, state-gathered statistics showed parochial school enrollments expanding at a rate that far outpaced the public sector—a trend brought to a temporary end by the financial Panic of 1893.[40] The fiscal demands of Rhode Island's localities trumped the commands of state laws.

Rhode Island was not alone in this regard. In Massachusetts as well, lawmakers struggled with implementing policies that alienated significant numbers of voters and taxpayers. Massachusetts's private school "approval" laws were rarely, if ever, enforced. Everyone from the Massachusetts commissioner of education to Catholic school advocates agreed that these regulations were a "dead letter," never acted upon and rarely mentioned. For much of the 1870s and 1880s, the law requiring public regulation of private schools went unheeded.[41]

By the late 1880s, however, Massachusetts Republicans began urging public officials to enforce, if not enhance, the regulations. The rise of parochial schools in the heavily Catholic state had sent lawmakers scurrying to find ways to dampen the competition. As concerns about parochial schools multiplied, legislators turned to the idea of strengthening the language in the compulsory attendance statute. In 1888, Massachusetts's governor, Oliver Ames, fired the first salvo in an address to the legislature that reminded lawmakers how much parochial schools threatened public education and weakened the very fabric of the nation. "Within the past few years many children of school age have been withdrawn from the public schools and placed in private schools," he began. "This has been done to such an extent as to cause some alarm. And there is reason for this alarm, for the perpetuity of our Republican institutions depends largely upon the education of all the children together in schools whose instruction is controlled by the State itself." Ames instructed the legislature to address the problem: by "making the public schools so good that all parents will insist on sending their children to them"; by ensuring that private schools have no access to public funds; by executing the existing compulsory attendance law and its requirements that private schools receive "approval" by the local school committee; and finally by amending or enacting a statute to enhance regulations affecting parochial schools. In sum, Ames sought to further Massachusetts's tradition as the nation's leader in compulsory attendance legislation.[42]

Legislators in 1888 answered Governor Ames's call. A special joint committee originally tasked with revising Massachusetts's child labor laws elicited an uproar when it produced a bill substantially revising the state's relationship with private schools. The committee recommended that private schools provide public officials with a list of their pupils and attendance records, that school committees be required to inspect all private schools and pass annual votes approving or disapproving each one, and that all private school teachers hold the same teaching certificates as public school instructors. The draft bill also added enforcement measures. Private schools that did not turn over their attendance records would be fined, the resulting revenues going to public schools. School officials would have full authority to inspect schools, with no prior notice necessary. Should the members of a school committee change their minds and deem a private school substandard, they could at a moment's notice vote to close it down. Through these provisions, the proposed bill sought to build stricter requirements and tougher enforcement mechanisms into the existing regulations.[43]

To the bill's opponents these measures represented the monopolization of education theorized by contemporary political economists. The majority of the bill's opponents argued that its intent was to harm parochial schools and weaken the competition they generated with public schools. The joint committee's lone dissenter, Michael McEttrick, a Catholic assemblyman, made the bill's anticompetitive regulations the focal point of his minority report. He warned against the bill's "tendency to give to the State a monopoly in the business of education" before making sweeping arguments on behalf of educational competition. "There is a competition, friendly, that can be maintained and eminently advantageous between public and private schools," he stated.

> As in the business world it may truly be said that competition is for the good of the community, may it not also say that in the business of education it may have its utility? . . . If you make the one the slave of the other, you throw away the possibility of generous rivalry, which is so beneficial in education and commerce. Competition is an American principle. Monopoly has not yet commended itself to the American people, because it secures its existence by a more or less arbitrary suppression of others' rights and privileges.[44]

Better to have legislation that would "promote fair, free, and friendly emulation between public and private schools," he concluded. Free competition and the rights of parents to direct their children's education became the rallying cry of the bill's opponents, who eagerly expressed their views in the public sphere.[45]

These encomiums to educational competition were not unusual, but rather part of a broader intellectual context in which Catholic school advocates pushed back against economists' attempts to define education as a natural monopoly. While nineteenth-century Catholics generally embraced regulatory measures like minimum wages and unionization, they frequently spoke out in favor of free-market competition within the sphere of education.[46] "Competition is good and healthy; without it education is deprived of its constant spur," editorialized the *Catholic World* in 1879.[47] "As competition is the life of trade, so also of education," a Jesuit priest and educator, James Conway, wrote in the *American Catholic Quarterly Review* in 1884. "And as State monopoly is prejudicial to any branch of business, so it must be to education."[48] A writer for the *Catholic World* in 1891 stated that "competition would bring to the front the real educators of real intrinsic merit; and those of inferior abilities would soon drop out of sight."[49] As Catholic schooling came under attack both domestically and in Europe during the late nineteenth century, the Catholic press frequently summoned the specter of "state monopoly" and praised its opposite: educational competition.

In a series of hearings in Boston, parochial school defenders drew on this language of competition in attacking the bill. A former Massachusetts school superintendent, August Small, echoed McEttrick as he spoke of the ways that "true competition is the life of trade and of education." Small argued that competition bred innovation—"new discoveries and inventions"—and that the best way to improve public and parochial schools would be to stimulate "rivalry" between them. "Emulation and self-interest are reliable guarantees of the healthiness of private instruction," he observed. "Statutory control of private schools would be costly, unprofitable, pernicious."[50] In a published response to the bill, Nathan Matthews Jr., an advocate for private academies and future Democratic mayor of Boston, said the value of a free, flourishing private school sector is precisely that it "afford[s] to our public schools that competition which is the indispensable prerequisite to progress in educational matters as in everything else; and partly by furnishing a means of educational experiment which would otherwise be wanting."[51] Even the notable Civil War veteran Colonel Thomas Wentworth Higginson spoke up against the bill. A Protestant, Higginson recounted his "first lesson in religious liberty" when as a child he stood by his mother's side watching a Protestant mob burn down a Catholic convent. This bill, part of that same tradition, would wrongly elevate the power of the state's "school committees and its superintendents" for the express purpose of making the "public schools models and drive the private schools off the track because the public are better." Educational innovation and competition, welcome in public and private schools alike, were under attack in Massachusetts, the bill's opponents insisted.[52]

The impressive degree of opposition to the bill effectively killed it. The law that eventually passed made superficial changes to the existing compulsory attendance statute, but nothing like the sweeping changes the Joint Committee had proposed. The *American Catholic Quarterly* suggested that Massachusetts politicians sufficiently feared the reprisals of Catholic voters that they refused to carry out the suggestions in the original bill.

Given the political consequences of upsetting parochial school advocates, the law's opponents believed that the existing regulations requiring private school "approval" would continue to go unenforced.[53]

That hope was largely fulfilled, though not without exceptions. In early 1889, the school committee in Haverhill, a town thirty miles north of Boston, decided to prosecute six Francophone parents whose children attended St. Joseph's parish school. The town had long been dominated by French-speaking workers, and public officials had expressed their disdain with the immigrants' unwillingness to assimilate. In the adjacent town of Lawrence, officials told stories of Francophone children even segregating themselves during recess.[54] The Haverhill superintendent remarked that "the movement for French parochial schools" was nothing less than "an attempt to establish a new France upon the soil of New England."[55] After inspecting the parochial school, the school committee refused to approve it, finding instruction dominated by French-language teachers, resulting in an educational product inferior to a typical public school. With these findings, the committee ruled that the parents who sent their children to the school violated the compulsory attendance law's English-language mandates. In February 1889, they charged six parents with illegally enrolling their children in an unapproved private school. Three of the parents contested the charges.[56]

Given the incident's proximity to the previous year's battle over private school regulations, the ensuing court battle drew wide attention throughout Massachusetts. The state's Catholic school advocates were relieved when the judge in the case, Henry Carter, ultimately ruled in favor of the Francophone parents. Carter reasoned that the legislature had intended the statute to apply to parents who "neglected" their children's education, not those who, out of fear of thrusting French-speaking students into English-speaking public schools, sought a different kind of education. The school committee had every right to approve or disapprove of schools, continued Carter, but they had no legal authority to close them or prosecute parents. Rather, respecting the "the private judgment of parents" was paramount. Similar to the opponents of the 1888 bill, Carter believed the regulations imposed by the school committee were excessively onerous, if not outright injurious, to maintaining educational quality.[57]

The failure to convict the Haverhill French parochial school parents only reinforced lawmakers' desire to make private schools more accountable to public officials. In February, the assemblyman S. R. Gracey, a Methodist minister, introduced a new compulsory attendance bill that made the previous year's efforts look tame. The bill's language largely repeated the terms of the 1888 measure, but it added provisions obviously aimed at Catholic priests by barring individuals from pressuring parents to withdraw their children from public schools. This bill too occasioned widespread controversy and was debated at a total of sixteen heavily attended hearings in March and April.[58]

Yet as with the previous bill, members of the heavily Republican State House balked when given the choice to sponsor it in the legislature. Preferring to achieve tougher regulations without the stain of passing this particular bill, they urged the Massachusetts

Supreme Court to render an official opinion on the meaning of the existing laws—hoping that the Court would at least overturn Judge Carter's interpretation. After the Court refused to weigh in on the controversy, the legislature superficially amended the compulsory attendance law in June 1889, but few felt the new legislation would make any difference. As the *Journal of Education* put it, the amended law was "a compromise . . . in the interest of peace and harmony."[59] It was "the least objectionable, because it appeared to do the least."[60]

For all the controversy surrounding parochial school regulation in Massachusetts, the inspection and approval system made very little difference. Many private school advocates feared that it would result in diminished educational competition, but as the Haverhill case demonstrated, it proved exceedingly difficult to close even one school. As state officials knew, local school committees were far more inclined to let parochial schools go uninspected, or to approve them so as to avoid controversy. The Massachusetts school controversy generated religious and ethnic tension but barely influenced actual policy implementation.

Three factors especially account for why Massachusetts's laws affecting parochial schools failed to halt their growth. First, as in Rhode Island, local school administrators knew that reducing parochial school attendance could lead to dire consequences for the public treasury and the public schools. "We may say what we like about parochial schools," a Boston alderman acknowledged in early 1889, "but if it were not for the recent withdrawals from the public schools of pupils who have been sent to the parochial schools we would be badly cramped for room. That is the only thing that has relieved us."[61] When the *Boston Daily Advertiser* surveyed nearly forty local school superintendents in 1889, they discovered that few public officials wanted to experiment with throwing thousands of parochial school students into the public schools, cramping existing conditions and placing pressure on taxpayers to fund additional buildings. In Boston, the parochial schools "have to a large degree removed this pressure" of overcrowding, the paper reported. In Springfield, the superintendent contemplated that if parochial schools closed, the city would have to open "at least one or two new public schools and make additional appropriations to defray the expense." In Hampshire County, the superintendent admitted that the "town would have needed more schools had the parochial schools not been established." In Malden, local officials estimated that the parochial schools saved the city about $15,000 a year. Were it not for the parochial schools, the superintendents of Cambridge and New Bedford told the paper, dozens of new public school teachers would be needed.[62] The collective message sent by the school superintendents was clear: attempts to stifle private school growth needed to be reconciled with a full accounting of their public benefits. Indeed, the savings were so widely acknowledged that some individuals in Massachusetts joked about them. In a series of hearings in Boston over a proposed property tax increase Nathan Matthews Jr. told the city council that the best way to keep taxes low would be for public schools to continue to discriminate against Catholics and push them into parochial schools![63] Given that Boston citizens already had among the nation's highest tax burdens, city officials knew that, like all jokes, there was an element of truth to what Matthews said. The financial cost of closing parochial schools outweighed the perceived benefits.[64]

A second, and related, reason that public school advocates feared regulating parochial schools too harshly was that new laws might lead to more fervent calls among Catholics for access to public funds. As the tax exemption battles in the 1870s and 1880s demonstrated, Catholic school authorities were often willing to exchange greater state oversight for access to public subsidies. To Catholics and Protestants alike, laws requiring that parochial schools resemble public schools could very well justify access to the same public money. This interpretation of public regulations proved so powerful that when news of the 1888 bill first broke, newspapers accounts considered the possibility that the new regulations would *benefit* parochial schools. Was the bill "aimed at parochial schools, or is it a measure intended ultimately to promote their interests?" the *Boston Daily Globe* wondered. Several Catholics interviewed by the newspaper believed that the law would aid parochial schools. "If it 'approves' the schools, it . . . so 'approves' what is taught in them," one Catholic clergyman argued. He reasoned that "if the parochial schools be given the same standing as the public schools, then they will be entitled to claim a share of the public school appropriations."[65]

Prominent public school advocates agreed. As the anti-Catholic *Boston Evening Transcript* put it, even members of the State Board of Education believed that tougher regulations would not only "awaken hostility from the Catholic element, but practically recognize the parochial establishments as State schools, and thus logically lead to the demand for a division of the school tax in their favor."[66] One public school principal was so alarmed by the threat of parochial schools accessing the school fund that he spoke out publicly against the bill. "If you supervise them, then, of course, you give them a claim for a division of the school fund," the principal, J. W. McDonald began. "If private schools can compete with us let them do it; we ask for no favors. There is only one way you can injure us, that is by legislating private schools into popularity by adverse legislation."[67] The prospect of public funding for parochial schools suggested that the bill's regulations would increase educational competition—the exact opposite of its stated intention.

Finally, insofar as the regulations threatened to "awaken hostility" from Catholics, public officials feared voter retribution. Catholic parents could decide to enroll their children in parochial schools, but they still voted in local public school committee elections, in addition to other local and statewide races. Lawmakers who sponsored laws threatening parochial schools risked payback at the polls. Worse for many Protestants was the threat that such legislation might produce a solid Catholic voting bloc increasingly alienated from the Protestant governing elite. Catholic voting power was no imagined phenomenon: Bostonians had elected their first Catholic mayor, Hugh O'Brien, in 1885, and by 1888 the city's school board was evenly split between Protestants and Catholics. After a bitter controversy erupted over an anti-Catholic textbook used by a public school teacher in 1888, Catholic (and anti-Catholic) women in Boston registered in droves to vote in the next school board elections.[68] Charles Eliot, the president of Harvard College, regarded Catholic voting power as the central reason to oppose the 1888 bill. In his public remarks to the joint committee he testified that "those of us who are Protestants may reasonably look with some apprehension upon the possible [electoral] results in those Massachusetts communities where the Catholics are in the majority, or are rapidly approaching a majority." Eliot argued that the bill, if passed into law, would "enlist every conscientious Catholic in the support of parochial schools."[69] Republican legislators in 1888 and 1889 knew that stringent parochial school regulations risked turning an entire generation of French-descended Catholics into Democrats.[70] Their refusal to pass the parochial school inspection bills into law reflected this fear. Nativist and anti-Catholic political agitation remained a fixture of Massachusetts politics throughout the 1890s, but Catholic voting power there, and elsewhere, made it highly unlikely that stringent regulations affecting parochial school attendance would be passed and enforced.[71]

Because opposition to the Massachusetts bills defeated them before they became law, the prospect of massive voter revolts never materialized and so remained an untested theory. In Wisconsin and Illinois, however, new state compulsory attendance bills were indeed passed into law, and the reaction was significant enough to temporarily realign party loyalty in the state. Wisconsin's "Bennett Law" and Illinois's "Edwards Law," both passed by Republican legislatures in 1889, were in some ways more moderate than the bills proposed in Massachusetts. Almost all of their provisions resembled Massachusetts's 1873 law that required "approval" of private schools, and defined "schools" as those that taught in the English language.[72] In other ways, however, the bills went beyond any existing state law. The Bennett Law, for example, had a clause requiring children to attend school in the district in which they lived, a provision that opponents feared would force children educated in a parish outside district lines to move or abandon their parochial school.[73]

Compared with Massachusetts, the origins of Wisconsin's private school regulations lay more strictly in ethnic, rather than religious, politics, since the law equally affected the state's large German-Protestant (Lutheran) community and its private schools. Together, the Catholic and Lutheran Germans of Wisconsin made up half of the state's foreign-born population in the late nineteenth century. By 1890, Wisconsin's parochial schools, many of which featured instruction in German, educated more than 15 percent of the state's school-attending children.[74] In large Catholic centers such as Milwaukee, well over one-third of school-going children attended these private schools.[75]

Over the course of the 1880s the state's public education organ, the *Wisconsin Journal of Education*, expressed increasing concerns about the rising attendance in German-speaking schools. Public school authorities in Wisconsin, as in New England, had long looked upon private school competition with some degree of suspicion. In 1879 the *Journal* reprinted an address that O. B. Wyman, the superintendent of the Vernon County public schools, delivered to the State Teachers' Association on the "Compulsory Educational Law." Like his counterparts in Rhode Island and other states, Wyman believed that compulsory attendance legislation led inexorably, as well as productively, toward educational monopoly. "The history of the past teaches, among many other lessons, that when the education of the masses is left to individual enterprise, or to private societies, that the training given too often tends to limit the understanding," he wrote. For Wyman, "the strong arm of the law" ought to eliminate educational competition as swiftly as possible.[76]

The *Journal* itself gradually came to endorse this view. In 1879 its official position was that German-language private schools fulfilled compulsory attendance laws. Even "the most despotic government in Europe does not attempt to compel education through one language only, where several languages are spoken," it proclaimed.[77] By 1882, however, its position began to shift. The *Journal* reported that in one city, "the attendance at a private denominational school is greater than the aggregate attendance at any three of the public schools," and English was quickly "becoming a dead [language]."[78] By 1889 the *Journal* announced that "it has come to light that the teaching of English is either utterly neglected or very imperfectly conducted in a large number of parochial schools," and referred to these trends as "a very serious evil." When, that same year, an obscure Catholic Republican state legislator, Michael Bennett, proposed a bill compelling attendance in schools taught in English, the *Journal* endorsed the measure. So, too, did Wisconsin's governor, William Hoard, who signed the bill into law in April 1889.[79]

The state's Catholic and Lutheran leaders reacted furiously to the Bennett Law. Acknowledging national trends, Milwaukee's *Catholic Citizen* accused Hoard of "circulat[ing] in this State the bad money that has done duty in bigoted Boston."[80] Wisconsin's three German-American Catholic bishops joined the Wisconsin Lutheran Synod in denouncing the measure publicly as an assault on parental and religious freedom. In a rare display of unity, Scandinavian Lutherans joined German Lutherans, and German Catholics joined Irish Catholics. Most importantly, Catholics and Lutherans— far from historical allies—united in their opposition.[81]

These new multiethnic and religiously diverse coalitions temporarily transformed local and state politics, blunting the Bennett Law's effects. In Massachusetts, Protestant Republicans had anticipated drastic electoral consequences for anti-Catholic legislation, and in Wisconsin those fears quickly became reality as the law's opponents decamped to the Democratic Party. Given that "every obnoxious law against Catholics and their Church, passed in the Wisconsin legislature, has originated with the Republican Party," the *Catholic Citizen* warned, the Bennett Law alone would "be reason enough for every Catholic voter to vote the Democratic ticket."[82] Even many Lutherans, long reliably Republican voters, agreed. One German Lutheran publication declared it the special duty of the "German citizen who is willing to assert the freedom of conscience and the rights of the German parochial schools to enter his protest by voting against the Republican party."[83] These hopes and predictions soon came true as Republicans, who had dominated the state for decades, went down in defeat. In April 1890, a Democrat, running in opposition to the Bennett Law, won Milwaukee's mayoral race for the first time in fifteen years.

Later that year, despite pledging to amend the law, Republicans met an even greater voter revolt. Save for one congressional seat, the Republicans lost every major office, along with their majority in the state legislature. Wisconsin's Lutheran and Catholic voters, meanwhile, trounced Governor Hoard at the polls and elected a Democratic governor for only the second time since 1856.[84] As a result of this swift and impressive political mobilization, the Bennett Law barely, if at all, made a dent in private school attendance. The incoming Democrats fulfilled their campaign promise and immediately repealed the law. When the legislature passed a new compulsory attendance bill in 1891, it no longer included language referring to residency and English-language requirements.[85]

In Illinois, the similarly motivated and worded Edwards Law also met stiff resistance and, ultimately, defeat. As in Wisconsin, little evidence exists that the regulations embedded in the Edwards Law had a significant impact on school attendance. Between 1889, when Republicans in the legislature approved the law, and 1893, when Democrats repealed it, newspapers reported few cases of enforcement. As in Wisconsin, the law made a greater impact on elections than school attendance. By the 1892 state elections, even the Republicans endorsed the Edwards Law's repeal. In their platform they stressed that parents should be "left absolutely free to choose in what schools" they enrolled their children, and that public officials never be given the authority "to interfere with private or parochial schools." Despite Illinois Republicans' attempts to avoid the fate of their colleagues in Wisconsin, voters ousted them from their majority in the Senate, and, in the land of Lincoln, elected their first Democratic governor since 1856. Once in power, the Democrats immediately repealed the provisions in the Edwards Law mandating English-language instruction and granting school board authority to approve private schools.[86] Democratic politics proved once again capable of overwhelming attempts to stifle parochial school attendance.

Compulsory attendance enforcement in Rhode Island, Massachusetts, Illinois, and Wisconsin reveals the gap between statewide officeholders and local ideologues, who saw compulsory attendance laws as politically popular, and local school officials, who had a more intimate knowledge of school finance and politics. This particular sensitivity to local conditions was on display at a meeting of the National Council of Education, a prestigious body of the larger National Education Association. There, in 1891, educational administrators from around the nation met to discuss the controversies surrounding compulsory education laws. Attendees heard blustery rhetoric praising increased state oversight of dangerous, foreign parochial schools. A paper produced by a committee chaired by the Saint Paul, Minnesota, public school superintendent barely concealed its anti-Catholicism. The committee accused those opposed to the Bennett and Edwards laws as an "un-American religio-political movement," close to a "foreign scheme, to be supported by foreign governmental and ecclesiastical influence." The report attacked parents who sent their children to foreign-language parochial schools and ended by suggesting that such parents lose their voting rights.[87] At the meeting, as at other gatherings of public school officials in the 1880s and 1890s, anti-Catholicism was heavily on display.[88]

The committee, however, did not have the last word. In a discussion following the paper, a group of public school superintendents rose in defense of parochial schools—not out of any particular affinity with Catholic education, but out of expediency. "To war on private schools in any way," Kansas City's Frank Fitzpatrick claimed, "is not in the providence of the public school." Fitzpatrick noted that "in my city it would require an increase of fifteen per cent in the taxes to provide accommodations in the public schools for all the children." Cincinnati's superintendent, Emerson White, agreed, arguing that states should acknowledge the difficulties with providing English instruction in communities where most of the teachers were foreigners. Better to focus first on the *public* schools that illegally instruct in foreign languages, White argued, and to use greater caution in supervising private education. "It is now hazardous and unnecessary to couple with [the question of compulsory education] the control of private schools," he concluded.[89] The audience of administrators erupted into cheers. While harassing parochial schools through burdensome regulations may have been the priority of a few nativist zealots, mainstream urban school administrators rejected that approach.

The educational competition introduced by parochial schools did produce a swift backlash, and the efforts to inspect and approve parochial schools often proved immensely divisive. Strikingly, however, attempts to restrict private schooling had almost no effect on attendance. Few schools were ever closed due to inspections, and still fewer parents convicted for aiding truancy. While greater numbers of parochial schools might have been pressured to close in more inconspicuous ways, most local school committees abstained from upsetting local ethnic groups. Despite the adversarial rhetoric and legislation of Republican state officials, compulsory school laws did not reduce attendance in parochial schools. On the contrary, because of other provisions in these laws, they facilitated their continued expansion.

5

Creating the Educational Marketplace

AS CATHOLIC SCHOOL systems grew and matured in the decades surrounding 1900 they, along with government regulation, created modern school choice. By the 1920s, Catholic schools represented a systematic alternative to public education, and millions of parents began exercising complex choices within the context of a tightly regulated education market. Parochial school attendance continued to surge between 1900 and 1930, as Catholic immigrants flooded into American cities from Southern and Eastern Europe. The number of Catholics in the United States more than doubled between 1890 and 1915, rising to sixteen million. Immigrant populations were particularly noticeable in urban areas, where, by 1916, Catholic communicants composed majorities in thirty-one cities with more than 100,000 residents.[1] In large cities such as Cleveland, Milwaukee, Cincinnati, Buffalo, Boston, and Pittsburgh, more than 40 percent of children attended Catholic schools.[2] As public and parochial school systems competed for Catholic students, their governance structures increasingly mirrored one another. For public schools in this age of dramatic educational change, the triumph of a bureaucratic "one best system"—of publicly financed, standardized, and state-supervised schools—marked the era's dominant reform agenda.[3] For Catholic schools the aims and means were remarkably similar: expanding the system, centralizing administration in offices of diocesan school superintendents, and standardizing curriculum across the parishes.[4] Essential differences remained between the two systems, from the religious content of parochial schooling to the increased emphasis on manual and vocational training in public schools. But in large and small cities alike, the existence of two distinct, competing systems was impossible to miss.[5]

The systematization of public education that linked increasingly centralized local districts with state standards, funding, and laws also included private schools. The nineteenth-century rise of laws regulating private schools had blurred distinctions between public and private in education entirely. The more Catholic educational systems became fixtures of urban life, the more state legislatures required that parochial schools align with centralized, "public" priorities—a process known as educational "standardization." Efforts to create a single system of legal authority over public and parochial schools arose because Catholic children did not typically attend either institution exclusively. Instead, pupils often transferred between them, reflecting a more urban America where parents had access to educational choices and a larger "marketplace" of schools. As reformers witnessed millions of Catholic parents exercising monthly and annual choices over their children's schooling, they sought ways to regulate that marketplace.

Unregulated school choice posed two problems, in particular. First, officials complained that compulsory attendance laws could not be enforced properly if cities lacked mechanisms to track attendance shifts between public and private schools. So long as parochial schools declined to voluntarily report attendance to public officials, truant officers could not maintain accurate enrollment statistics. Moreover, Catholic parents and children seeking to evade attendance mandates could simply transfer to the parochial school in order to avoid the truant officer's watchful eye. Laws that addressed parochial school attendance thus became a rallying cry for reformers during the Progressive Era. State legislators crafted new regulations forcing parochial schools to coordinate their attendance systems with local public schools. In addition, urban school boards constructed vast bureaus of attendance to manage transfers between school systems, tying together public and parochial school governance in ways unthinkable during the nineteenth century.

Transfers between rival systems also posed instructional problems, what one Chicago researcher in 1912 termed "the difficulty of harmonizing two courses of study having diverse aims and methods."[6] Because almost all Catholic dioceses lacked secondary schools of their own, students were often first educated in the parish elementary school and then attended a public high school. Catholic and public officials alike sought ways to ensure that parochial schools met minimum standards and that their graduates were adequately prepared for public high school curricula. As a response, in addition to the minimum requirements written into compulsory attendance statutes, school boards in several cities during the Progressive Era began accrediting pre-secondary parochial schools. Students graduating from parochial schools officially "approved" by school committees received privileges in their applications to public high schools not afforded to those from unaccredited schools. Graduates from approved schools, for example, could be admitted to public high schools without taking an entrance examination, a common requirement throughout the nineteenth century, thus facilitating access to institutions increasingly crucial to upward mobility. Parochial school officials calculated, accurately, that parents would spurn their institutions if they did not comply with accreditation standards.

Because urban areas had ethnically and religiously diverse neighborhoods, new regulations and administrative bureaus arose to govern otherwise dizzyingly chaotic, competing school systems. Indeed, public regulation, as it had in previous decades, actually fostered increased competition. Regulatory reforms satisfied public and parochial school authori-ties' desire for "modern" administration and encouraged better school attendance in the dueling systems. Over the first two decades of the twentieth century Catholic educators willingly, even happily, complied with state laws that required them to report attendance information to public officials. Accreditation and the raised standards that came with it, meanwhile, satisfied Catholic concerns that secondary schools and labor markets would treat parish institutions as equivalent in quality to public schools. By the 1920s, cities and states regulated public and parochial schools to a degree unfathomable a half-century earlier. A tightly regulated educational marketplace had been born.

The push to regulate Catholic parents' school choices and the educational marketplace those choices created fit comfortably within the broader agenda of municipal and state reformers between the 1890s and 1920s. Public regulation of private behavior was not new to the period, but as the United States in the late nineteenth and early twentieth century shifted from a predominately rural to an urban society, more Americans felt the strengthened hand of the regulatory state. Because of their tremendous growth, concen-trated wealth and poverty, and cultural diversity, cities became the focus of regulatory reform. Cities had a surfeit of social concerns that captivated reform-minded citizens. Reformers targeted the machine bosses and *padroni* (exploiters of immigrant labor), men who victimized the uneducated masses with false promises of future rewards.[7] Their vision involved corruption-free, efficient municipal government, run by the wisdom of experts rather than desperately impoverished and illiterate voters. Urban reformers pro-moted clean government and attacked vice wherever it existed. Whether out of religious or secular motivations, laws regulating private "vices" proliferated, including restraints on Sunday alcohol consumption, prostitution, racial mixing, miscegenation, divorce, and polygamy.[8] Reformers and so-called child savers targeted commercial amusements such as vaudeville and motion pictures, concert saloons and dime museums—each of which could lead children and men into temptation.[9] By 1890, virtually every state in the nation had anti-lottery laws. State censorship boards, along with new municipal zoning laws, emerged to "protect" children and neighborhoods from the corrupting influence of par-ticular industries, such as films and publishing.[10]

Police power regulation surged at the state level, as the locus of public policymaking shifted from local to state jurisdiction.[11] At the turn of the twentieth century, twenty-eight states limited child factory labor; in 1917, thirty-nine limited women's work hours. By 1914, every state licensed dentists and pharmacists. New York, the most populated state, averaged more than 1,000 new statutes per session during the Progressive Era.[12] Between 1860 and 1900, the Empire State's expenditures for regulatory agencies grew 1,800 percent, from $50,000 to $900,000.[13] In those decades New York established a railroad commis-sion to regulate rates, a board of health to investigate disease and enforce pure food laws, and boards and bureaus to inspect factories, bakeries, sweatshops, and farms.[14] Wisconsin soon led other states in pioneering banking and insurance regulations and civil service reform, and the state passed the first income tax and workers' compensation laws.[15]

Urban school reform was a central component of this rising regulatory state. Beginning in the nineteenth century, compulsory attendance laws transformed school attendance from a private concern to one heavily regulated by states and administrative agencies. While other spheres of American life witnessed immense statutory revision, education stood out as a primary locus of reform. The Chicago reformer Sophonisba Breckinridge believed that "there are few branches of the law which have been more completely revolutionized by statutory amendment" than education, thanks to compulsory attendance legislation.[16] Illinois's state superintendent favorably compared attendance laws to eminent domain and public health standards.[17] New York City's Attendance Bureau director, John Davis, asserted in his 1915 report that compulsory attendance enforcement perfectly encapsulated the period's yearning for public solutions to private problems. For Davis, compulsory attendance joined pure food and drug laws, banking oversight, and occupational licensing as central regulatory reforms of the early twentieth century. In education, he remarked, the "state has interfered more and more" by "assert[ing] . . . the superior rights of the child and that of the State . . . against parental neglect."[18] The vast administrative apparatus Davis oversaw to enforce these laws supported his claim. In New York City, over one hundred truant officers employed by the Bureau of Attendance investigated 375,000 cases of truancy in one year (1916–17) alone.[19] An entire system of municipal courts—the Domestic Relations Court and the Children's Court—existed in part to prosecute parents and commit children to truant schools.[20] The rise of an administrative state was perhaps nowhere more visible than in the realm of public educational regulation.

Public regulation of school attendance formed only one of the poles supporting a broader tent of school reform. In the Progressive Era, urban school reformers demanded that public laws rationalize the educational decisions made by a host of "inexpert" actors, including families, political bosses, ward representatives, and school boards. In cities throughout the country Progressive Era reformers—a coalition that frequently included elite and grassroots organizations—replaced the lay, "political" educational leadership with a smaller corps of administrative professionals. By World War I urban school boards no longer exhibited the same extent of occupational and economic diversity that they had in the nineteenth century. Thanks to smaller school boards and city-wide (rather than ward) elections, educational governance lay in the hands of metropolitan elites, a more distant group of policymakers.[21] With increasing vigor school boards compelled attendance, enforced district boundary lines, standardized curriculum, certified teachers, and centralized school governance.

Courts, meanwhile, both accommodated and accelerated governmental policing of private parental prerogative. With greater frequency judges ruled in favor of public schools over challenges by parents. State courts held that legislatures had the right to compel attendance in public and "approved" private schools. Insofar as they could compel attendance, courts reasoned, schools could also compel vaccinations. Parents and teachers who expressed curricular and pedagogical preferences contrary to state guidelines also found decreasing sympathy from courts, as judges decided that states could proscribe instruction in politically "radical" subjects and in foreign languages.[22] Even parents seeking legal redress for tort liability discovered that courts sided with schools over families. Providing education constituted the clearest of "public duties," a Massachusetts judge wrote, which private individuals had no recourse to redress.[23] Courts thus represented an important actor in what one Catholic commentator in 1915 referred to as a larger, "generous shifting of the responsibility of the parent to the state," one that emphasized public administration guided by professional expertise.[24]

Progressive Era administrators focused on schools as key sites of reform and regulation because, echoing nineteenth-century common school reformers, they believed education could lead the way to reforming the polity. More than other institutions, they argued, schools had the potential to improve the lives of individuals and strengthen families.[25] In the absence of a strong domestic welfare state, they provided a social safety net and public services for working-class children.[26] Administrators ultimately helped transform schools into more social institutions. Beginning in the 1890s parents, voluntary associations, and local governments tasked schools with performing a dizzying variety of new roles. Schools provided children not only with academic instruction but also vocational training, medical care, and hot meals.[27] They stayed open at night to teach immigrants English and to serve as venues for political and social activities.[28] Whether public or parish-based, schools became critical community centers. Reformers hoped that this transformation of the school would beget an assimilated and productive populace. As Americans expanded their ideas about what schools should do, reformers aimed to shape and direct parental choices over education by defining which schools children could attend, when, and why.

Effective public regulation of urban schools would have been vastly simpler if all children attended public schools, and if all families lived permanently in one neighborhood. Neither, however, was the case. Geographic mobility was a familiar feature of urban life, and families moved regularly. In response, legislators and school boards tried to shape parental decisions about school attendance. Catholics were not passive amid this state activity. Churches and dioceses designed their own educational guidelines, while parents negotiated this complex world of competing schools and policies as the situation allowed, making decisions deemed in their family's best interests. Indeed, private educational authority and parental choice frustrated policymakers' attempts to regulate school attendance as they saw fit. As Catholic parents continued to exercise choices over where to live and where to send their children to school, reformers accordingly pushed for stronger laws to regulate the very act of choosing—or transferring—between schools.

Catholic parents, like all parents, never made educational choices free from the constraints imposed by circumstance and by custom. The Catholic Church was central to the lives of millions of urban residents and remained a ubiquitous force in promoting parochial schooling. Diocesan schools, for example, had their own set of rules, codified by church hierarchs as "statutes," and just as public school officials shaped attendance zones by district or ward, so too did Catholic officials carve out school boundaries. The very term "parochial" cultivated geographic images and linear enclosures, which Catholic churches treated as expressions of canon law. Dioceses limited Catholic school attendance to within the parish boundaries. They mandated that Catholic children attend parochial school unless their parents provided the bishop with a reasonable excuse—the most common being that a family resided more than three miles from the nearest parish.[29] Diocesan regulations often required priests to refuse absolution to parents whose children attended the public schools. Fearing the monopoly that public laws had on school attendance, the Catholic Church thus imposed its own constraints on parishioners.[30]

Church regulations that arose from inside or outside of the parish could even contain content strikingly similar to state laws. When immigration restriction and nativism reared its head in the years immediately following World War I, American-born Catholic bishops believed that Church-led Americanization efforts would protect immigrant parishioners from outside attacks. As a result, in large and diverse dioceses where immigrant (or "national") Catholic parishes had distanced themselves from the American-born hierarchy, Catholic bishops in the early 1920s often pursued centralized policies aimed at assimilation. Church leaders often aided state efforts to prohibit foreign-language instruction in private elementary schools. George Mundelein, Chicago's Catholic leader, was particularly unafraid to challenge that archdiocese's longstanding policy of accommodating national parishes. Shortly after becoming the new archbishop in 1916, Mundelein prohibited new national parishes and tried to impose English into immigrant church services. Equally as controversial, he mandated that all parochial schools in the archdiocese use English-language textbooks in the major subjects.[31] Buffalo's diocesan superintendent pursued a similar measure.[32] In these manifold ways, Catholic school systems asserted their own private regulations.

In addition to these official rules, Catholic communities with high rates of parochial school attendance exerted informal mechanisms to direct children away from public schools. In a study on patterns of school attendance completed in 1897, the University of Chicago social scientist Daniel Folkmar emphasized that the parents he had studied decided which schools, if any, their children attended, according to their "wish to live in accordance with the social demands of the community or to obey the law which the community demands."[33] The Irish-American writer James T. Farrell, in his 1932 novel *Young Lonigan*, added that mothers feared "what the neighbors would think" if their sons did not attend a Catholic school.[34] Even lapsed Catholics who did not attend church could not always escape pressure to send their children to Catholic schools. When diocesan officials canvassed neighborhoods to obtain parish demographic data, one of the first questions asked regarded parochial school attendance. As one census-taker reported in 1924, when parents indicated that their children attended public school he "argued the matter out with them."[35]

Finally, the Catholic press in the early twentieth century stressed the need to attend parochial schools. Each summer, the conservative Jesuit magazine *America* published articles with titles such as "School-Picking Time" and "What School for Your Child," highlighting the extent of choices, and the importance of choosing the Catholic school.[36] Editorials in *America* equated Catholic parents who sent children to public schools with Judas, warning of a "fearful reckoning" in the afterlife.[37] The foreign-language press added to the pressure. When a Chicago-based Polish-language newspaper asked readers, "which of the two schools shall we select: public or parochial?" the answer was obvious.[38] Catholic parents could quickly discover that while public laws compelled school-going, private rules and pressures often framed what school children attended.[39]

The power of Catholic authorities to shape educational policy disturbed many public school advocates, who argued that public regulations should have the exclusive power to compel attendance. In a debate on the role of Catholic schools in America sponsored by the National Educational Association in 1889, the public school champion Edwin Mead centered his remarks on church policies that forced children into parochial schools. Mead aimed to turn Catholic arguments about the coercive nature of public schools and compulsory attendance laws on their head. It was the Catholic Church, he insisted, that truly interfered with "parental freedom" and the ability "for parents to choose such schools for their children as they believe best." The state, he insisted, "cannot for a moment permit any church to coerce any citizen into the support of its own denominational schools."[40] In the same year as Mead's address, antipathy toward Catholic educational policy appeared in legislation as well. The Massachusetts legislature debated a bill that, though it was never signed into law, threatened to prosecute any priest who pressured children to enroll in parochial over public schools. Wisconsin's Bennett Law, meanwhile, notoriously required children to attend school in the public school district in which they lived, presumably prohibiting attendance in parochial schools outside of state-imposed lines.[41] As early as the 1880s, then, public school advocates saw fit to challenge private educational policy with state power.

Despite attempts by public and church officials to shape where children attended school in the early twentieth century, parental choice in education remained a prominent feature of urban life wherever there were large numbers of Catholics. Millions of Catholic parents each year defied official church rules requiring that their children attend parochial schools. Sociological studies of urban Catholic life in the early and mid-twentieth century listed dozens of reasons that Catholic parents elected public over parochial school, or vice versa. Catholics were divided by ethnicity and language, and parents cared to different degrees about the academic reputation of particular schools, parochial or public, that their children might attend. Which schools seemed to have better teachers, or better discipline, or smaller class sizes?[42] Behind the abstract percentages of Catholic children attending public schools lay thousands of individual stories: a mother who believed the public school offered better services for her sickly child; a father's memory of how cruelly he was treated at the parish school; a father who feared that sending his child to the parochial school would unravel the secrecy of his marriage outside of the church.[43]

Catholic parents who sent their children to parochial schools were not necessarily following priestly mandates: some parents hoped that their children could lead a religious life, or become prosperous, or attend the school closest to home. Some parents enrolled their children until they received their First Communion, others until Confirmation.[44] Catholic children, in turn, could attempt to influence their parents, or could be perplexed by the mysterious decisions of their guardians. Consider the responses a Minnesota researcher and school inspector received from children in the 1920s when he inquired why their parents sent them to a private (likely Catholic) high school: "I just have to hang out at this dump," "Because it's a jail," "Haven't the slightest idea," "Don't ask me," "I have often wondered," "No one knows," and "None of your business."[45] Decision-making by parents often seemed opaque. Undoubtedly for most, if not all, parents, choices about their children's schooling intersected with a tangle of other concerns, as Catholics navigated the economic opportunities, cultural expectations, and religious norms of the urban environment that surrounded them.

While cost proved to be a central factor in determining where parents sent their children to school, geography was also crucial. Parents valued schools near their homes, and so long as public policy and parish rules structured attendance according to residence, where one lived was central to determining where one went to school. Residential choices, in turn, frequently reflected urban ethnic identity, wealth, and the prejudices of landlords. By the late nineteenth century, new mass transit systems, together with mass industrial production, had erased many existing neighborhood boundaries, annihilating the formerly close relationship between home and workplace and the enclosures set by rivers and hills. Instead, urban areas featured a series of neighborhoods delineated by their racial and ethnic character, each one fiercely (often physically) defensive against individuals who dared cross an invisible border. More so than other religious groups, Catholics were deeply rooted in physical communities, a consequence of their spiritual ties to the parish. Where Protestants and Jews generally relocated their churches and synagogues to wherever they chose to move, Catholic parishes were, by custom and church law, immobile. As a result, Catholic immigrant groups invested substantially in property near their churches and identified their neighborhoods by parish ("St. Stanislaus," "Holy Redeemer").[46] Ironically, deep ties to parish and ethnicity occasionally produced swift demographic changes when new migrants threatened to upset homogeneity. The brutally violent ethnic enclaves of 1916 Chicago fictionalized in James T. Farrell's *Young Lonigan* (1932) recalled a world where street battles between Irish, African-American, and Jewish youths were common, and where the encroachment of a single "undesirable" family over a commonly recognized neighborhood boundary line could trigger mass hysteria and neighborhood turnover.[47]

Despite ties to the parish, geographic mobility was a constant feature of urban life, including for Catholics. Working-class families seeking employment or cheaper rent moved, both from and within a given city, as the demand for labor, and the supply of housing, shifted.[48] Socially mobile families sought larger accommodations and safer neighborhoods. The historian Stephen Thernstrom famously described the nineteenth-century Irish workers of Newburyport, Massachusetts, as "permanent transients," relocating in order to pursue the dream of stable work and suitable accommodations.[49] In late nineteenth-century Omaha, Nebraska, more than 75 percent of the city's young families moved locations within the city every five years.[50] Rates of residential mobility in Pittsburgh were similar.[51] While home ownership varied considerably across cities and between different ethnic groups, estimates are that around three-quarters of urbanites lived in rented quarters during the late nineteenth century, ready to move at the next promise of an improvement for their family.[52] In this context of swirling population movements, children migrated frequently from place to place every year, changing schools in the process. In New York City, the sociologist Le Roy E. Bowman noted in 1925, such ethnic patterns of mobility had rendered "one school, ten years ago 99 per cent Jewish . . . now 99 per cent Italian."[53]

Parental educational preferences, along with residential and demographic shifts, also meant that Catholic children alternated between public and parochial schools. Scores of school reports and studies from the late nineteenth century onward contained accounts of children attending two schools, one parochial and one public, even during the same year. "Children go not only from one school to another, but from one school system to an entirely different one," wrote Edith Abbott and Sophonisba Breckinridge in a study of school attendance in Chicago. They "go constantly back and forth between [the neighborhood] school and near-by parochial schools."[54] Another in Chicago noted "the great fluctuations of population through immigration and exodus" and the "transfer of pupils to and from parochial and private schools."[55] The Woonsocket, Rhode Island, superintendent noted in 1898 that "pupils are continually changing from public to private, and from private to public . . . just as the mood of the parent happens to be."[56] In Pittsburgh, one observer referred to a "constant migration to the public schools, as well as in the reverse direction, an ebb and flow occasioned by the requirements of confirmation."[57] In New Orleans, a school official noted, "in hundreds of cases children . . . are removed from school to attend temporarily the parochial or other private schools."[58] New York City officials estimated that well over 10,000 children transferred from public to parochial schools in 1911 alone, a number that surely underestimated the additional thousands who went uncounted in a city lacking efficient pupil accounting practices.[59] In Philadelphia, the number of transfers between public and parochial schools generally hovered around eight or nine thousand each year.[60]

This situation alarmed early twentieth-century social scientists, who feared that such instability disrupted productive lives. The University of Chicago sociologists Robert Park and Ernest Burgess deemed the consequences of mobility "subversive and disorganizing." In neighborhoods where migration and dislocation were common, they claimed, so too were poverty, crime, delinquency, suicide, and other ills.[61] When the nation's leading sociologists gathered in 1925 to discuss the state of urban society, this high degree of urban mobility emerged as a central theme. The University of Minnesota professor M. C. Elmer noted that an important characteristic of the Twin Cities was so-called zones of transition, or areas with "a high percentage of mobile population, such as temporary boarders and roomers, unsettled families, persons moving up the social scale, and persons moving down the social scale."[62]

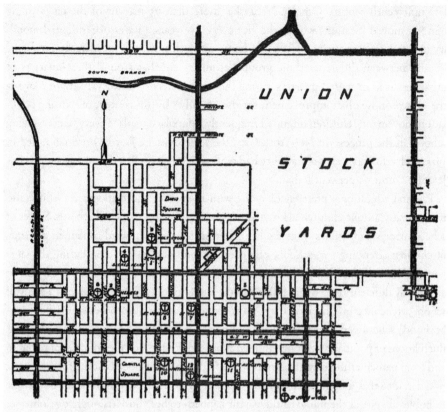

MAP SHOWING THE LOCATION OF PUBLIC AND PAROCHIAL SCHOOLS

1. Seward Public School.
2. Hedges Public School.
3. Hamline Public School.
4. Sacred Heart, Polish Catholic School.
5. St. Joseph, Polish Catholic School.
6. St. John of God, Polish Catholic School.
7. St. Rose of Lima, Irish Catholic School.

8. St. Michael, Slovak Catholic School.
9. Holy Cross, Lithuanian Catholic School.
10. S. S. Cyrill and Methodius, Bohemian Catholic School.
11. St. Augustine, German Catholic School.
12. St. Martinni, German Lutheran School.
13. Lake Public High School.

School transfers were particularly common in Chicago's "Back of the Yards" neighborhood, which was home to an array of public and parochial schools.
Reproduced in Louise Montgomery, *The American Girl in the Stockyard District*, University of Chicago Press, 1913

Reformers particularly feared the effects of urban mobility on children. To some educational experts, school reform would be unrealized if children did not remain in stable neighborhoods and a single school. In 1898 the Woonsocket, Rhode Island, school superintendent declared it "certainly detrimental to the true interest of the child to move him about thus, from place to place."[63] In his widely read 1909 jeremiad on the failures of American education, *Laggards in Our Schools*, Leonard Ayres deemed it "manifest that children are bound to suffer more or less when they leave one school to attend another." Ayres's book linked transfers between school and the "laggards" of his title—the frequently held-back children who were not performing at grade level. He explained that given "our shifting population such changes are so frequent as to effect a considerable part of the children attending school."[64] The belief was widespread. A Chicago doctor studying children in public and parochial schools remarked in 1912 that "not only was retardation caused by differing standards in the schools, but by days and weeks where it was possible to be out of school during the process of transfer."[65] As late as 1926, a Teachers College dissertation described such transfers as a "source of serious educational loss."[66] Studies of juvenile delinquency claimed close correlations between mobility and truancy. One report found that 170 families with truant children had moved households a combined 425 times, with sixty-seven of the families having moved more than three times.[67] In an urban context of constant dislocation and mobility, consistent school attendance—and, therefore, effective urban education—always seemed just out of reach. Parents could still elect to send their children to school, but frequent relocations and school transfers rendered the education less than optimal.

For school officials charged with tracking and enforcing attendance, mobility posed significant practical problems. The Wisconsin Bureau of Labor and Industrial Statistics implored school officials in 1911 to undertake a great "system of registration of children" in a context of constant upheaval: "Parents move from one district to another, families move in from different states. Children enroll in one parochial school for a time, and leaving it enroll in another, or in the public school. Children in the [public] school withdraw and enroll in a private or parochial school."[68] Tracking attendance in this endless maze of transfers was no simple task. When New York City's head of attendance enforcement recommended a permanent census to track school transfers in 1907—"necessary because of the migratory characteristics of a larger part of the city's population"—he noted that hundreds of thousands of children changed schools every year. "Many people move from place to place, often two or three times within a school year," the administrator noted, leading to "non-attendance and truancy."[69] Compelling attendance under these conditions would be impossible unless city officials had mechanisms to follow children from school to school, ensuring that they had properly enrolled and that attendance officials did not count them twice.

Within densely populated cities filled with parochial schools the dilemmas posed by transfers became more acute. Parents and children who transferred schools to avoid attendance and evade truant officers became targets for criticism in reports issued by reformers and school officials. A popular belief among administrators, echoed by the Cleveland superintendent in 1902, was that "pupils who do not wish to attend school register with the parochial schools and almost immediately cease attendance and spend their time as they wish, either upon the streets or at work."[70] Skeptical truant officers frequently discussed finding children on the street only to be told they "belonged to a Catholic school," "transferred to the Catholic school," were off for a "religious holiday," or were free because the parochial school "teacher is sick."[71] A truant officer in Maryland reported that "there have been so many cases of this kind that I could spend my entire time . . . and be kept busy."[72] One attendance official from York, Pennsylvania, grew so concerned about all the children in the streets claiming to be from Catholic schools that he worried about his job safety and, writing to the superintendent, suggested that children from private schools wear official badges on days their schools were closed.[73]

Social workers echoed these accounts, targeting immigrant Catholic parents for using parochial schools to shield their children from receiving a formal education. A 1906 study by Gertrude Howe Britton, a social worker in Chicago, recounted several of these examples. She discussed James G. of the Goodrich School, a twelve-year-old boy and "one of many who use the device of being transferred from the public school to the parochial school and from the parochial school to the public school to cover their absence from both." James, like his mother, told truant officers that he "belonged to a Catholic school," which Britton believed to be a lie. The mother of seven-year-old Alice L. similarly deceived school authorities into thinking the child was enrolled in the parochial school, as did Maggie T.'s mother, who enrolled her child in the parochial school under the belief that social workers could no longer "interfere with her." Throughout Chicago, she noted, "the loop-holes afforded by the transfer system are made use of to escape attendance in either school."[74] In a report issued eight years later, settlement house workers in Chicago found little had changed, noting a "serious problem" created by "transfers from public and parochial schools."[75] While no quantitative evidence suggested that the majority of children who transferred between public and parochial schools did so to avoid enrollment, anecdotes like these were used to persuade a legion of child welfare workers to reform the attendance system.

Attendance reformers sought to regulate what they viewed as private vices. While many reformers would like to have seen mobility decreased substantially, the only realistic legal option was to have it managed and ordered. City and state school officials believed that the solution to the transfer problem lay in superior bookkeeping. Beginning in the 1880s, state superintendents began insisting that private schools turn over their attendance registers to public officials. Without these returns, reformers argued, officials could not determine precisely how many children outside of public schools received any education at all. Wisconsin's state superintendent of public instruction endorsed forcing parochial school officials to hand in attendance reports three times in his annual reports in the late 1880s.[76] In 1891, when the U.S. Commissioner of Education, William T. Harris, asked Rhode Island's State Commissioner of Education, Thomas Stockwell, to comment on the "relation of the State to private schools," it was precisely this need for statistics that dominated the discussion. Stockwell called for a series of accounting mechanisms: accurate enrollment data for private schools buoyed by the use of uniform registers and annual returns by private schools. Amid the "chaos and ignorance" of school attendance in the state, Stockwell wrote, only an "accurate statement of facts" by private schools would suffice.[77]

Legislatures responded to these pleadings by incorporating reporting requirements into their school codes. In Ohio's compulsory attendance statute, passed in 1889, the legislature mandated that private schools provide local attendance officers with their enrollment data. As one Ohio official recounted the law's aim: "Suppose [the truant officer] finds on the street or in a factory a boy thirteen years old, and he says, 'My boy, have you attended a school one hundred days?' He says, 'Yes, sir.' 'Where?' 'At Father Quigley's, at

St. Francis de Sales.' It is necessary for the officials charged with the enforcement of that law to know whether that is true or not."[78] As more children attended parochial schools, states required more accurate attendance data. Connecticut, Rhode Island, and New York also passed laws in the 1880s and 1890s requiring private schools to maintain attendance records and furnish them to local officials. By 1925 Illinois, Indiana, Iowa, Maine, Massachusetts, Michigan, Nebraska, New Hampshire, New Jersey, Pennsylvania, South Dakota, Washington, West Virginia, and Wisconsin had enacted similar provisions.[79]

Reporting requirements aimed to regulate the act of choosing schools itself. In other words, they sought to mitigate the perceived dangers of parallel urban school systems with high rates of mobility between them. To school superintendents across the country, such requirements fulfilled a glaring need, as one Rhode Island superintendent put it, to "adequately gover[n] frequent change of school relations."[80] These laws "would answer the question where the child really belongs," a Pennsylvania city superintendent wrote.[81] They would "determine the degree of effectiveness with which the compulsory attendance law is being enforced," one study found.[82] A Wisconsin official added that, by addressing the transfer process itself, reporting requirements would "prevent . . . the whimsical changing from one school to another so common in the parochial schools."[83] Once school officials solved the "poorly worked-out system for keeping track of the child," compulsory attendance statutes could be properly enforced, and the chaos produced by parallel school systems properly coordinated.[84]

As administered by superintendents and attendance officers, new transfer laws devised mechanisms with which to follow children from school to school. When the laws initially were passed in the 1880s and 1890s, truant officers employed blunt policing methods to obtain the data they sought. In Toledo, Ohio, in 1890, a truant officer simply walked into a parochial school and demanded that the priest turn over a list of enrolled pupils. When the priest, Reverend Patrick Francis Quigley, indignantly refused the request—believing it an assault on the church's privacy rights—the officer had him jailed and, ultimately, criminally prosecuted.[85]

In the ensuing decades municipalities and states developed more sophisticated methods to track and enforce attendance. Amateur truant officers engaged in less policing of individual children and schools; rather, they became professional members of "attendance services" and, using the tools and rhetoric of emerging social sciences such as sociology and criminology, focused more heavily on prevention, persuasion, and bureaucratic welfare services for "maladjusted" children.[86] The process for determining attendance statistics itself shifted. Cities in the nineteenth century had administered an annual "school census" to register how many children lived in the city and attended school annually.[87] While state departments of instruction used these statistics primarily to distribute annual state appropriations, reformers focused on compulsory attendance found the census woefully inadequate, since it failed to account for the frequent residency changes throughout the year. To address the reality of shifting populations, cities in the early twentieth century gradually adopted permanent or continuous censuses. New York State's 1908 permanent census law stipulated that parents of school-aged children report to authorities when their children reached compulsory school age, or when they moved addresses or schools. State legislatures also wrote the continuing census into their compulsory attendance statutes, mandating that children who moved from one school to another report the transfer to local authorities.[88]

Once equipped with more accurate demographic data, cities then implemented increasingly strenuous pupil accounting practices. School districts created uniform attendance procedures, ensuring that children who transferred schools within the state—whether within the public system or between public and parochial schools—would be tracked efficiently. A cottage industry of administrative experts arose, producing new standard forms and mechanisms for superintendents and attendance officers to track students.[89] Typically, students leaving one school for another received a "transfer card" to present to their new school. A copy of the transfer card would then be sent to the attendance department, which would update the student's permanent record card. If the child was absent at the new school for three or four days, attendance departments would alert the truant officers, triggering an investigation. One researcher studying 346 cities found that 245 required private schools to cooperate with attendance officers.[90]

More stringent, bureaucratic attendance mechanisms legally mandated the compliance of parochial schools. Resistance of the sort that got Father Quigley jailed in Ohio dissipated as parochial school administrators increasingly found reasons to comply with, even embrace, public oversight over attendance. Thus, while the Cleveland superintendent still found "no willingness displayed on the part of [parochial] schools to furnish us" with data a decade after the Father Quigley incident, by the 1910s and 1920s such

To more efficiently monitor transfers between public and private schools, cities established large attendance bureaus in the early twentieth century. In a photo included in a Bureau of Compulsory Education report, an officer goes door to door taking a census of school enrollments.

The Board of Public Education, School District of Philadelphia, Bureau of Compulsory Education, *Report for the Year Ending* June 30, 1926

expressions among public officials were uncommon.[91] Experts on compulsory attendance laws and their enforcement noted that Catholic schools generally followed attendance procedures. In one of the Progressive Era's most detailed and sweeping analyses of compulsory attendance enforcement, published in 1921, Forest Chester Ensign described how, in New York City, "parochial schools, formerly distinctly suspicious of any law or ruling which touched their interests, now welcomed the assistance and supervision of the State Department, thus marking one more advance in the direction of unification in the educational activities of the state."[92] New York City's director of school attendance frequently identified the "close cooperation" between city officials and parochial schools, and he claimed that the latter provided assistance "cheerfully."[93] As evidence for such cooperation, he described how the number of children formally listed as "discharged" to the public schools—that is, those who exited the attendance department's accounting system entirely—had dropped by more than half between 1911 and 1918. The director surmised that the drop was due to "an assimilation of the procedure of the public schools by the parochial schools," creating a common system of attendance.[94]

Catholic officials in New York City and elsewhere corroborated these accounts. The superintendent of Brooklyn's Catholic parish schools, Joseph McClancy, remarked in 1916 that the city's attendance officials "handle . . . the manner at once creditable to themselves and cordial to the Catholic school officials."[95] Even Catholic officials in Toledo had moved past the bitter relationships between city officials and parochial schools typical in Father Quigley's day. In 1912, Toledo's bishop, Joseph Schrembs, told a gathering of Catholic school authorities that "we ought to meet the stand[ards] of the State in the spirit of kindliness in all matters pertaining to the general welfare of the child, and I can see no good reason for refusing certain elementary politeness." He urged "greater compliance in Catholic schools in general," and also admonished his colleagues to refrain from "excessive criticism of the public school."[96] Catholics and public school officials alike observed the change in attitudes toward state regulations.

Why did Catholic school authorities eventually comply with new attendance regulations? Many observers noted that compliance was a crucial means of increasing attendance. Parochial school enrollments, after all, benefited from public attendance officials who enforced orderly transfers and enrollments. Parochial schools, one public official assured an audience of Catholic educators, "have access to the attendance officers, thereby giving them the same facilities for a high percentage of attendance as the public schools."[97] Ellwood Cubberley, the widely read Stanford University education professor and critic of private education, also acknowledged that extending compulsory attendance laws to parochial schools placed the latter "on the same plane as public schools in the matter of school attendance, and . . . extends to them the public facilities for enforcing attendance."[98] Letters from Catholic school officials suggest that they understood the benefits of compliance clearly. Philadelphia's diocesan superintendent, Philip McDevitt, frequently corresponded with the city's chief attendance officer, urging him to provide assistance with parochial school truants in return for Catholic compliance with all reporting requirements.[99] Insofar as Catholic schools gradually came to recognize the accrued benefits of consistent, orderly transfer practices, they complied with state laws mandating attendance reporting.

Catholic schools also complied with complex reporting requirements because the data compiled for them symbolized modern education.[100] As the superintendent of Pittsburgh's parish schools, Reverend Paul E. Campbell, acknowledged, "we live in an age devoted to the scientific study of education," where "meticulously we apply statistical method to the study of educational data."[101] Catholic school administrators, not surprisingly, echoed their public school colleagues in searching for new methods of child accounting. Meetings of the National Catholic Educational Association featured long discussions of the subject, as did dissertations produced by graduates of the Catholic University of America's Department of Education—each sprinkled with citations to the latest works on educational psychology and accounting.[102] In Philadelphia, Superintendent McDevitt urged parochial school principals in 1910 to "keep accurately and faithfully the records of enrollment and attendance, in order that the Annual Report of the parish schools may have both value and authority." Together with his admonition four years earlier, via order of the city's archbishop, that principals "co-operate with the officials of the Bureau of Compulsory Education" wherever possible, Catholic school officials received the message that data and public compliance were essential to furthering the aims of the system.[103] Ultimately, then, while some Catholic educators quietly lamented how "modern public taste in matters educational is more concerned with adequacy of records than with skill in teaching," they dared not resist it.[104] As parochial schools continued to grow, becoming ever more centralized and bureaucratic, Catholics' demand for educational measurement kept pace with public school reformers'.

Managing and measuring transfers between parochial and public schools, in sum, enabled administrators to coordinate the existence of dual, parallel systems. Yet administrators were not the sole group to benefit from a closer articulation between public and parochial schools: Catholic parents and their children also had good reasons to push parochial schools toward greater compliance with public mandates. Children had much to gain from a private school that met modern, state standards. The vast majority of students attending parochial schools who aspired to attend high school had to transfer to the public system. As increasing numbers of Catholic parents sought to enroll their children in secondary schools, parochial primary schools benefited from cooperating with state officials.

Catholic parents and children, like most Americans, turned to public high schools with growing vigor in the decades surrounding the turn of the twentieth century. High school attendance in the United States doubled every decade from 1890 to 1930, spurred by increased urbanization, stronger compulsory attendance and child labor laws, the gradual decline in the youth labor market, and the literacy, numeracy, and vocational skills required by twentieth-century industrial jobs.[105] High school attendance and attainment varied dramatically by class and ethnicity, and Catholic families from more rural, traditional cultures such as southern Italy were particularly resistant to the institution.

By the 1930s, however, the high school fulfilled its reputation as the "people's college," becoming the normative experience for American teenagers and, as those who graduated from high school discovered, a ticket to the skilled professions.[106]

While Catholic parents and children sought access to secondary education, parochial secondary institutions were scarce. Costs, in many cases, were prohibitive. Public high schools originated, by design, as expensive enterprises. Their mid-nineteenth-century advocates believed that physically imposing structures and well-paid instructors would attract middle-class parents away from the private toward the public sector.[107] Cities in the early twentieth century constructed similarly grandiose edifices. New high schools featured science laboratories, elaborate vocational training programs, state-of-the-art gymnasiums, and swimming pools. By World War I, 79 percent of the public high schools accredited by the Midwest's North Central Association had manual training programs, 83 percent had cooking classes, and 68 percent had courses in typing.[108]

Immigrant Catholic communities, in contrast, struggled to fund parochial primary schools, despite estimates that costs averaged only $8 per pupil.[109] As a result, according to one report written at the turn of the century, only 53 Catholic parishes had official "high schools" attached to their larger elementary branches, enrolling a total of less than 2,000 students nationwide. More than ten times that number attended "private" institutions: tuition schools run by religious orders or Catholic colleges for the benefit of the middle classes, in contrast to the legions of parish schools that aspired to universal Catholic attendance.[110] While the number of Catholic high schools would increase considerably over the next three decades, they would never educate Catholic children in proportions similar to parochial elementary schools. The vast majority of Catholic parents who aspired to send their children to secondary schools had little choice but to elect public high schools.[111]

To ensure seamless matriculation between private primary and public secondary schools, parents demanded that parish institutions as closely as possible conform to local and state standards. Since their inception in the early nineteenth century, public high schools had imposed numerous requirements for admission, usually in the form of written entrance examinations. As urban public schools grew into standardized and centralized systems, and as the demand for secondary education burgeoned, most high schools gradually dropped these requirements, assuming that graduates of public primary schools met the standards.[112] Private primary schools, however, were another matter: many urban school systems in the late nineteenth century continued to require private elementary school graduates to pass an entrance exam in order to enroll in a public high school.[113]

Around the turn of the century, growing numbers of high schools chose a new method for assessing parochial school quality, one that colleges used for high school graduates: accreditation.[114] The development of Milwaukee's school laws was a case in point. In the 1880s and 1890s the city's schools permitted public elementary school graduates to enroll in the Milwaukee public high school "without further examination." The school board did not extend that allowance to private school students, however, who in addition to taking the exam needed to produce a certificate indicating that their course of instruction was "equivalent to that of the public schools."[115] In 1901, the board changed course and began to admit private school students into city high schools without an examination, provided that their schools met the "equivalency" standard.[116] A school board committee on course instruction soon began judging the schools that met this standard, adding their names to a growing list of approved or "accredited schools."[117] A similar process characterized Chicago, as well as other cities, where small committees composed of public school teachers and administrators would visit private schools, produce a report, and recommend accreditation or not.[118]

With this stamp of official approval, children who graduated from accredited parochial schools had the advantage of attending public high school without the added strain of an entrance exam, or the "stigma" of attending a nonaccredited institution. A study of Chicago parochial schools in the 1920s found that "nonaccredited [parochial] schools experience some difficulty in retaining pupils who intend to enter public high schools." The author attributed the exodus of students from seventh and eighth grade in large part to the desire "to avoid the examinations they would have to take to enter the public high school if they graduated from a nonaccredited parochial school."[119]

In the increasingly crowded urban marketplace of schooling, diocesan officials understood that regulations caused parents to seek schools that resembled one another, conforming to the same standards. As early as 1904, Buffalo's diocesan school superintendent, E. F. Gibbons, told a gathering of Catholic school administrators that raising standards to conform with public expectations was essential to attract students and parents hoping to attend high school. "There are the children and their parents, who are only too apt to place the modest little [parochial] school in damaging contrast with a fine public school, with its complete staff of teachers, free books, and every inducement to pupils," he announced.[120] By the 1920s, administrators talked openly about a "Catholic educational market" amid the new educational demands imposed by parents. One administrator noted that "Catholic parents are becoming increasingly aware of the handicaps under which the graduates of non-accredited schools labor," particularly for those students anxious about eventually attending Catholic high schools.[121] Reverend Daniel Richard Sullivan, who led a Catholic high school, was particularly colorful about how students and parents yearned for state approval of Catholic schools. Speaking in front of the Catholic Educational Association of Pennsylvania in 1923, he remarked that

> young women at least, like their mothers, have an eye for standard quality both in toilet articles and in education, and will take what bears a recognized stamp and no other. The very first questions they ask you are "what is the rating of your school? Is it approved? How do its graduates stand with my state board and with the professional schools?" . . . They, and not the pastors, are in a position to recommend schools to their pupils, and they evaluate schools in terms of the standardizing agencies and not otherwise.[122]

Other contemporaries agreed. In 1925, when George Johnson looked back on the previous several decades of Catholic education, he noted that "Catholic parents [have] expected the same type of education from us that the children of their neighborhood receive in the public school across the street."[123] Three years later, a Catholic woman from Buffalo, writing privately to the editors of *America*, argued that its exhortations regarding universal parochial school attendance were meaningless unless Catholic schools "are brought up to a high standard." "Catholics do not want their children's education branded as inferior to others," she wrote. Catholic school graduates from institutions with low standards "feel bitter about such things, when they find they are unable to compete with others in the educational and business and professional world."[124] Parental and student demand for Catholic education, in other words, had clear limits. Parochial schools that failed to meet local and state standards were unable to compete with public schools that guaranteed parents an automatic bid to the high school and, so it seemed, the job market.

To assuage these parents, Superintendent Gibbons recommended enhancing standards, which would "protect our graduates when they present themselves for matriculation in higher schools." In New York State, the examinations offered by the regents of the state education system afforded just such a possibility. Gibbons argued that the exams, given to students hoping to attend the state's high schools and colleges, "offer at least one great advantage to our parish schools, viz., a common ground upon which our pupils can meet those of the public schools, and prove their ability to measure up to the public-school or State standard." Like other parochial school administrators, Gibbons welcomed both the exams and the accreditation process because they pressured parochial schools to raise their standards. In addition, publicly sponsored examinations gave diocesan and parish authorities the ability to quantify and publicize the quality of their institutions to Catholic parents. "We must advertise in this age of advertising," he remarked. "We shall display our wares if we wish to draw customers."[125] Accreditation offered the stamp of state approval that diocesan administrators knew would appeal to ambitious, upwardly mobile Catholic parents.[126]

A savvy and pragmatic administrator, Gibbons admitted that such standards, when imposed from outside Catholic authorities, might resemble "ignominious slavery," but he acknowledged that there was little parochial schools could "do to escape" from public standards. "It seems to me that in New York we must be careful not to adopt any plan that would be out of harmony with that of the state schools," he concluded. "Our schools simply have to measure up to their requirements."[127] State standards could thus provide parochial schools with the opportunity to publicize their quality. As another Catholic educational leader noted, conforming to the "same standards" as public schools "would seem the part of wisdom, if only for the protection of our reputation and prestige."[128] Catholic schools had every incentive to meet the various voluntary and involuntary standards states and localities hoped to impose on schools through accreditation and other regulations.

Accreditation and parental demand thus forced Catholic administrators to raise their standards, even though they often resented the pressure. As one Catholic educator put it in 1917, schools seeking accreditation did so "as a necessary means of subsistence, or as a consequence of competition for local patronage" rather than as a "matter of election or choice."[129] A speaker at the National Catholic Educational Association's 1907 meeting similarly admitted that parochial schools were raising standards and centralizing administration not for an intrinsically good reason, but "in order to compete with the public schools."[130] Accreditation and state regulation, these administrators acknowledged, made Catholic schools more, not less, competitive.

The Catholic push for state standards reached its apex in Michigan in 1921, when an Irish Catholic state legislator and parochial school graduate, Vincent P. Dacey, introduced a bill to supervise and enforce new teacher quality standards in private schools. The bill placed parochial schools under the supervision of the state's superintendent of public instruction. It allowed state officials to investigate parochial schools and inspect their enrollment records. More significantly, it mandated that parochial school instructors possess teaching licenses equivalent to those of their public school counterparts, excepting those who had taught for at least ten years. Michigan's Catholics overwhelmingly supported the bill. Some of the state's bishops believed that it would ward off more severe regulations; others hoped that it could help them force laggard schools into modernizing their instruction.[131] Michigan's large second-generation Polish community, eager to direct their children into quality high schools and good jobs, also weighed in to support the bill's passage.[132] So, too, did the National Catholic Educational Association. A. C. Monahan, the association's director, referred to the Dacey bill as "sympathetic to Catholic education." Because "Catholics of the State in large number supported this Bill," he continued, it "indicates to the general public that [Catholics] have confidence that their schools are satisfactory as any other schools in the State." As for the possibility of anti-Catholic enforcement of the law, Monahan knew that the public officials would not dare antagonize the state's large Catholic population. "The inspection which will result will probably be sympathetic," he added, "as the State Department of Education is a political office and can not afford to antagonize the Catholics of the State without great cause."[133] As a result of Catholic support, the Dacey bill passed overwhelmingly into law.

Most, but not all, Catholic school officials spoke favorably of the tighter state standards in bills such as Dacey's. Some bishops, particularly those closer to the more conservative American hierarchy, were much more skeptical about state involvement in Catholic education. Monahan's superiors in the National Catholic Welfare Conference (NCWC), for example, reacted with fury after learning about his comments in the Catholic press. In a series of internal letters and telegrams, Father John Burke, the NCWC's general secretary, called Monahan's actions "disorderly" and a "mistake." Burke declared that Monahan's support for the Dacey bill, which American Catholics could confuse for the NCWC's own endorsement, "has done much harm and has been the cause of much misunderstanding."[134] Monahan quickly offered to resign, and the controversy ended, but the conflict revealed ongoing disagreements among Catholic officials over the extensiveness of state regulation.[135]

Ultimately, however, most Catholic educators recognized the positive value of complying with new state standards. A 1930 study found that public schools continued to place transfers from parochial schools into lower grades, but that standardization tended to lessen the "danger of discrimination in the event of transfer."[136] Dissertations by Catholic University students in the 1930s and 1940s argued that Catholic compliance with accreditation had been "highly desirable."[137] On the subject of fledgling Catholic high schools one even remarked that the "pressure exerted by accrediting agencies has done more to raise the standards" than "any action taken within the Catholic body itself."[138] Without this voluntary "pressure" by local and state authorities, Catholics would not have patronized parochial schools in such consistently large numbers. In an age where Americans saw educational attainment and advanced schooling as central to upward mobility, Catholic schools responded to state regulation and accreditation by raising their standards. In doing so, they attracted students to their schools, before sending them off to public high schools with the proud stamp of state approval.

When Charles Lischka, a researcher for the NCWC, set out in 1924 to compile and publish a short pamphlet on state laws regulating parochial schools, the list of laws quickly began to fill more than a hundred pages. The book featured long lists of often intricate, state-imposed guidelines on private school attendance, accreditation, teacher certification, curriculum, accounting, student health, buildings, and many other policy areas. In the preface to his text, Lischka declared that even Americans steeped in school law would find it a "revelation" to read the variety of regulations and restrictions affecting private schools. States required medical inspection and fire drills. In twenty-three states local school committees certified or inspected private schools. A still larger number required courses on the Constitution, civics, and patriotism, and English had to be the official language of instruction in the school. Michigan, Nebraska, and South Dakota mandated that teachers in parochial schools obtain the same occupational license as those in public schools. States "consider private schools not merely a part of the educational resources of the state," he wrote, "but practically a part of its educational system, subject to indefinite regulation and restriction." Private schools, according to Lischka's survey, were barely private at all.[139]

As Catholic school authorities like Lischka understood, Progressive Era regulations produced a diocesan system decidedly more "public" than ever before. With new transfer and accreditation policies, two urban systems "under quite distinct management" became vastly more coordinated and standardized.[140] State laws and urban administrators pressured diocesan officials to link their students and records with public schools. Catholic educators, understanding the importance parents placed on public institutions and public approval, complied with increasing alacrity. By the 1920s, the nation's two million Catholic school students attended institutions whose curriculum, instructional methods, building design, teacher credentials, and health codes reflected the public school's own standards. In an ideal world, urban children transferring from parochial to public systems felt the effects of this coordination when they arrived at their new school.

Their new teacher would have an enrollment card with the child's name, old school, and grades. The child would be familiar with American history and civics and be comfortable with a teacher instructing in English. He or she also would be familiar with fire drills, medical inspections, and vaccinations. Most importantly, coming from a school with similar standards, the child was ready to learn, at the same ability level as his or her peers.

Standardized public and parochial educational systems enabled Catholic parents to choose between schools that were roughly equivalent academically. With middle-class success increasingly tied to educational attainment—attendance at high schools, and even colleges—Catholic parents and administrators relied on this regulated system of schooling. They yearned for forms of state endorsement that could expand the system, make it easier to compete with public schools, and attract the approval of public high schools. The continued expansion and increasing competitiveness of parochial school systems in the Progressive Era was inextricably linked to the dense texture of laws and administrative procedures that enveloped them.

6

Fighting the Educational Monopoly

IN THE 1920S, conservative Protestants staged the most concerted campaigns since the origins of public school systems to prohibit private education. In more than a dozen states they tried but failed to prohibit attendance at private schools, while in Oregon they successfully enacted a law compelling students to attend public schools exclusively. These campaigns emerged from a post-World War I context rife with nativist, anti-Catholic sentiment. In Oregon and throughout the North, membership in a reconstituted Ku Klux Klan spiked. In Congress, lawmakers sharply restricted immigration from southern and eastern Europe, and they debated establishing a federal department of education capable of dramatically increasing Americanization programs in public schools.

But even as states sought to eliminate educational competition, federal courts began to protect it. The Supreme Court, in its 1925 decision in *Pierce v. Society of Sisters*, struck down Oregon's law. By monopolizing schooling, the Court reasoned, Oregon violated the Fourteenth Amendment's guarantee that no "state shall deprive persons of life, liberty, or property without due process of law." The state had deprived private school operators of their "property" (their schools), and parents of their "liberty" to choose such schools for their children. Children are not "the mere creature of the state," read the unanimous opinion, authored by Justice James C. McReynolds. Rather, parents had a "fundamental," substantive right to elect private schools for their children. *Pierce* represented one of the federal government's most significant interventions in state educational policy to that time. With its decision, the Supreme Court gave immediate national sanction to the educational marketplace forged during the previous half-century.[1]

The meaning of the *Pierce* decision has been much debated, but it remains misunderstood. Judges and legal historians have usually highlighted *Pierce*'s broadly defined "liberal" qualities, stressing that the decision contributed to human freedom by limiting discriminatory government policies.[2] Supreme Court justices in the 1930s cited *Pierce* to justify increased judicial scrutiny of laws infringing on basic civil liberties.[3] Then, in 1954, Chief Justice Earl Warren cited *Pierce* in an early draft of *Bolling v. Sharpe* (the Washington, DC companion case to *Brown v. Board*), drawing on the decision's rhetoric of the "fundamental" rights to education and liberty.[4] In the 1960s and 1970s the Court relied on the broad, unenumerated liberties enunciated in *Pierce* to expand women's rights to contraception and abortion in *Griswold v. Connecticut* and *Roe v. Wade*.[5]

Since the 1990s, however, revisionist historians have subjected the decision to greater criticism. They have noted how the opinion appeared to draw from the same jurisprudential doctrines of "substantive due process" and the "liberty of contract" that conservative judges used to strike down a range of progressive regulatory policies, from state laws limiting working hours in the early twentieth century to federal economic policies during the New Deal. It was precisely because of *Pierce's* association with these ideas of economic liberty and laissez faire that Earl Warren, under pressure from his colleagues, removed the citation from his opinion in *Bolling*.[6] Studies of the individuals involved in the *Pierce* litigation support the view that the decision reflected "conservative" beliefs. William D. Guthrie, the lead attorney for the National Catholic Welfare Conference (NCWC), who represented the Society of Sisters of the Holy Names of Jesus and Mary and their parochial schools, was a corporate lawyer and constitutional scholar renowned for his defense of private property and his contempt for federal progressive legislation such as the income tax and child labor laws. Meanwhile, Justice McReynolds, who authored the opinion, was a racist and an economic conservative who became notorious during the 1930s as one of the "Four Horsemen" of the Court, perennially striking down New Deal legislation.[7]

Interpretations both favorable and unfavorable to *Pierce* agree that the ruling carved out a greater space for private enterprise and parental authority at the expense of an activist state. Liberal and libertarian scholars who praise the decision cite the Court's protection of parental freedom in the case.[8] Some modern libertarians even assert it is one of the greatest Supreme Court decisions of all time.[9] *Pierce's* critics, on the other hand, observe how the ruling foreclosed the possibility that government could aggressively use education to mitigate class stratification and protect children's rights. This latter interpretation highlights the democratic and egalitarian promise of mass—even compulsory—public schooling, and scorns the manner in which the rhetoric of "parental rights" neglected the autonomous needs of children.[10] Ultimately, therefore, scholars on both sides of the debate over the merits of *Pierce* agree on the decision's meaning: that the Court expressed hostility to government intervention in private life, protecting private corporations, religious associations, and parents. "Antistatism" is the word most frequently used to encapsulate the Court's legal philosophy in the case.[11]

This interpretation, however, has obscured how the ruling was originally understood. Catholic officials in 1925 viewed the decision differently, seeing *Pierce* as a profound approval of state regulation. Far from removing states' ability to regulate parochial schools, in fact, Catholics believed the opinion reaffirmed such authority. The unanimous decision explicitly upheld "the power of the State reasonably to regulate all schools, to inspect, supervise and examine them, their teachers and pupils; to require that all children of proper age attend some school, that teachers shall be of good moral character and patriotic disposition, that certain studies plainly essential to good citizenship must be taught, and that nothing be taught which is manifestly inimical to the public welfare."[12]

To regulate, inspect, supervise, examine, and compel—in one sentence the Supreme Court countenanced the vast array of state laws and administrative agencies that had developed over the previous decades. Indeed, several high-ranking Catholic educational authorities expressed disappointment with the Court's obeisance to existing state regulations. As Father John Burke, the NCWC's general secretary, wrote in a private letter, the opinion's treatment of these laws "should sober those who are inclined to be drunk with enthusiasm over this decision."[13] Worried that further regulation might nonetheless hamper Catholic education, Burke concluded that parts of the decision "do not give us so much comfort."[14] *Pierce* protected parochial schools from state abolition, but at the expense of approving the scores of laws regulating nearly every aspect of their existence.

In reality, deference to state regulation was central to the legal arguments proffered by his own side, the NCWC, and its lead counsel, William D. Guthrie. At the core of Guthrie's briefs and oral arguments was a distinction between regulation on the one hand and prohibition on the other. Where Oregon had every right to engage in the former, Guthrie reasoned, it crossed the boundaries established by the Fourteenth Amendment when it exercised the latter. Moreover, Guthrie argued, the notion that the state could achieve its educational goals only through abolishing parochial schools was utterly unreasonable: sound laws regulating parochial schools negated the very rationale for prohibition in the first place. As he asserted in his brief, "where regulation is so completely adequate, prohibition is unnecessary and constitutes mere arbitrariness and wanton abuse of power."[15] Under the state's police powers, he reasoned, Oregon—like any state— possessed substantial tools to shape its parochial schools.

Guthrie's arguments highlighted the ways in which public regulations had grown to become part of the rationale for parochial schools. Far from threatening the existence of private education, state regulations provided Catholic lawyers with the arguments necessary for its survival. The irony of *Pierce*'s "antistatist" protection of parents and corporations from government interference was that the decision also represented a profound assertion of state power. Much as federal courts in the late nineteenth century helped forge a national, interstate commercial market, so the Court in *Pierce* gave federal sanction to the emergent educational marketplaces within states.

Prior to the ruling in *Pierce* the fate of private education in the United States was in doubt. For William Guthrie, a devout Catholic, the stakes were even larger. "The Catholic Church ha[s] never before since the foundations of our National Government faced so dangerous and far-reaching a crisis," he wrote of the Oregon law in 1924. Other state legislatures were in the process of debating similar measures, making it "quite evident that the contagion of the movement was likely to spread." Even more alarming, the mass abolition of private schooling—what Guthrie considered the "greatest possible menace"—could potentially be upheld by the courts. In Iowa, Nebraska, and Ohio, state courts recently had sustained laws that made it a criminal offense for private school instructors to teach subjects in a foreign language. Now Guthrie wondered if state courts might uphold state abolition of private education altogether. A successful legal challenge to the Oregon law would likely have to reach the federal courts, on a federal claim grounded in the liberties protected by the U.S. Constitution. The immediate threat of the Oregon law may have been relegated to the northwestern corner of the nation, but its implications and solutions were national in scope.[16]

As one of private enterprise's greatest defenders, Guthrie was accustomed to making sweeping claims about federal power and constitutional rights. A former partner in the storied Wall Street law firm of Seward, Guthrie & Steele (known today as Cravath, Swaine & Moore), Guthrie had midwifed American business through a period of immense transformation and growth. As U.S. Steel, Standard Oil, and Union Pacific grew into corporate behemoths during the 1890s, lawyers such as Guthrie drew up the contracts, facilitated the mergers, and managed the vast legal intricacies of corporate finance. Guthrie's inventory of clients, contacts, and arguments in front of the Supreme Court reads like a list from a textbook on the Gilded Age. He represented Andrew Carnegie, J. P. Morgan, and the Vanderbilt family, railroads and banks. In the 1890s, as Congressional majorities sought to redistribute income through taxation and expand the scope of federal regulation, Guthrie forcefully stood in the way. He argued against a federal income and excise tax in the famed cases *Pollock v. Farmers' Loan and Trust Company* (1895) and *McCray v. United States* (1904). In 1920 he disclaimed the constitutionality of alcohol prohibition in *The National Prohibition Cases*.[17]

With mansions on Park Avenue and on Long Island neighboring those of America's business magnates, their physical proximity reflecting tight intellectual bonds, Guthrie held views that merged seamlessly with his clients' interests and his own background. He opposed income taxes and antitrust laws both on principled as well as on pragmatic grounds, since these measures were calculated to harm his clients, and he disdained child labor laws since his own humble beginnings as a Catholic child growing up in New York City had not blocked his path to fame and fortune.[18] Oregon's compulsory education law represented everything that Guthrie abhorred: ugly American anti-Catholicism mixed with senseless abolition of private property and individual rights.

The law Guthrie challenged in *Pierce* grew from sources both new and old. It not only drew on elements of the state regulatory policies forged between the 1890s and the 1920s but also emerged in a different context, with distinct aims. It simultaneously tapped into older, nineteenth-century traditions deeply suspicious of private schooling, as well as the renewal of white, Protestant values among the populace in the 1920s. In particular, drives for compulsory public school attendance combined a mixture of motives intensified by World War I. The rise of German militarism and Russian radicalism revived fears about immigrant education, recalling the animated political battles surrounding compulsory attendance laws in the 1880s.

Catholic school authorities had responded to the domestic fallout of World War I by supporting the war effort. Guthrie had enthusiastically backed relief efforts of U.S. allies after the war, giving his time and financial resources to beleaguered Catholics in France.[19] He applauded the "splendid record . . . of patriotic service and in the Army and Navy" of American Catholics, especially parochial school graduates, whom Americans perennially suspected of being "un-American." Catholic participation in the war "refuted all the slanders and libels of the past," he wrote, auguring a new era of comity between Catholics and Protestants in the nation.[20]

But the politics of school reform both during and immediately after the war quickly disillusioned Catholic authorities, many of whom watched in horror as the federal government assumed new powers over education. The war created the will and administrative capacity to produce vast reforms of the nation's schools, both public and private. War mobilization also fanned deep American anxieties about school quality, particularly in comparison with Germany, a nation whose efficient educational systems observers touted worldwide.[21] Many Americans, including the renowned educational philosopher John Dewey, believed that the triumph of American democracy over Prussian militarism depended as much on the public school systems at home as on the troops overseas.[22]

The federal government assumed unprecedented powers during the war, enabling it to engage in sweeping educational reforms. Federal officials in Washington, for example, nationalized American railroads and became more intimately involved in promoting the war in local school systems. The Treasury Department and Food Administration inundated state and local officials with propaganda materials and dramatically increased spending on educational programs.[23] In 1917, Congress enacted the first major federal educational program: aid for vocational education in high schools. A year later, to augment war mobilization, the House and Senate nearly approved the Smith Act, which would have created a federal Department of Education capable of dispensing $100 million to the states as carrots to induce higher educational quality. As the United States entered the war the impulse, will, and capacity to fundamentally reform American education breathed with renewed vigor.[24]

Private schools had always rested uncomfortably in the ideological matrix of reformers who focused on public education systems. In the context of war, fears about immigrant private schooling and radical education spiked. States responded to concerns about German-speaking Americans with xenophobic restrictions on the schools they attended. By the early 1920s twenty-nine states required English as the principal, if not exclusive, language of instruction in both public and private primary schools. Two dozen states passed laws mandating that private schools teach courses on the Constitution, civics, or patriotism.[25] Following the armistice, as fears of Kaiserism turned into fears of Bolshevism, public officials began rooting out private radical schools. In 1921, only months after a group of anarchists exploded a bomb on Wall Street that killed thirty-eight people, the New York legislature banned instruction in schools that promoted the "doctrine that organized governments shall be overthrown by force, violence or unlawful means." A state appellate court upheld the law the following year.[26]

As Congress debated stringent immigrant restriction laws, federal school officials commented with aplomb on the need to regulate private schools. The U.S. Commissioner of Education, P. P. Claxton, echoed the call for English-language instruction in private schools, writing in 1920 that "it is the duty of the State to make such inspection of all private and parochial schools as may be necessary to make sure that . . . they offer instruction in those subjects which are generally considered necessary for good and intelligent citizenship and for successful living in a democracy."[27] In the proposed but never enacted Smith-Towner bill, states receiving federal money were required to Americanize their foreign-born residents by emphasizing instruction in English.[28] Guthrie, writing as an interested Catholic as well as an expert in constitutional law, called the bill an unconstitutional recipe for the "complete nationalization of education" and a threat to religious education throughout the nation.[29]

The Smith-Towner bill also elicited enormous protests among certain members of the NCWC and an interlocking organization, the National Catholic Educational Association. The NCWC, which would lead the legal effort against the Oregon law several years later, was itself a product of Catholic support for the war. Originally named the National Catholic War Conference, the NCWC created a unified national organization led by a committee of bishops. Following the armistice, these bishops helped transform the NCWC into a powerful, centralized lobbying force for Catholic interests, with offices in Washington. One of the NCWC's first tasks was to mobilize Catholics against Smith-Towner. Together with the Catholic press, the NCWC complained that increased federal authority in education would raise the status of public schools at the expense of private ones. It would result in a greater centralization of education along the very Prussian lines that had led Germany down its path to war. It would unfairly raise taxes for Catholics who, by virtue of their commitment to private education, would not see the fruits of new public projects. It would violate the federalist principles embodied in the Tenth Amendment of the Constitution, which left unenumerated powers (such as education) to the states. Finally, it would harm Catholic schools' ability to compete with public alternatives. Because the public purse was better endowed than parish coffers, Catholic schools would be hard pressed to keep up with public systems' modern buildings, school buses, and free textbooks. The more the federal government spent on public schools, the less Catholic authorities could defend the superiority—in secular matters, at least—of parochial institutions. In large part due to the NCWC's opposition, the Smith-Towner bill ran aground after two aborted attempts in the early 1920s.[30]

The more menacing, short-term threat to Catholic education in the immediate postwar years was not federal intervention, but rather state abolition of parochial schools. Anti-Catholic social movements in Michigan and elsewhere fought to outlaw attendance in parochial schools. As early as 1918 a Detroit-based organization calling itself the Wayne

County Civic League proposed an amendment to the state legislature compelling attendance exclusively in public schools. When that measure was defeated, the group—now named the Public School Defense League—gathered the required number of signatures to place compulsory public school attendance on the 1920 ballot, subjecting it to popular referendum. In response, a coalition of Catholics and Lutherans organized to oppose the measure and soundly defeated the amendment. Once again, in 1924, the Public School Defense League, together with the local Ku Klux Klan, gathered the requisite number of signatures to place it on the ballot, which Michigan voters again rejected, this time even more resoundingly.[31]

Political movements in more than a dozen states attempted to follow Michigan's lead by passing similar legislation. Only in Oregon did such a measure succeed. There, the Scottish Rite Masons cooperated with the Klan to introduce a compulsory public school bill in 1920. Unlike in Michigan, where the law would have produced an economic calamity by suddenly throwing large numbers of parochial school students into the public system, Oregon had only a small Catholic school population of roughly nine thousand Catholic students, two-thirds of whom resided in Portland. This low attendance in Catholic schools diminished economic arguments against increased public school attendance.[32]

In order to court the local Klan's political support, Oregon's Democratic gubernatorial candidate Walter M. Pierce supported compulsory public education. When the bill, along with Pierce's candidacy, appeared on the ballot in the fall of 1922, a majority of Oregon voters supported both. Set to take effect in 1926, the law compelled children ages eight to sixteen to attend public school, exempting children physically unable to attend school, children living at too great a distance from a public school, and children who received private tutoring, so long as they received annual written permission from the county superintendent and sat for a quarterly examination. Noncompliant parents faced heavy fines and imprisonment.[33]

Efforts to abolish parochial schooling unified and mobilized American Catholics to a nearly unprecedented extent. Nearly 100,000 protesters gathered in Detroit's baseball stadium to express their dissent against Michigan's 1920 compulsory public school attendance law. Responses to the Oregon bill came from across the nation, as churches, newspapers, and advocacy groups flooded local Catholic groups with tracts and, eventually, funds for legal defense. Coming in the wake of World War I, those on both sides of the argument stressed the "foreign" nature of their opponents. While proponents of the law insisted that only public schooling could ensure an America free from radical and antidemocratic forces, the Catholic press assaulted it as a proposed "state monopoly" reminiscent of the very Prussian, or Bolshevik, school systems that Americans had fought to defeat.[34]

NCWC officials quickly sought to distinguish these existential threats from the much longer, and more sanguine, history of state regulation. Harrisburg's bishop, Phillip McDevitt, drew a line between the "enlargement of civil authority over private schools" and "legislation that would make education the exclusive function of the State." Educational regulation, McDevitt stated, was distinct from the creation of a "State monopoly of education."[35] A. C. Monahan, the National Catholic Educational Association's director, went even further, arguing that support for state regulations affecting parochial school attendance, teaching licenses, and curriculum standards was essential to maintaining their existence. He wrote that "the attitude that the Parochial school is a private institution, and not a public utility, which has been assumed by a few of our Catholic authorities, is bound to create unjust suspicion toward them and their work, and result either in their abolition or in their complete control by public authorities." If Catholic schools had the state's stamp of approval they were less likely to meet with public suspicion. It was better to support a strong regulatory regime in the short term, Monahan believed, than to risk Catholic education's long-term abolition.[36]

When William Guthrie constructed his legal argument in defense of parochial schools, he opted to foreground this insight that regulation could be private schools' salvation. That public regulation occupied a central place in Guthrie's argument in the first place might seem peculiar: Guthrie's biography, after all, conforms with classic depictions of the early twentieth-century legal establishment as a bastion for laissez-faire ideas. In nearly all of the Supreme Court cases that Guthrie argued, he represented private individuals or firms battling against state and federal legislatures that had allegedly overstepped their constitutional authority. His views reflected the broader jurisprudential agenda of the so-called *Lochner* era, in which several notable decisions struck down state and federal regulatory laws under the due process clause of the Fourteenth Amendment. In *Lochner v. New York* (1905)—a case that critics believed defined the Court's ideological stance until the 1930s—the Supreme Court ruled that a New York statute imposing maximum working hours for bakers was unconstitutional, in part because it violated an unenumerated "liberty of contract." When the legal scholar Benjamin Twiss began researching the origins of judicial conservatism amid the obstructionism of the New Deal Supreme Court, he focused on Guthrie, a standard bearer for the "outstanding triumph of laissez faire" during the period.[37] While legal historians have revised this facile understanding of the *Lochner* era, Guthrie's name continues to appear with the words "laissez faire" attached.[38]

Guthrie's legal conception of public regulation—his view of "police powers jurisprudence"—was decidedly more complex than the rigid absolutism of laissez faire. In general, he felt that courts should strike down government regulation under two conditions: when it discriminated against one individual or group and favored another, or when a regulation's provisions were arbitrary or unnecessary. Like some of the members of the *Lochner* Court, Guthrie also believed that the due process clause of the Fourteenth Amendment guaranteed a substantive, "fundamental right" to property and contract.[39] But nowhere did he suggest that individual and corporate activity could be unrestrained by public regulation. Indeed, many of his concerns about government interference with private property were procedural in nature, stemming from his conviction that federal courts, rather than state legislatures, should be the primary arbiter of "reasonable" police powers. For Guthrie, courts played an essential role in structuring the most contested sites of public regulation in the late nineteenth century: the relationship between labor and capital and between private enterprise and the state. Understanding Guthrie's juris-prudential philosophy, as well the legal context that surrounded it, is essential to redis-covering the forgotten regulatory emphasis of *Pierce*.

Guthrie's ideas about the Fourteenth Amendment and the role of federal courts were emblematic of the immense transformation in American law ushered in by Northern victory in the Civil War. The Fourteenth Amendment, ratified in 1868, brought to the forefront of American law an interlocking yet unwieldy set of ideas about individual rights and centralized governance. Republicans proposed the amendment as a way to codify civil rights legislation and to protect African Americans from racially discrimi-natory Southern state laws—the Black Codes—passed immediately following the Civil War. Where the Fifth Amendment's due process clause protected Americans from dis-criminatory federal laws, the due process and equal protection clauses of the Fourteenth Amendment applied these protections to Americans from the several states. Free African Americans would now have the same rights to life, liberty, and property, including the right to contract, as white citizens.[40] Indeed, all Americans could now invoke due proc-ess rights when seeking redress from discriminatory or arbitrary state uses of the police power, including laws that affected their private enterprises.[41] The titles of the great legal treatises on police power in the late nineteenth century captured these new constitutional checks on state regulatory authority: Thomas Cooley on the *Constitutional Limitations which Rest upon the Legislative Power of the States* (1871); Christopher Tiedeman on the *Limitations of Police Power in the United States* (1886); and Ernst Freund's subtitle to his book *The Police Power: Public Policy and Constitutional Rights* (1904).[42]

Protecting individual rights from state governments, ironically, required even greater federal judicial authority, and federal courts became the primary agency to protect lib-erty and property. Beginning in the 1840s, successive political generations empowered federal courts to restrain interstate rivalries and forge a more fluid, national marketplace. In 1842 the Supreme Court ruled in *Tyson v. Swift* that federal courts could decide which common-law rules applied in cases involving parties from different states. The *Swift* doc-trine set in motion a body of federal common law that undermined states' efforts to pro-tect particular local enterprises from interstate competition. In 1867 and 1875 Congress passed laws further extending the reach of the federal courts, granting them greater juris-diction to hear state cases in which a party felt it could not receive a fair hearing from local judges. Republican lawmakers believed these judicial reforms would assist African Americans seeking fair trials and, indeed, these acts became essential—if imperfect—tools for racial and ethnic minorities, along with women, pursuing civil liberty within their states.[43]

Multistate corporations also benefited from heightened federal review, and their remonstrations proved immensely successful in removing barriers to enter into individual state markets. As the U.S. economy grew more integrated in the 1870s and 1880s, the Court aggressively protected interstate commerce from protectionist state laws, striking down state licensure, inspection, and taxation regimes that attempted to keep "foreign" goods and salesmen from entering the state. The federal government, with the Supreme Court leading the way, stood poised to impose greater uniformity in legal arenas across American life.[44] *Pierce* was a direct result of this legacy.

In the realm of state regulation (the subject of *Pierce*), the Fourteenth Amendment's due process clause became the primary means to enforce these dual commitments to private rights along with greater federal judicial power. Guthrie, an active and lifelong Republican, became one of the Amendment's most prominent exponents. In a variety of prominent venues Guthrie defended judicial independence and the rights of federal judges to strike down state legislation that he deemed unconstitutional.[45] In addition to his arguments in front of the U.S. Supreme Court, he served as president of both the New York State Bar Association and the Association of the Bar of the City of New York. His personal ties to wealthy donors and trustees opened doors to the most prestigious chaired lectureships and professorships in America law. He delivered the esteemed Yale Law School's Storrs Lectures in Constitutional Law in 1907 and in 1909 became the Ruggles Professor of Constitutional Law at Columbia Law School.[46] In his widely read *Lectures on the Fourteenth Amendment*, published in 1898, he referred to the Fourteenth Amendment as America's "new Magna Charta," a "bulwark" on which citizens would protect themselves from the "growing tendency to invade the liberty of the individual and to disregard the rights of property."[47]

Guthrie's enunciations of individual liberty, however, did not signify an opposition to all, or even most, of the emerging regulatory state. For Guthrie the Fourteenth Amendment's protections rendered only particular types of laws unconstitutional. State regulations would be upheld so long as they fulfilled two basic conditions: that they be neutral in their classification and enforcement, and reasonable in their scope.[48] Like most prominent lawyers and judges trained in constitutional law during the late nineteenth century, he believed that the due process clause gave citizens and businesses alike substantial freedom from the burden of unequal laws. Populists and progressives at the time feared the de facto powers that private business owners wielded over defenseless workers, forcing them to labor in underpaid, exacting, and dangerous conditions. Guthrie, however, feared the de jure authority that legislatures possessed to shape private enterprise in ways that benefited one group over another: "class legislation" that used the police power to take from one party and give to another. Neither taxes that soaked the rich nor building codes that disproportionately affected the immigrant poor could be countenanced by a Constitution that mandated strict neutrality and equality in conflicts between social groups. Courts therefore had the responsibility to strike down all public regulations that discriminated against particular classes, whether workers or owners, immigrants or natives. Minimum wages, maximum hours, and income taxes that arbitrarily singled out particular groups tended to fit in this category of "class legislation."[49]

The maximum hours law for bakers at the heart of *Lochner*, Guthrie believed, was one such law. In a 1912 address on "Constitutional Morality" given before the Pennsylvania State Bar Association, he defended the *Lochner* ruling as exemplifying the proper role of federal courts "in protecting the individual and the minority against unconstitutional enactments favoring one class at the expense of another." In *Lochner*, he said, the legislature's maximum hours law discriminated against owners, who would be prosecuted for the actions of their employees.[50] In other cases, however, owners were the favored class. In describing the 1885 New York case *In re Jacobs*, Guthrie discussed how the owners of large tobacco factories in New York had colluded "to destroy the competition of cigar manufacturers who worked at home" by pressuring the legislature to prohibit tobacco production in tenement houses. The small business owners and workers had as much of a right to their liberty and property, he argued, as did the bakery owners in *Lochner*. Reasonable police powers ought to be neutral in their impact. When public regulations served particular private interests they violated the constitutional protections afforded by the Fourteenth Amendment.[51]

For state regulations to be constitutional, according to Guthrie, they had to be not only neutral in their intended impact but also reasonable in their scope. Legislatures could regulate railroad or grain elevator rates, for example, but they could not set those rates so low as to deprive businesses of property without due process. Federal courts, then, had the responsibility to draw the line between "reasonable" regulation and "unreasonable" (and unconstitutional) deprivation. Guthrie was fond of quoting Chief Justice Morrison Waite's pronouncement that the "power to regulate is not a power to destroy, and limitation is not the equivalent of confiscation."[52] In his *Lectures* he favorably transcribed the portion of the majority opinion in *Lawton v. Steele* (1894), which insisted that regulations be "necessary for the accomplishment of the purpose, and not unduly oppressive."[53] When the Supreme Court overturned a state regulation as having ventured into the territory of confiscation—as it did in *Chicago, Milwaukee and St. Paul Railway Company v. Minnesota* (1890)—Guthrie eagerly showered the judges with praise.[54]

Guthrie therefore was hardly a zealot for unbridled capitalism. So long as regulations were neutral and reasonable, he deemed them permissible. He believed that judges would rightly uphold public police authority most of the time, recognizing that states required flexibility in order to govern.[55] Like the Supreme Court of the *Lochner* era—which *upheld* more than 99 percent of the social and economic regulations that came before it between 1887 and 1911[56]—Guthrie had no constitutional objections to the vast majority of public regulations. "The truth is that our constitutions, national and State, do not stand in the way of any fair and just exercise of what is called the police power," he wrote in 1912. "They do not prevent reasonable regulations tending to protect the health of the community; and that they certainly do not prevent the enactment of proper and reasonable factory Acts or proper and reasonable workmen's compensation Acts." New York's general Public Health Law, which prevented food manufacturing in unsanitary places, was a perfect example of a regulation "clearly within the police power of the legislature." It

protected workers and consumers in a way that did not discriminate against one particular class, unlike the unconstitutional bakery law the legislature enacted to single out a
particular group of workers.[57]

Guthrie's defense of state police powers was not mere rhetoric. Five years before *Pierce*,
he defended New York's right to impose emergency rent ceilings during the housing
shortage following the outbreak of World War I. Guthrie took the case for free, at the
pleading of a colleague.[58] Amid the "extortionist" rents being charged by landlords, and
the war industry's immense hunger for housed workers, he submitted a brief arguing for
the "ever-existing police power and *duty* of the State to legislate by fair and appropriate
means to secure the protection, safety and general welfare of the community." In the context of the war emergency, the brief read, "the rights of property . . . are not so absolute
as to necessitate any such self-destructive and suicidal policy of government."[59] The rent
controls, in other words, were perfectly reasonable given the exigencies created by the
war. Such support for state police powers stunned Guthrie's friends. His corporate lawyer
colleagues upbraided him privately, inquiring politely whether he had lost his mind.[60]
The secretary general of the NCWC's National Catholic Educational Association,
Francis Howard, barely concealed his astonishment after Guthrie sent him the brief.[61]
Despite these pressures to reconsider his position, Guthrie persisted, seeing little contra-
diction between his general advocacy of property rights and his support for reasonable
state police powers when merited by circumstance.

When Oregon voted to outlaw attendance in private schools in November 1922, Guthrie
was the NCWC's obvious choice to lead the legal battle against it. Francis Howard had
immense respect for Guthrie's longstanding devotion to the Catholic Church and to private property—both victims of the Oregon law. The two had corresponded extensively in
early 1920 amid the controversy over the Smith-Towner bill, sharing their concerns about
the growth of the federal government and the assault on private enterprise, including in
education.[62] In March 1923, four months before the NCWC filed suit against the Oregon
law in federal court, it officially named Guthrie lead counsel in the case.[63]

Guthrie had already been at work pressuring the Supreme Court, with its attention
now drawn to another private school case in Nebraska, to turn toward Oregon. That 1923
Nebraska case, *Meyer v. Nebraska*, marked the most prominent regulatory dispute involving a parochial school to reach the U.S. Supreme Court. The spark that ignited the case
occurred on an otherwise average Tuesday in May 1920. When the school superintendent
of Hamilton County, Nebraska, some seventy miles west of Lincoln, paid a visit to the
Zion Evangelical Lutheran parochial school he found its teacher, Robert Meyer, leading
the class in German. Teaching primary school in a foreign language was illegal in Nebraska,
as it was in several states that had passed English-only laws in the wake of World War I. The
state convicted Meyer, who, joining with the Lutheran Missouri Synod, soon appealed. The
Synod's lawyer, Arthur Mullen, claimed that the law violated Meyer's property rights—his
right to work—as protected under the Fourteenth Amendment. Furthermore, insofar as
foreign languages were not, per se, inimical to the public welfare, they did not constitute

a "legitimate subject for prohibitory legislation."[64] The U.S. Supreme Court agreed to hear *Meyer* in 1922, which it bundled together with a handful of similar lawsuits emanating from Catholics and Lutherans in Nebraska, Iowa, and Ohio.[65]

Guthrie was undoubtedly disturbed by the Nebraska law but publicly chose to withhold his opinion. The English-only statutes were minor affairs when compared with the Oregon law, which, after all, abolished all instruction within private schools. To draw the justices' attention to what he saw as the more significant issue, Guthrie and his law partner, Bernard Hershkopf, submitted an amicus brief in *Meyer*. There, Guthrie struck at the distinction made by Justice Waite between regulation and abolition, arguing that while the Nebraska law might pass constitutional muster, legislatures did not have limitless police powers over private schools. He acknowledged that Nebraska and Oregon's laws were not equivalent, but maintained that if the Supreme Court affirmed the English-only law in *Meyer* it must draw the line there. Abolishing private education interfered with the natural rights of parents, he wrote, similar to how Plato's *Republic* envisioned a utopia where children would be raised communally. Equally important, Guthrie insisted, was how Oregon's law violated private schools' property rights, a claim shared by Meyer's lawyers. A private school, Guthrie wrote, was "an ordinary and honest business" employing "many worthy citizens," subject just as much to due process protections as the other private enterprises he had defended.[66]

Guthrie's amicus brief proved immensely influential. Arthur Mullen had mentioned the specter of private school abolition during oral arguments, but that topic did not appear in the Lutheran Synod's brief. Guthrie placed private school abolition front and center. The thin line he introduced between prohibition of foreign-language instruction and abolition of private schools likely moved the justices. As they learned during the oral arguments, the Nebraska legislature passed its language law only after a measure to ban private education entirely had failed by a single vote.[67] The majority opinion, written by James McReynolds, adopted the property rights arguments introduced by Mullen and Guthrie in noting how the law "interfere[d] with the calling of modern language teachers." It placed itself squarely within the post-Civil War jurisprudential movement, championed by Guthrie, to have federal courts protect "those privileges long recognized at common law," including the right to contract, hold employment, and receive education. In a more direct reference to Guthrie's brief, McReynolds referred to the overweening educational policies in Plato's *Republic*, establishing a clear link between Nebraska's regulation and Oregon's abolition.[68]

Ultimately, the Supreme Court ruled 7–2 that language laws like Nebraska's violated the Constitution. Justices Oliver Wendell Holmes and George Sutherland dissented, citing the reasonableness of the English-language laws given the desirability "that all citizens of the United States should speak a common tongue."[69] When the NCWC legal team learned of the Court's majority ruling in *Meyer*, they filed their challenge to the compulsory education law in the Oregon federal district court. McReynolds's opinion hinted that the Supreme Court would likely be receptive to their cause.[70]

Pierce v. Society of Sisters was perfectly suited to Guthrie's litigation experience. Unlike Robert Meyer, the Society of Sisters of the Holy Names of Jesus and Mary was a corporation, owning and operating six schools throughout Oregon and educating more than 865 students. It was exactly the sort of legal entity, with the exception of being a nonprofit corporation, that Guthrie had defended his whole life.[71] Others in the NCWC feared that a corporate plaintiff would harm their case, and even Guthrie at first was concerned about establishing a legal argument on the basis of property rights rather than religious and parental liberty.[72] John Burke, for example, worried that an individual would have a stronger claim to Fourteenth Amendment due process protections. Others grew anxious that the Court might hold, as it did a mere fifteen years earlier in *Berea v. Kentucky*, that states had ample right to regulate the private educational corporations they chartered.[73]

Guthrie quickly assuaged any concerns about corporate rights. As an eyewitness to the growth of corporate power and consolidation in the late nineteenth century, a movement aided by the Supreme Court, he reminded Burke that "it is the settled rule that the word 'persons' as used in the [Fourteenth] Amendment includes corporations and that corporations are entitled to the protection of its guaranties."[74] As for the precedent in *Berea*, Guthrie responded that if an individual brought suit it "might create the impression on the court that we were fearful that the doctrine of the *Berea College* case applied," which could potentially expose the Catholic Church itself to future litigation. *Berea* was nothing to be feared, as nowhere did it "go to the length of permitting a State to prohibit parents, guardians and custodians from sending children to any properly conducted school, corporate or otherwise."[75] Kentucky was regulating, not prohibiting, private schools, and public regulation was not the legal issue.

On March 31, 1924, Judge Charles Wolverton of Oregon's federal district court delivered a decision striking down the state's compulsory attendance law. In a sentence that Guthrie no doubt was pleased to read, Wolverton's opinion noted that the state's "exercise of the police power is subject to judicial review, and property rights cannot be ruthlessly destroyed by wrongful enactment." Oregon's law violated due process in part because it discriminated against private schools despite there being no evidence that private education was particularly harmful. More importantly, however, the law went far beyond the reasonable scope of valid state police powers. The state "destroy[ed] the business and occupation of the complainants' schools," exceeding the "limitations of its power" and therefore depriving the aggrieved parties of their property without due process of law.[76] While Wolverton's decision proved only temporary, and Oregon's attorney general quickly filed an appeal, the reasoning mattered. As Guthrie prepared his arguments for the Supreme Court, he employed the distinction between regulation and abolition, cited by Wolverton, to the Sisters' advantage.

Public regulation, Guthrie insisted time and again in his Supreme Court brief, was not at issue in *Pierce*. Catholics and private school operators, after all, tolerated many kinds of laws. To punctuate his point, Guthrie submitted an appendix to his Supreme Court brief with a 156-page list of state laws regulating private schools. Throughout his brief he referenced this list, demonstrating to the justices that Oregon's private schools were not challenging state regulations. "At the outset, it should be clearly understood that the private and parochial schools of Oregon are not in court complaining of any *regulatory* measure," he wrote. "Private and parochial schools in Oregon are, and long have been, subject to inspection by the State Superintendent of Public Instruction, and anything prejudicial to the public welfare could easily have been prevented by proper and reasonable supervisional regulation."[77]

> As Appendix II further shows, the education laws of the various states provide for varying degrees of regulation and control by the state of private schools, their several curricula and teachers. Provision has, for example, been made that representatives of the state shall inspect private schools, that their standing under the compulsory school laws and otherwise shall depend upon approval by the state authorities, that general standards laid down by the state authorities shall control the curriculum of the private school, that certain subjects inculcating patriotism shall be taught, such as courses related to the Constitution, civic duties, etc., that elementary courses shall be conducted in English, that the flag shall be displayed about the schoolhouse, that teachers in private schools shall obtain certificates from the state and be required to be citizens of the United States or to take the oath of allegiance, that private schools shall furnish reports and statistical data to the state authorities in connection with the compulsory school laws and otherwise, that private schools shall be subject to state regulation as to medical, health and sanitary matters, and that no doctrine subversive of the authority of the state shall be taught in private schools.[78]

"These statutory provisions," Guthrie concluded, "show how far the control of the state over private education may reasonably extend and how unnecessary it is to suppress all private and parochial schools in order to insure unobjectionable methods of teaching and courses of study, or the inculcation of patriotism in the minds of American children." Guthrie returned to this argument repeatedly, insisting that Catholics were not challenging the dozens of reasonable state regulations affecting private schools.[79]

Precisely because of these regulations, Guthrie argued, abolishing private education was unreasonable, a deprivation of property without due process. "In such a system of regulation, there is no element of total and indiscriminate prohibition," he added. "It is not reasonably necessary to destroy the private and parochial schools conducted by this appellee, which has scrupulously obeyed the law." After all, "where regulation is so completely adequate, prohibition is unnecessary and constitutes mere arbitrariness and wanton abuse of power." If Oregon schools truly failed to fulfill basic American principles, then "they can be made to do so by proper regulation." In this reading, regulation was not so much the oppressor of Catholic schools in Oregon as a means to its survival. Public law negated the need to abolish private schools.[80]

On June 1, 1925, the Supreme Court unanimously struck down the Oregon law. As in *Meyer*, Justice McReynolds authored the opinion. As in *Meyer*, he admitted the close connection between private schools and other private enterprises. He likened parents to "customers" and referenced "property" or "business" eleven times. In a fourteen-paragraph decision, McReynolds used one to explain how the law violated the "fundamental theory of liberty" of parenting that he had asserted earlier in *Meyer*. The aspects of the case relating to corporations' property rights, on the other hand, occupied four paragraphs. McReynolds defended the view that corporations, like individuals, could seek protection under the Fourteenth Amendment, and that a court injunction was reasonable—despite the law not yet having taken effect—since it was necessary to "protect business enterprise against interference with the freedom of patrons or customers."[81]

The opinion situated the case exactly where Guthrie said it belonged: in the annals of corporate rights and unreasonable state police powers. But McReynolds's decision, like Guthrie's brief, also asserted that corporate autonomy had its limits. Guthrie had mentioned countless times that states had a wide array of tools to regulate corporations and, just as McReynolds had borrowed the language of Plato's *Republic* from Guthrie's *Meyer* brief, so in *Pierce* McReynolds drew upon Guthrie's arguments about reasonable state regulation. In a remark that echoed Guthrie's elongated sentences about proper state police powers, McReynolds wrote that nowhere did this opinion prevent the "power of the State reasonably to regulate all schools, to inspect, supervise and examine them, their teachers and pupils; to require that all children of proper age attend some school, that teachers shall be of good moral character and patriotic disposition, that certain studies plainly essential to good citizenship must be taught, and that nothing be taught which is manifestly inimical to the public welfare."[82] Here were the three decades' worth of state laws that Guthrie had summarized in his voluminous appendix.

With McReynolds's decision, the Supreme Court, by virtue of its ultimate federal jurisdiction, affirmed on constitutional grounds the regulated educational marketplaces of American states. On the one hand, the ruling prohibited states from eliminating educational competition. Majorities could not mandate public school monopolies, nor, as McReynolds would reiterate two years later in a case about foreign-language schools in the U.S. territory of Hawaii, could the Constitution justify wantonly regulating private schools out of the existence.[83] On the other hand, state regulation of private schools would continue unabated. When states and localities failed to uphold this federal mandate courts would act as a quasi-"super" board of education, capable of maintaining educational competition throughout the nation.[84] As the NCWC's executive director, James H. Ryan, observed shortly after the decision, even when "discriminatory legislation [is] enacted in isolated instances, the private schools always can have recourse to the courts."[85] In striking down state laws in *Meyer* and *Pierce*, the Court did not diminish the power of the government to shape education: at the state level the Court affirmed it, and at the federal level, the Court dramatically enhanced it.

Responding to the decision, Catholic officials within the NCWC acknowledged its assertions of state police power. "*Regulation* is normal, *prohibition* is *drastic*," was the summary of NCWC's legal expert Charles Lischka.[86] Guthrie, for one, always had recognized the potential pitfalls of his own arguments elevating state regulation, at one point writing in private that he was growing "apprehensive that the court may stress the feature of the power of regulation, which is so open to abuse and oppression." He had tried to prevent this abuse through a "constant use of the word 'reasonable' in that connection," but the opportunity for the Court to make broad claims about public regulation was always present.[87] Fortunately for Guthrie, McReynolds had indeed used the qualifier "reasonably" in his discussion of state regulation in the opinion. When the NCWC's John Burke read that portion of the decision, he remarked that "the word 'reasonably' saves the paragraph." Nonetheless, Burke recognized that the decision was anything but the paean to private property that some critics concluded. "I am inclined to believe that legally the paragraph in its decision dealing with State supervision settles nothing," he wrote. "The paragraph on its face betrays the disposition and mind of the Court and shows that it would not be willing to declare a law unconstitutional which prohibited schools wherein, for example, the teachers were not of patriotic disposition and wherein certain studies, plainly essential to good citizenship, were not taught."[88] A lawyer corresponding with Burke agreed, claiming that the decision "leaves open, of course, the extent to which specific examination questions may be insisted upon and how far inspection and supervision in general may go."[89] James H. Ryan remarked optimistically that Catholic schools were "prepared and even anxious to meet all the just demands" and regulations the decision portended.[90] NCWC officials, though ecstatic about the decision, understood that the Court did nothing to remove the state's heavy involvement from their schools.

Other legal observers outside the NCWC also recognized the decision's approval of state regulation. When a doctoral student at American University in Washington, DC read through the case materials in *Pierce* several years later, he saw state power everywhere. *Pierce* "recognizes that the state has the unequivocal right to determine and prescribe the subjects to be thus taught and to supervise and regulate this instruction," he concluded. "It is difficult to see wherein the states could ask for any broader authority to regulate rightfully the secular education in private and parochial schools than is afforded by the decision in the Oregon case."[91] Interpretations stressing the regulatory implications of *Pierce* even found their way into the other major 1925 court case involving schools, *The State of Tennessee v. John T. Scopes*, about whether the state could prohibit teaching the theory of evolution in its public schools. Arguing for the State of Tennessee, William Jennings Bryan had intended to read excerpts of *Pierce* aloud, especially McReynolds's pronouncements on "the right of the state" to "direct what shall be taught and also forbid the teaching of anything 'manifestly inimical to the public welfare.'" Although *Pierce* dealt with private school regulation, and *Scopes* with public schools, Bryan believed the emphasis "fits this case exactly."[92] Those searching for statist justifications in *Pierce* found them easily.

State courts, instead of highlighting *Pierce*'s enunciations of parental liberty, seized upon the decision's regulatory emphasis. Four years after *Pierce*, in *State v. Oscar Hoyt*, the New Hampshire Supreme Court relied on McReynolds's opinion in upholding a state statute that prohibited home schooling. The decision quoted verbatim his paragraph on the state's ample police powers over education, reasoning that "attendance at some school may still be required, and that the state may supervise the school attended." Ultimately, the court found that this "power to supervise necessarily involves the power to reject the unfit, and to make it obligatory to submit to supervision," an authority the local statute did not exceed.[93] Likewise, courts in New Jersey (1937), Virginia (1948), New York (1950), and California (1953) cited McReynolds in upholding prosecutions of parents who violated compulsory attendance statutes, usually through home schooling.[94] For many parents yearning for the liberty to school their children in alternative ways, *Pierce* was a dead end. While the decision protected private schools across the nation from abolition it also sanctioned a federally applied ceiling of permissive educational regulation, whose heights states did not often approach.

Given the strong assertion of public power in *Pierce,* why today is it seen as fundamentally antistatist? The story of how judges and scholars came to ignore the decision's regulatory emphasis began in the federal courts and the liberal press. As a rising tide of liberal reformers sought to defeat *Lochner* era jurisprudence, they succeeded in discarding and discrediting *Pierce*. For American progressives, *Pierce* needed to be thrown out with the rest of the conservative jurisprudential bathwater. As a result, the state power inherent in the *Pierce* decision was forgotten as quickly as it was asserted.

As early as 1925, some American progressives began interpreting *Pierce* as an attack on the regulatory state. In a series of articles published in the *New Republic* shortly after the ruling, liberals seized on the Court's use of *Lochner* era police-powers jurisprudence. They attacked McReynolds's reliance on substantive due process—that the Society of Sisters had a right to its property—all the while ignoring his strong defense of state educational regulation. In an unsigned editorial entitled "School, Church and State," one *New Republic* writer asserted that "no question . . . of the quality of the educational training of parochial schools is even bruited" and that "the right of the state to stipulate what education its children shall receive is hardly mentioned." The writer denounced the very basis of the decision in property rights.[95]

In a letter to the magazine, the legal scholar Morris R. Cohen echoed these remarks, writing that the Court had "stretched the term property" to well beyond its traditional meaning.[96] Harvard Law School professor Felix Frankfurter offered a more nuanced reading than his colleagues, at one point acknowledging that the decision left ample room for regulatory activity. Yet, while Frankfurter approved of the outcome in *Pierce* he was uncomfortable with how it provided yet another example of a conservative Supreme Court overturning a state law. According to Frankfurter, insofar as *Pierce* involved striking down the will of the people, it formed part of the dangerous turn in the American judiciary, epitomized by *Lochner*, toward usurping the authority of democratically elected legislatures. Damning the decision with faint praise, he wrote that "a heavy price has to be paid for these occasional services to liberalism."[97]

For decades *Pierce* strained under the portrait that Frankfurter and others painted of it as an example of conservative judicial activism. As a rising tide of liberal appointments displaced the Court's pre-New Deal majorities, criticisms of *Pierce* abounded. Frankfurter continued to assault the decision when he became a justice in 1939. When his colleague Wiley Rutledge decided to cite *Pierce* in a 1944 opinion dealing with the rights of Jehovah's Witnesses, Frankfurter informed him that he would not join the opinion. He told Rutledge that Holmes's dissent in the *Meyer* companion cases "remained compelling," and that the Court would "rue the implications of *Pierce*."[98] In 1949, Justice Hugo Black, a Franklin Roosevelt appointee to the Supreme Court, wrote that the "due process philosophy" used in *Pierce* and other cases "[has] been deliberately discarded."[99] Black urged Chief Justice Earl Warren to remove any mention of *Pierce* from Warren's 1954 opinion in *Bolling*, which struck down legally enforced school segregation in Washington, DC. Bowing to the dominant mood on the Court at the time, Warren obliged.[100]

Indeed, *Pierce* became so stigmatized by its association with conservatism that, by the 1960s, in order to resurrect its protections of liberty a lawyer arguing in front of the Court in the contraception case *Griswold v. Connecticut* had to explicitly sever *Pierce* from the "line of due process decisions exemplified by *Lochner*."[101] When the majority opinion in *Griswold* agreed with the lawyer's use of *Meyer* and *Pierce*, Justice Black again dissented. "The reasoning stated in *Meyer* and *Pierce* was the same natural law due process philosophy which many later opinions repudiated," Black wrote, "and which I cannot accept."[102] As midcentury American jurisprudence decisively broke with the *Lochner* era, lawyers and judges found it almost impossible to untether *Pierce* from its roots in the "discarded" philosophy of substantive due process. Today, legal scholars on both sides of the ideological spectrum generally treat *Pierce* much as its liberal critics did from the 1920s through the 1960s: as a decision constricting the scope of the regulatory state. The decision's strong affirmation of public regulation has been lost.

A final irony of *Pierce*'s legacy is that while the case was a decision about corporations and private property, scholars since the 1960s almost entirely discuss it in the context of education and religion.[103] Much as *Dartmouth College v. Woodward* had revolutionized the relationship between state governments and private corporations generally, so scholars initially drew on *Pierce* to continue to define the scope of corporate rights. Legal scholars writing during the 1930s and the 1940s cited *Pierce* in articles entitled "Corporations as Persons, Citizens, and Possessors of Liberty," "Non-Natural Persons and the Guarantee of Liberty under the Due Process Clause," and "Is a Corporation Always Entitled to Due Process of Law."[104] Similarly, as New Deal programs dramatically expanded the scope of public activity, legal scholars in the 1930s turned to *Pierce* to search for how the Supreme Court managed conflicts between public and private enterprise. Thus did *Pierce* appear in articles on "Municipalities in Competition with Private Business," "Power of the Federal

Government to Compete with Private Enterprise," and "Standing of Public Utilities to Challenge the Constitutionality of the TVA."[105]

William Guthrie most likely would have been surprised to see *Pierce* exclusively discussed as a case about religion. His career had exemplified the close legal ties between corporations and schools. As Guthrie knew well, private parochial schools were more than creatures of religious expression: they were institutions near the center of enduring arguments among Americans about the relationship between private enterprise and the state.

In a nation where educational policymaking legally devolved to states and localities, the Supreme Court's decision in *Pierce* was decidedly national in scope. Just as the Gilded Age Supreme Court had shifted American law toward constituting a national commercial market, so the Court, beginning in the 1920s, defined the legal contours of the educational marketplace, albeit at the state level. The educational arena, the Court ruled, must accommodate private sources of schooling as well as public ones. States had to permit educational competition, and state-mandated educational monopolies were unconstitutional. But local schooling and educational competition were not the legal realms of laissez faire. As William Guthrie had demonstrated, the compiled laws affecting private schools in the American states now filled up hundreds of pages of text. These regulations, as he asserted and the Court agreed, were essential to the very fabric of a competitive educational marketplace. By compelling attendance and ensuring a minimum standard for all schools, they obviated the need for compulsory public schooling. Because of public regulation, private schools would not be prohibited, but would be given federal recognition.

Epilogue

PUBLIC PROBLEMS AND PRIVATE EDUCATION IN

THE POST-WORLD WAR II ERA

AS SCHOOL CHOICE and competition became increasingly central education issues in the post-World War II era, the long history of educational markets became as relevant as ever. Private schools, after all, have long been tools of public policymaking. In the late nineteenth and twentieth centuries states bestowed indirect subsidies to parochial schools in the form of property tax exemptions, which state and federal judges protected. States also provided truancy officers, at public expense, to compel private school attendance. Public regulations made it easier, and more legitimate, for students to transfer to and from parochial schools, while new public standards raised their academic quality and, more importantly, their reputation in the eyes of prospective parents. It was the very existence of these regulations that had enabled parochial schools to avoid abolition in the 1920s. A half-century later, in 1979, the *Harvard Law Review* would note that "the degree of regulation of private education by state and federal authorities suggests that the government in some sense operates as a 'partner or even a joint venturer in the [private school's] enterprise.'"[1]

The close ties between public regulation and private enterprise both reflected and contributed to the development of American political economy more generally. Law, regulation, and public investment had been used as tools to achieve private economic growth throughout the nineteenth century. Local regulations had established the very rules and structures for outdoor marketplaces. States and the federal government lent their treasury money and lands to build canals and railroads. The Supreme Court facilitated interstate commerce and, as a result, legalized large interstate corporations by proscribing states from passing laws that discriminated against outside firms. In the twentieth century, as the federal government responded to two world wars and economic depression, public economic planning and stimulus only deepened. American private enterprise did not emerge naturally, solely by dint of innovation and individual initiative; like the marketplace of urban schooling, it was the product of law and public policy.[2]

Just as private schools benefited from public regulation, so too did they contribute to the development of America's regulatory state. Tax codes and compulsory attendance laws inserted government into private affairs in unprecedented ways, bringing state inspectors into church schools and truant officers into homes. Supreme Court cases involving private schools also shaped the relationship between state legislatures and private enterprise. In *Dartmouth v. Woodward* and *Pierce v. Society of Sisters*, the Court defined the legal boundaries surrounding the autonomy of private enterprise and prohibited states from penetrating those private rights. *Pierce* not only established new constitutional protections from government intervention, but also affirmatively recognized broad state police authority over private education. In the following decades, for example, judges relied on *Pierce* to uphold convictions of parents who had violated compulsory attendance regulations by home schooling their children.

Private schools became crucial tools of public policy because state and local government officials relied on mass attendance in them to govern more effectively. Public education was the most expensive, if not most important, service of state and local government.[3] Were it not for the "double taxation" faced by millions of Catholic families who paid taxes to support public schools they did not attend, public systems would have suffered even more from drastically overcrowded and underfinanced schools. Public officials understood this dynamic well. They often protested, or refrained from enforcing, laws that would result in thousands of students suddenly being shifted into public schools, and used fiscal policy to relieve demands on the public treasury. Property tax exemptions for parochial schools never met serious challenges after the 1870s in large part because private schools served this public function. Better to deliver backdoor fiscal subsidies to private schools, legislators believed, than to see parochial schools close and their students enter public schools en masse. Public officials thus learned that they could expand education during the Progressive Era by relying on private schools. With greater public oversight, private schools grew.

In the second half of the twentieth century, private schools took on increasingly public roles. Legislators, policymakers, and intellectuals proposed dissolving public school systems altogether, replacing them with various schemes to support private education. In the North, a diverse group of intellectuals proposed voucher programs intended to unleash religious freedom, educational competition, and accountability. In the South during the long aftermath of *Brown v. Board of Education*, governors and state legislators proposed replacing public systems with private schools. The motivations for these proposals were vastly different, although each viewed private schooling as a solution to the perceived failures of publicly provided education. Millions of white Southerners saw private schooling as the vehicle to protect racial segregation from court-ordered public school desegregation. Northern policymakers and intellectuals, meanwhile, believed that privatized schooling would address many of the problems that appeared to plague American life, from urban decay to overly ossified bureaucracies.

Recent school choice proposals have nonetheless relied on the older methods of public regulation. Drawing on the traditions forged in the late nineteenth and early twentieth century, proponents of privatization continued to accept the role of public regulation in ensuring the financial stability, quality, and growth of market-based alternatives. In an age of greater privatization and deregulation, in other words, Americans continued to believe that mass education necessitated heavy public intervention. It was impossible to sever private schools from public policies.

Voucher proposals that emanated from the North in the 1950s and 1960s aimed to expand private schools with public funds. Catholics proposed tuition grants or tax credits that would pay for attendance in parochial schools, while free-market economists and sympathetic policymakers aimed to revolutionize public education with a voucher system that would increase parental choice and market discipline. By the mid-1960s several prominent liberal and New Left voices, discontented with the perceived failures of public school systems in inner cities, also promoted vouchers and greater educational competition as a means to achieve higher-quality schools.[4]

Virgil Blum, a Catholic priest, anti-Communist, and professor at Marquette University in Milwaukee, was one of the most outspoken 1950s adherents of greater educational competition. Born in Iowa in 1913 and educated in parochial schools, Blum had observed the anti-Catholic crusades of the 1920s with horror. Well into the 1950s he continued to think of Oregon's compulsory public education law as recent history, and as an example of why Catholics needed to be eternally vigilant about protecting their rights.[5] Blum fashioned himself as a civil rights advocate for American Catholics and framed his struggle as a fulfillment of American values on the world stage.

Blum's attempts to secure public funding for private schools came amid a series of gradual, though significant, Catholic school successes in obtaining additional subsidies. Starting in the Great Depression, Catholic schools in various cities received public money (including federal dollars) in order to avoid closing down and burdening public schools with more students.[6] In that same decade, some states used tax dollars to provide free textbooks and transportation services for children who attended private schools, practices that the Supreme Court generally upheld.[7] In the 1960s, finally, the National Catholic Welfare Conference and other private school advocates successfully lobbied Congress to allow federal education funds to flow to children attending parochial schools.[8] While courts and lawmakers justified these measures as benefiting individual children, rather than private (religious) schools, their effects on private education specifically were substantial. Absent these public laws and responsibilities, Catholic private schools would have experienced far less dramatic growth, and in some states perhaps outright closure.

For Blum, these gains were half-measures. States, he argued, discriminated against Catholics by burdening them with the additional costs of sending their children to parochial schools. Thus, while he praised the *Pierce* decision for giving Catholic parents the choice to send their children to private schools, he urged Catholics to recognize that they were never truly free to choose. Catholic parents with children in parochial schools faced the burden of being taxed for public schools they did not attend. They witnessed public school students riding on free buses, receiving free hot lunches, reading free textbooks, and receiving free medical attention.[9] In his 1958 book *Freedom of Choice in Education*, Blum proposed a voucher or federal tax credit for parents electing to send their children to private schools. His plan received a wide audience. The prominent Jewish theologian Will Herberg wrote a foreword to his book, which also garnered attention in national publications such as *U.S. News and World Report* as well as in Catholic journals. Blum sent pamphlets that condensed his arguments to powerful figures in American politics and religion, from congressmen in Washington to Catholic bishops throughout the country.[10] In 1959 he helped organize the Citizens for Educational Freedom, whose mission was to propagate educational vouchers. The same year that Blum died, 1990, the Wisconsin legislature enacted the nation's first public voucher program, operated in Milwaukee—a symbolic, if not direct, tribute to Blum's advocacy.[11] In using the language of religious rights, Blum helped achieve direct public subsidies for private schools.

Blum's proposal, though rooted in his Catholicism, also drew on the work of a rising chorus of voucher advocates in university economics departments. The University of Chicago economics professor Milton Friedman was particularly influential. In a 1955 essay entitled "The Role of Government in Education," Friedman suggested eliminating public education altogether, replacing it with a system where states gave students tax-funded vouchers that they would use to attend tuition schools. Blum cited Friedman's essay in his book, and in 1959 he received an invitation to participate in a seminar led by Friedman on free-market economics.[12] The rhetoric of market competition pervaded Blum's *Freedom of Choice in Education*. He talked about an "educational market place" in which private schools, given their financial disadvantages, could barely compete, and referenced the need for Catholics to "appeal to the competitive spirit of free enterprise" in the United States.[13] The language of unleashing the free market in education, and removing public regulation, pervaded both Blum and Friedman's writings.

Friedman's reasoning was especially radical, breaking with scholars' conventional wisdom, stable since the nineteenth century, that education was best provided by public authorities. He explicitly rejected late-nineteenth-century "natural monopoly" arguments for public schooling as anachronistic, asserting that the rise of densely populated cities and urban transportation networks made educational competition more feasible. In a market economy, Friedman believed, vouchers reflected important liberal values. In addition, they would more effectively allocate educational opportunity. In education "as in other fields," he wrote, "competitive private enterprise is likely to be far more efficient in meeting consumer demands than either [state] enterprises or enterprises run to serve other purposes."[14] Friedman's proposal thus recaptured the market ideas and metaphors of the early nineteenth-century classical economists.

And yet, despite Friedman's reputation for advocating free markets and private schools, government was far from absent in his voucher proposal. Friedman argued that governments should intervene in financing the education of the poor and even compelling attendance. These measures were necessary because schooling was largely a public good given its "neighborhood effects," or positive externalities, whereby one child's education produced discrete social benefits, including a greater proportion of law-abiding, productive citizens. It was because of these neighborhood effects, Friedman noted, that governments could compel education as well as the taxation to pay for it.[15]

Indeed, Friedman's essay went beyond even this limited vision of public regulation. Unlike most nineteenth-century classical economists, Friedman did not propose limiting government interventions only to compulsory attendance and taxation; rather, he suggested that governments should regulate educational quality as well. In this regard, Friedman's essay did not propose an "unregulated" voucher system, as several of his interpreters later stressed.[16] For Friedman, states had to "require a minimum level of education" for all children. They would limit vouchers to those redeemed for "approved educational services." They would ensure that "schools met certain minimum standards such as the inclusion of a minimum content in their programs." Schools would arise to fulfill niche preferences, Friedman acknowledged, but he was confident that schools could instill a "common core of values" provided that they "satisfied specified minimum standards." Friedman's remarks more closely resembled the views of the Progressive Era legislator than the classical economist.[17]

Friedman's proposal, far from envisioning a stateless educational system, drew from a distinctive, even robust, regulatory tradition. While his plan arose as a response to public education's bureaucratic nature, he believed, ironically, that it was precisely America's administrative structures that made a voucher system feasible. Nineteenth-century cities and school districts, Friedman surmised, may have implemented voucher systems of their own had they possessed "an efficient administrative machinery to handle the distribution of vouchers and to check their use." The twentieth century had witnessed precisely the "development of such machinery," thanks to the "enormous extension of personal taxation and of social security programs." Though Friedman did not spell out this machinery in detail, its effect in education was omnipresent, particularly in the vast attendance bureaus that could identify and track hundreds of thousands of urban students. For Friedman, voucher ideas had risen in tandem with these "modern developments in governmental administrative machinery that facilitate such arrangements." They owed their very existence to the public administrative agencies at the local, state, and federal level forged during the Progressive Era and New Deal.[18]

Following Friedman, other more left-wing voucher advocates further emphasized the importance of strict governmental controls of private schools. Left-liberal support for vouchers emerged in the 1960s and 1970s as public school systems appeared unable to stem the tide of urban segregation, poverty, and decay. Vouchers, they argued, could empower minority parents while diminishing the segregation produced by public school attendance zones and high property taxes. Not surprisingly, left-liberal voucher proposals stressed that vouchers could achieve egalitarian outcomes only through abundant public regulations.[19] In the late 1960s, the Harvard education professor Christopher Jencks and other liberal education reformers drew up a voucher plan for the Center for the Study of Public Policy, winning a grant from the U.S. Office of Economic Opportunity. The plan contained complex regulatory mechanisms. Their proposal stipulated how schools accepting public money admitted students, distributed vouchers, maintained educational quality, and informed consumers.[20] John E. Coons, a product of Catholic parochial schools and a prominent University of California law professor, made a similar argument in his influential treatise on school finance, published in 1970. There, he (alongside two co-authors) wrote that a tightly regulated voucher system was the most efficient way to produce equal educational opportunities in the United States consistent with the principles of local control.[21] Other liberal and left voucher advocates, including Harvard Graduate School of Education Dean Theodore Sizer, offered additional ideas about how a carefully regulated voucher program could benefit the disadvantaged and prevent discrimination.[22]

These left-liberal intellectuals sought to distinguish their own voucher plans from Friedman's approach, even if they had a significant amount in common. In particular, they were critical of Friedman's proposed regulations for not preventing vouchers from going toward segregated schools.[23] Jencks listed seven distinct education voucher plans currently in circulation, ranging from what he termed an "Unregulated Market Model" (where he placed Friedman's proposal) to a "Regulated Compensatory Model" (which closely resembled his own).[24] Jencks argued that proposals like Friedman's represented "an unregulated system [that] would have all the drawbacks of other unregulated markets," producing racial and economic segregation and great income inequality. As a result, his plan detailed how poor children's vouchers "would have a somewhat higher redemption value" in order to encourage their attendance in socioeconomically integrated schools.[25] Likewise, Coons argued that Friedman's proposal, ironically, was "not conservative enough" in truly guaranteeing "freedom of choice" because it did nothing to prevent wealthy parents from using their financial power to supplement vouchers with personal funds.[26] Partly in order to popularize their ideas among other liberals, voucher advocates like Jencks and Coons drew clear, if exaggerated, lines of demarcation between their proposals and Friedman's.

The differences between Friedman on the one hand and Jencks and Coons on the other should not obscure their fundamental agreement that governments must play a significant role in regulating private education. As Jencks himself admitted, all of these "diverse voucher schemes" were simply "different approaches to the regulation of the educational marketplace." When the economist Henry M. Levin surveyed different voucher proposals in 1968 he noted that, even including Friedman's, "it is important to point out that all of the advocates of the market approach view basic schooling as a public function" where—albeit to varying degrees—the political process must sort out issues of educational standards, accountability, and funding. While support for vouchers by the late 1970s had come to include some "strange bedfellows" across the political and ideological spectrum, as the sociologist James Coleman observed in the late 1970s, intellectual commitments to public regulation remained.[27]

The origins of this consensus around regulated vouchers lay as much in the past as in the present. After all, in the previous century cities and states had developed laws and mechanisms to supervise private school quality. While the voucher proposals of the 1960s and 1970s ambitiously sought to create an equitable and regulated system, their means were thus decidedly unoriginal. The Jencks plan established seven requirements for determining whether a school could be approved to accept vouchers. Three of the criteria had their origins in the late-nineteenth-century laws that regulated parochial schools: to "agree to make a wide variety of information about its facilities, teachers, program, and students available . . . to the public," to "maintain accounts of money received and disbursed," and to "meet existing state requirements for *private* schools regarding curriculum, staffing, and the like."[28] The regulated educational marketplace envisioned by school reformers drew on a nearly century-old tradition of overseeing and approving private schools.

White Southerners in favor of racially segregated schooling in the post-World War II years also made robust attempts to use government to promote private schools. Prior to the late 1950s and 1960s, when Southern public school segregation came under attack, private schooling in the South was far less widespread than in the North. The chief reason was that Catholic schools, which in the North fed private education's growth, existed in far fewer numbers in the South. Southern states experienced less European Catholic immigration in the nineteenth and twentieth centuries than their Northern counterparts. Outside of the large Catholic populations in cities like New Orleans, Baltimore, and Louisville, the vast majority of Southerners attended public schools. Whereas nearly one child out of every five in the Northeast attended a private school in the 1950s, in the South it was one in twenty.[29]

The social and economic structures of Southern life also contributed to low private school attendance. Southern society was more divided along racial, rather than ethno-religious lines, diminishing sectarian motivations for establishing private schools. Economic concerns produced by a racially segregated and unequal system also drove lower attendance in private schools. Whites and blacks already needed to support two parallel systems. Black public schools, consistently underfunded, often required additional private contributions from black families.[30] For whites, too, segregation had its costs: the commitment to segregated schooling meant two school buildings in towns where one larger one would suffice, along with two school transportation systems for black and white students. This burden made financial support for private education more difficult, especially in the Upper South, where black school facilities were generally better funded than in the Deep South. The Swedish sociologist Gunnar Myrdal observed of the South in 1944 that segregated systems had a "profound effect on costs."[31] In Washington, DC, a Southern newspaper editor commented, "the continuing effort to superimpose a rigidly segregated school system upon a rapidly shifting residential pattern has made crises, financial and otherwise, the norm." The added costs of the system in Washington were estimated at between $7 million and $8 million per year, "more than one-fourth of the entire school budget."[32] Southern county officials in practice went to great lengths to ensure that white schools, at black schools' expense, had superior facilities. But the economic burden of a dual system was never far from the surface. According to Thurgood Marshall, the NAACP's Legal Defense Fund pursued a strategy of forcing school districts to equalize their schools under the theory that the "extreme cost of maintaining two 'equal' school systems would eventually destroy segregation."[33] With the fiscal burden of paying for a dual public system, white Southerners were less able to afford private school tuition payments.

Gradual public school desegregation orders, begun with *Brown v. Board* in 1954, changed these dynamics drastically, ushering in a new and significant role for private education. Southern states responded to that and later desegregation rulings with evolving strategies of "massive resistance." One form of resistance entailed state support for "private" schools that could maintain segregation. Southern states enacted laws closing down or penalizing public schools (and families) that participated in integration, and they provided publicly funded tuition grants for whites to attend segregated private schools. Just as Northern state legislatures had sought to ensure private school quality through public regulation, so too did Southern whites believe that heavy state involvement was the key to maintaining their desired public outcome of continued segregation. Legislatures often designed these "private schools" to be the same public schools as before, with the buildings essentially given away to a "private" group to operate. In Louisiana, for example, the very same counties (or "parishes") that had governed public schools before would continue to manage the "private" schools. Ultimately, Alabama, Arkansas, Georgia, Louisiana, Mississippi, North Carolina, South Carolina, and Virginia adopted tuition grant schemes.[34] As a result, counties throughout the South that previously had no private schools rapidly saw their numbers climb. In the twelve-state southeastern region between 1961 and 1971 attendance in private schools increased by 242.2 percent. From 1964 to 1970, in Mississippi alone, the number of whites-only private schools grew from 17 to 155. Throughout the South in 1970, estimates placed the number of children in such "segregation academies" at 400,000.[35] Advocates of Southern segregation academies thus believed that "public" goals of white supremacy and racial apartheid could be advanced through state-supported private schools.[36]

Yet, precisely because whites-only private schools were dependent on state subsidies, they came under attack by civil rights advocates, who quickly challenged them in the courts. Civil rights groups argued that segregationist schools using public grants should be subject to desegregation mandates. Federal judges agreed, viewing whites-only private schools as a barely disguised public system and thus subject to the same decrees as the state systems they had replaced. The Fourteenth Amendment's guarantee that "no state shall . . . deny to any person within its jurisdiction the equal protection of the laws" implied that defendants needed to show discrimination supported by "state action." State action was everywhere, the courts ruled. As the judges in one Mississippi tuition grant challenge wrote in 1969, "what is involved here are legislative enactments which 'will significantly encourage and involve the State in private discriminations.'"[37] Encouraging the spread of segregated private schools through state-financed tuition grant programs violated the spirit of *Brown v. Board of Education*, they argued. In a flood of cases emanating from around the South during the 1960s, judges found these state-activated schemes unconstitutional.[38] Precisely because these private schools were deeply implicated in public policies, they could not escape federal judicial oversight.

Beyond direct subsidies like tuition grants, judges determined that indirect subsidies, including tax exemptions, also supported illegal, segregated schools. Like nineteenth-century Catholics, Southern segregationists in the second half of the twentieth century knew that tax exemptions were an essential public subsidy for perpetuating private schools. Not only did private schools avoid local property taxes, but federal exemptions allowed their donors the right to deduct contributions from their gross income taxes. By 1970, one study estimated, federal and state tax deductions, together with local tax exemptions, contributed 13.8 percent of total nonpublic school income.[39] When civil rights organizations challenged the privileged tax status of segregationist private schools, they highlighted this public subsidy frequently.

In 1969, a group of African-American parents in Holmes County, Mississippi, brought a class action suit requesting the courts to enjoin the Treasury Department from granting tax exemptions to three new whites-only private schools in the state. Although the Internal Revenue Service (IRS) had already been flagging such schools for their policies, whites in Mississippi who made charitable contributions to private school tuition scholarships and capital financing for buildings could deduct these gifts from their gross income tax. Tax exemptions were a more indirect form of public subsidy than a voucher, but the judges hearing the case in the U.S. District Court of the District of Columbia nonetheless believed that they constituted substantial government involvement. Evidence submitted in the case showed that the tax deductions were central to these private schools' very existence. As one school implored its donors, "unless we receive substantial contributions to our Scholarship Fund there will be many, many students, whose minds and bodies are just as pure as those of any of their classmates and playmates, who for financial reasons alone, will be forced into one of the intolerable and repugnant 'other schools' or into dropping out of school entirely." The letter then emphasized that "donations to the school are deductible from your gross income for tax purposes."[40]

Ruling in favor of the African-American plaintiffs, in *Green v. Kennedy* (1970) the District Court ordered a preliminary injunction denying the tax exemptions for Mississippi's whites-only private schools; it was permanently upheld on the merits a year later. The judges found that "the tax benefits under the Internal Revenue Code mean a substantial and significant support by the Government to the segregated private school pattern." Segregationist whites saw private schooling as a haven from the reach of the federal government, but as the District Court pointed out, these schools' very existence depended on federal, state, and local tax policies.[41]

Private school resistance to new and more aggressive IRS policies in the 1970s highlighted their reliance on these indirect subsidies even more. Following the District Court's ruling in *Green*, the Nixon administration in 1970 announced a new IRS policy removing tax exemptions nationwide from private schools that practiced racial discrimination. In 1975 the IRS published a new revenue procedure that required private schools to adopt a nondiscriminatory policy, to refer to this policy in all brochures and catalogues, and to publish the policy annually in a newspaper, radio, or television advertisement. Three years later it sought to strengthen enforcement even more by specifying the percentage of minority students that private schools required to avoid IRS scrutiny. Private Protestant schools, which had been growing dramatically in numbers, were particularly resistant to the new IRS policies. While some Christian schools had their origins entirely in segregationist principles, others by the late 1970s sought to create a Protestant alternative to increasingly secular public schooling. Concerned about how these proposed regulations might affect Christian school finances and religious freedom, evangelicals flooded Congress and the IRS with upwards of a half-million protest letters.[42]

For these schools, the financial stakes alone involved in their tax status were crucial. After the IRS officially revoked the tax-exempt status of Bob Jones University, a Christian college in South Carolina, in 1976, they claimed the institution owed it $489,675.59 for unpaid federal unemployment taxes, plus interest. For Goldsboro Christian Schools, a fundamentalist Christian academy in North Carolina under similar orders, the IRS ordered it to pay $160,073.96 in unpaid social security and unemployment taxes, including interest and penalties. When legal challenges to these two IRS decisions reached the Supreme Court, the judges ruled 8–1 in favor of the IRS. The judges stated that the university could not be a legitimately charitable institution, since it engaged in racially discriminatory policies that violated the public policy of the United States. That policy, the majority held, citing the Fourth Circuit's opinion in the case, was against "subsidizing racial discrimination in education, public or private."[43]

Evangelical Christian schools like Bob Jones University obtained a reputation for being isolated from public policies and mainstream America, but their steady push for public aid suggested a different story. As demand for evangelical private schooling grew both in the South and throughout the nation, Christian lobbyists in the 1980s continued to advocate for various forms of public subsidies, including tuition tax credits. While American Protestants once "assailed private alternatives" to public schools, the historian William J. Reese observed in 1985, they now "champio[n] marketplace competition as a cure for modern educational ills." Some evangelical private school operators understood that these subsidies would produce the same forms of government oversight that had followed Catholic schools throughout the twentieth century, and racially discriminatory private schools in the 1970s. "Anytime there is a subsidy, it opens the door to interference," one Baptist minister stated. Christian school leaders such as Jerry Falwell did seek public support without the regulations that accompanied it.[44] In some cases, Christian lobbyists succeeded in obtaining public aid while eliminating forms of private school regulation such as minimum standards and teacher licensure. More often than not, however, significant public subsidies did not arrive, and public regulation of private schools continued.[45]

The marketplace in which Southern and evangelical private schools hoped to participate had already been deeply shaped by public policies. Government aid, in the form of vouchers and tuition tax credits, launched thousands of private schools following desegregation orders. In the 1970s and 1980s, tax exemptions became crucial to Christian schools' survival in the South and elsewhere. Even government attempts to require more integrated private schools at least in part contributed to more diverse Christian schools. Between 1991 and 1994 black enrollments in conservative Christian schools nearly doubled, rising to 71,399, or roughly 12 percent of the total Christian school population.[46] Through these battles over public subsidies and regulations, alternatives to public schooling once again were intimately dependent on public policies.

Ironically, efforts to increase parental choice in education during the late twentieth century occurred precisely as Catholic schools, which long had dominated private education, underwent a precipitous decline. Altogether, nearly 2,700 Catholic schools closed between 1970 and 1990, the result of diminished demand amid "white flight" to the suburbs and increased costs as expensive lay teachers replaced tens of thousands of low-cost nuns.[47] These declines, coupled with perceptions of public school failure, produced enthusiasm for using public vouchers to support beleaguered Catholic schools in the 1970s and 1980s. In 1972, a panel convened by President Richard Nixon at the behest of Daniel Patrick Moynihan, his urban affairs assistant, recommended tuition tax credits for poor and minority students to attend urban Catholic schools.[48] A decade later, James Coleman produced a widely read study purporting to demonstrate the superior academic achievement produced by Catholic secondary schools, and he relied on these findings to call for a "reorganization of the public sector."[49] This renewed attention to Catholic education, however, failed to prevent massive parochial school closures.

In the 1990s and 2000s, enrollments continued to decline as urban Catholic schools often found it difficult to compete with publicly funded but privately managed charter schools.[50] In late 2012, charter schools surpassed Catholic schools in total enrollments.[51] For the first time in a century and a half, Catholic schools no longer represent the largest K-12 educational sector outside of traditional public schools.

Much like urban areas in the 1870s and 1880s, American public schools today face new educational competitors in the form of charter schools and voucher programs. Unlike nineteenth-century Catholic school proponents, though, today's advocates of educational competition do not speak in the language of religious piety and ethnic solidarity.

As increasing numbers of students attend private and charter schools, conceptions of public and private in American education are once again shifting. But as more students seek to attend private schools, the more publicly accountable those schools are likely to become. Like the Catholic schools from a century ago, charter schools and voucher programs today are subject to a range of public regulations. State legislatures, together with the federal government, have the potential to exercise immense regulatory controls over charter school operators and their authorizers—the agencies that approve, supervise, and hold charter schools accountable. Seeing this potential, scholars have proposed detailed model legislation to use charter schools "to further goals of equal educational opportunity."[52] Researchers, meanwhile, have examined the relationship between charter school quality and the extent of state regulations.[53] Acknowledging that private school attendance, curriculum, and quality can be substantially shaped through public regulation is a historical lesson that contemporary debates about school choice would do well to heed.

Reformers might succeed in privatizing much of the provision of education, but even if they fail, American definitions of public and private in education are sure to change in the future, as they have in the past. Certain continuities are likely to persist as well. As Catholic school authorities noted in the nineteenth century, and Milton Friedman acknowledged in the twentieth century, Americans view their schools as fundamentally public goods. Schooling in the twenty-first century United States will likely continue to reflect the designs of elected legislatures and departments of education. Educational change is inexorable, but the shape it takes is not. If history is any guide, Americans will maintain their desire for a strong public presence in their schools, and the future of American education will likely be structured as much by public policies and court rulings as by competition and the next round of educational innovations.

NOTES

INTRODUCTION

1. "Reports of School Commissioners and City Superintendents," in *Twelfth Annual Report of the State Superintendent of Public Instruction, of the State of New York* (Albany: C. Wendell, 1866), 111–17.

2. Rev. Israel Wilkinson, *Memoirs of the Wilkinson Family in America* (Jacksonville, IL: Davis and Penniman, 1869), 254–55; Carl F. Kaestle, *Pillars of the Republic: Common Schools and American Society* (New York: Hill and Wang, 1983), 75–103; William J. Reese, *America's Public Schools: From the Common School to "No Child Left Behind"* (Baltimore: Johns Hopkins University Press, 2005), 10–44.

3. Kaestle, *Pillars of the Republic*, 116–17.

4. U.S. Bureau of Education, *Report of the Commissioner of Education for the Year 1886–87* (Washington, DC: Government Printing Office, 1888), 90; U.S. Bureau of Education, *Report of the Commissioner of Education for the Year 1887–88*, 65.

5. *The Educational Times* 43, no. 348 (April 1, 1890): 186.

6. Roger Finke and Rodney Stark, *The Churching of America, 1776–2005: Winners and Losers in Our Religious Economy* (New Brunswick, NJ: Rutgers University Press, 1992), 113.

7. Timothy Walch, *Parish School: American Catholic Parochial Education from Colonial Times to the Present* (New York: Crossroad Publishing Company, 1996), 60; David P. Baker, "Schooling All the Masses: Reconsidering the Origins of American Schooling in the Postbellum Era," *Sociology of Education* 72, no. 3 (October 1999): 197–215.

8. Harold A. Buetow, *Of Singular Benefit: The Story of Catholic Education in the United States* (New York: Macmillan, 1970), 179.

9. "Religion and Schools," in *Notes of Hearings before the Committee on Education and Labor, U.S. Senate, on Joint Resolution S.R. 86,* 50th Cong., 1st Sess. (February 15, 1889), 46, 53, 70, 103.

10. Edwin D. Mead, "Has the Parochial School Proper Place in America?" *National Educational Association Journal of Proceedings and Addresses* (Topeka: Kansas Publishing House, 1889), 123–47.

11. J. B. Thayer, "Discussion," *National Educational Association Journal of Proceedings and Addresses* (Topeka: Kansas Publishing House, 1890), 199.

12. Harold A. Buetow, *Of Singular Benefit: The Story of Catholic Education in the United States* (New York: Macmillan, 1970), 179; John T. McGreevy, "Introduction," in *Catholics in the American Century: Recasting Narratives of U.S. History,* ed. R. Scott Appleby and Kathleen Sprows Cummings (Ithaca, NY: Cornell University Press, 2012), 4.

13. Daniel Carpenter, "Regulation," in *The Princeton Encyclopedia of Political History,* ed. Michael Kazin, Rebecca Edwards, and Adam Rothman (Princeton, NJ: Princeton University Press, 2009), 2:665. See also Daniel Carpenter, "Confidence Games: How Does Regulation Constitute Markets?" in *Government and Markets: Toward a New Theory of Regulation,* ed. Edward J. Balleisen and David A. Moss (New York: Cambridge University Press, 2009), 164–92.

14. See Elizabeth Clemens, "Lineages of the Rube Goldberg State: Building and Blurring Public Programs, 1900–1940," in *Rethinking Political Institutions: The Art of the State,* ed. Ian Shapiro, Stephen Skowronek, and Daniel Dalvin (New York: NYU Press, 2006), 187–215; William J. Novak, "The Myth of the 'Weak' American State," *American Historical Review* 113, no. 3 (June 2008): 752–72; William J. Novak, "Public-Private Governance: A Historical Introduction," in *Government by Contract: Outsourcing and American Democracy,* ed. Jody Freeman and Martha Minow (Cambridge, MA: Harvard University Press, 2009), 23–40.

15. On the "hidden" American state see Balogh, *A Government out of Sight*; Adam Sheingate, "Why Can't Americans See the State?" *The Forum* 7, no. 4 (2009): Article 1, 1–14.

16. For a summary of the existing literature see Nancy Beadie, "Toward a History of Education Markets in the United States," *Social Science History* 32, no. 1 (2008): 47–73.

17. Brian Balogh, *A Government out of Sight: The Mystery of National Authority in Nineteenth-Century America* (New York: Cambridge University Press, 2009); William J. Novak, *The People's Welfare: Law and Regulation in Nineteenth Century America* (Chapel Hill: University of North Carolina Press, 1996); Harry N. Scheiber, "State Law and 'Industrial Policy' in American Development, 1790–1987," *California Law Review* 75, no. 1 (January 1987): 415–44; Charles W. McCurdy, "American Law and the Marketing Structure of the Large Corporation, 1875–1890," *Journal of Economic History* 38, no. 3 (September 1978): 631–49.

18. As late as the 1790s the majority of entities holding the corporate form were non-business enterprises: governmental entities (cities, towns, and other units of local government), religious associations, educational institutions, and voluntary associations. Pauline Maier, "The Revolutionary Origins of the American Corporation," *William and Mary Quarterly* 50, no. 1 (January 1993): 53.

19. Carl Zollman, *American Civil Church Law* (New York: Columbia University, 1917), 78–79.

20. Timothy Walch, *Parish School: American Catholic Parochial Education from Colonial Times to the Present* (New York: Crossroad Publishing Company, 1996); James W. Sanders, *The Education of an Urban Minority: Catholics in Chicago, 1833–1965* (New York: Oxford University Press, 1977); JoEllen McNergney Vinyard, *For Faith and Fortune: The Education of Catholic Immigrants in Detroit, 1805–1925* (Urbana and Chicago: University of Illinois Press, 1998); James C. Carper and Thomas C. Hunt, *The Dissenting Tradition in American Education* (New York: Peter Lang, 2007).

CHAPTER I

1. H. H. Barney, *Report on the American System of Graded Free Schools, to the Board of Trustees and Visitors of Common Schools* (Cincinnati: Daily Times, 1851), 24.

2. *Seventh Biennial Report of the Superintendent of Public Instruction of the State of Illinois, 1867–1868* (Springfield: Illinois Journal Printing Office, 1869), 24–25. See also the Massachusetts politician and education secretary George Boutwell's *Thoughts on Educational Topics and Institutions* (Boston: Phillips, Sampson and Company, 1859), 42, 68, 152–63.

3. M. D. Leggett, "Origin of the Ohio School System," *Magazine of Western History* 7, no. 3 (January, 1888): 246.

4. Carl F. Kaestle, *Pillars of the Republic: Common Schools and American Society* (New York: Hill and Wang, 1983); Jurgen Herbst, "Nineteenth-Century Schools Between Community and State: The Case of Prussia and the United States," *History of Education Quarterly* 42, no. 3 (2002): 317–41; William J. Reese, "Changing Conceptions of 'Public' and 'Private' in American Educational History," in *History, Education, and the Schools*, ed. William J. Reese (New York: Palgrave Macmillan, 2007), 95–112.

5. Nancy Beadie, "Toward a History of Education Markets in the United States," *Social Science History* 32, no. 1 (2008): 47–73; Reese, "Changing Conceptions of 'Public' and 'Private,'" 97; Carl F. Kaestle, "Common Schools Before the 'Common School Revival': New York Schooling in the 1790s," *History of Education Quarterly* 12, no. 4 (1972): 465–500; Jon Teaford, "The Transformation of Massachusetts Education, 1670–1780," *History of Education Quarterly* 10, no. 3 (1970): 287–307; J. M. Opal, "Exciting Emulation: Academies and the Transformation of the Rural North, 1780s–1820s," *Journal of American History* 91, no. 2 (2004): 445–70.

6. Nancy Beadie, "Tuition Funding for Common Schools: Education Markets and Market Regulation in Rural New York, 1815–1850," *Social Science History* 32, no. 1 (Spring 2008): 107–33; William A. Fischel, *Making the Grade: The Economic Evolution of American School Districts* (Chicago: University of Chicago Press, 2009), 13–66; Claudia Goldin and Lawrence Katz, *The Race Between Education and Technology* (Cambridge, MA: Belknap Press, 2008), 140–41.

7. Benjamin Justice, "The Originalist Case Against Vouchers: The First Amendment, Religion, and American Public Education," *Stanford Law and Policy Review* 26, no. 2 (2015): 447; Nancy Beadie, "Market-Based Policies of School Funding: Lessons from the History of the New York Academy System," *Educational Policy* 13, no. 2 (May 1999): 299–300.

8. Hilary J. Moss, *Schooling Citizens: The Struggle for African American Education in Antebellum America* (Chicago: University of Chicago Press, 2009); Beadie, "Toward a History of Education Markets in the United States," 52.

9. Kaestle, *Pillars of the Republic,* 32–39.

10. Smith compared this dynamic to "a merchant who attempts to trade without a bounty, in competition with those who trade with a considerable one." Smith, *Wealth of Nations*, 3:133. Generally, see Smith, *Wealth of Nations*, bk. V, ch. I, pt. III, art. II–III.

11. Smith, *Wealth of Nations*, 3:133. See also E. G. West, "Private Versus Public Education: A Classical Economic Dispute," *Journal of Political Economy* 72, no. 5 (1964): 465–66; Margaret G. O'Donnell, *The Educational Thought of the Classical Political Economists* (Latham, MD: University Press of America, 1958), 74, 94.

12. Jean-Baptiste Say, *A Treatise on Political Economy; or the Production, Distribution, and Consumption of Wealth*, trans. C. R. Prinsep (Boston: Wells and Lilly, 1821), 3:230.

13. Francis Wayland, *Elements of Political Economy* (New York: Leavitt, Lord & Company, 1837), 457–58; Thomas Cooper, *Lectures on the Elements of Political Economy* (Columbia, SC: Telescope Press, 1826), 266–68. On antebellum political economy textbooks see Dorothy Ross, *The Origins of American Social Science* (New York: Cambridge University Press, 1991), 42–43.

14. Willard Phillips, *A Manual of Political Economy, with Particular Reference to the Institutions, Resources, and Condition of the United States* (Boston: Hilliard, Gray, Little, and Wilkins, 1828), 270–71.

15. Benjamin Rush, "A Plan for the Establishment of Public Schools and the Diffusion of Knowledge in Pennsylvania," in *Essays on Education in the Early Republic*, ed. Frederick Rudolph (Cambridge, MA: Belknap Press of Harvard University Press, 1965), 15–16; Richard D. Brown, "Bulwark of Revolutionary Liberty: Thomas Jefferson's and John Adams's Programs for an Informed Citizenry," in *Thomas Jefferson and the Education of a Citizen*, ed. James Gilreath (Washington, DC: Library of Congress, 1999), 91–102.

16. Kaestle, *Pillars of the Republic*, 33.

17. Samuel Knox, "An Essay on the Best System of Liberal Education," in *Essays on Education*, ed. Rudolph, 315.

18. Justice, "The Originalist Case Against Vouchers," 440.

19. Cooper, *Lectures on the Elements of Political Economy*, 264–66; Dorfman, *The Economic Mind in American Civilization*, 527.

20. Jefferson wanted them both as professors at the University of Virginia. See Herbert Baxter Adams, *Thomas Jefferson and the University of Virginia* (Washington, DC: Government Printing Office, 1888), 56–65.

21. Thomas Jefferson, "A Bill for the More General Diffusion of Knowledge," in *The Educational Work of Thomas Jefferson*, ed. Roy J. Honeywell (Cambridge, MA: Harvard University Press, 1931), 199–205.

22. James Madison to Thomas Jefferson, April 27, 1785, in *Letters and Other Writings of James Madison, Vol. I, 1769–1793* (Philadelphia: J. B. Lippincott 1865), 150.

23. Robert Coram, "Political Inquiries: To Which Is Added a Plan for the General Establishment of Schools throughout the United States" (1791), in *Essays on Education*, 138.

24. Justice, "The Originalist Case Against Vouchers," 456–67; Campbell Scribner, "False Start: The Failure of an Early 'Race to the Top'," in *The Founding Fathers, Education, and the "The Great Contest": The American Philosophical Society Prize of 1797*, ed. Benjamin Justice (New York: Palgrave MacMillan, 2013), 69–84.

25. Fischel, *Making the Grade*, 22–28, 58–60; Justice, "The Originalist Case Against Vouchers," 467–79; Gordon Wood, *Empire of Liberty: A History of the Early Republic, 1789–1815* (New York: Oxford University Press, 2009), 472.

26. Kaestle, "Common Schools Before the 'Common School Revival,'" 486.

27. William J. Reese, *America's Public Schools: From the Common School to "No Child Left Behind"* (Baltimore: Johns Hopkins University Press, 2005), 10–44; Kaestle, *Pillars of the Republic*, 75–103; Michael B. Katz, *Reconstructing American Education* (Cambridge, MA: Harvard University Press, 1987), 5–23.

28. Horace Mann, *First Annual Report*, in *The Republic and the School: Horace Mann on the Education of Free Men*, ed. Lawrence Cremin (New York: Bureau of Publications, Teachers College, Columbia University, 1957), 33; Mann, *Twelfth Annual Report*, in *The Republic and the School*, 87, 107.

29. Kaestle, *Pillars of the Republic*, 52–61.

30. Ibid., 116–17.

31. Ibid., 136–51.

32. Michael B. Katz, *The Irony of Early School Reform: Educational Innovation in Mid-Nineteenth Century Massachusetts* (Cambridge, MA: Harvard University Press, 1968; reprint, New York: Teachers College Press, 2001), 19–114.

33. Steven K. Green, *The Bible, the School, and the Constitution: The Clash that Shaped Modern Church-State Doctrine* (New York: Oxford University Press, 2012).

34. Goldin and Katz, *The Race Between Education and Technology*, 144.

35. Ira Katznelson and Margaret Weir, *Schooling for All: Class, Race, and the Decline of the Democratic Ideal* (New York: Basic Books, 1985), Chapter 2; William J. Reese, *The Origins of the American High School* (New Haven, CT: Yale University Press, 1999), 80–102; David Labaree, *The Making of an American High School: The Credentials Market and the Central High School of Philadelphia, 1838–1939* (New Haven, CT: Yale University Press, 1988).

36. "Report of the Committee on Education, Appointed by the Governor," *Journal of the State of Vermont, October Session, 1842* (Montpellier: E. P. Walton and Sons, 1843), 8–9.

37. Historians' estimations differ as to when this tipping point precisely occurred. See Lawrence A. Cremin, *The American Common School: An Historic Conception* (New York: Bureau of Publications, Teachers College, Columbia University, 1951), 179; Albert Fishlow, "The American Common School Revival: Fact or Fancy?" in *Industrialization in Two Systems: Essays in Honor of Alexander Gerschenkron*, ed. Henry Rosovsky (New York: John Wiley and Sons, 1966), 41, 54.

38. David Cutler and Grant Miller, "Water, Water Everywhere: Municipal Finance and Water Supply in American Cities," in *Corruption and Reform: Lessons from America's Economic History*, ed., Edward L. Glaeser and Claudia Goldin (Chicago: University of Chicago Press, 2007), 169–70; Mark Guglielmo and Werner Troesken, "The Gilded Age," in *Government and the American Economy: A New History*, ed. Price Fishback and Douglass C. North (Chicago: University of Chicago Press, 2007), 255–87.

39. Gail Radford, *The Rise of the Public Authority: Statebuilding and Economic Development in Twentieth-Century America* (Chicago: University of Chicago Press, 2013), 74–76; Daniel T. Rodgers, *Atlantic Crossings: Social Politics in a Progressive Age* (Cambridge, MA: Belknap Press of Harvard University Press, 1998), 130–59.

40. Carl C. Plehn, *Government Finance in the United States* (Chicago: A. C. McClurg 1915), 85–87.

41. See, e.g., Board of School Commissioners of Milwaukee, *Rules and Regulations of the School Board of the City of Milwaukee* (Milwaukee, 1884); *The School Manual: Containing the School Laws of Rhode Island; with Decisions, Remarks and Forms for the Use of School Officers of the State* (Providence, RI: Providence Press Company, 1873).

42. Albert Shaw, "The American State and the American Man," *Contemporary Review* 51 (May 1887): 698, 705–10.

43. Tracy Steffes, *School, Society, and State: A New Education to Govern Modern America, 1890–1940* (Chicago: University of Chicago Press, 2012); David Tyack, *The One Best System: A History of American Urban Education* (Cambridge, MA: Harvard University Press, 1974).

44. Henry Vethake, *The Principles of Political Economy* (Philadelphia: P. H. Nicklin and T. Johnson, 1838), 318.

45. Francis Wayland, *The Elements of Political Economy*, ed. Aaron L. Chapin (New York: Sheldon & Company, 1879), 114. Emphasis in the original.

46. Richard T. Ely, "Report of the Organization of the American Economic Association," *Publications of the American Economic Association* 1 (1887): 6–7.

47. Richard T. Ely, *Ground Under Our Feet: An Autobiography* (New York: Macmillan, 1938), 9. At seventeen Ely spent a year teaching in a common school. Edmund James and Henry Carter Adams were sons of ministers.

48. For collective biographies of these men see Robert Crunden, *Ministers of Reform: The Progressives' Achievement of American Civilization* (Urbana: University of Illinois Press, 1984); Nancy Cohen, *The Reconstruction of American Liberalism, 1865–1914* (Chapel Hill: University of North Carolina Press), 143–76; Ross, *The Origins of American Social Science*, 101–8; Rodgers, *Atlantic Crossings*, 85; John Rutherford Everett, *Religion in Economics: A Study of John Bates Clark, Richard T. Ely and Simon Patten* (New York: King Crown Press, 1946).

49. This view reflected the broader Progressive Era agenda that Robert Wiebe has described in *The Search for Order: 1877–1920* (New York: Hill and Wang, 1967). See also Crunden, *Ministers of Reform*.

50. Sumner at one point suggested that each social class should provide for its own children's education. See William Graham Sumner, *What Social Classes Owe to Each Other* (New York: Harper & Brothers, 1883), 95.

51. Richard T. Ely, *The Past and the Present of Political Economy* (Baltimore: N. Murray, 1884), 26.

52. John B. Clark, *The Philosophy of Wealth: Economic Principles Newly Formulated* (Boston: Ginn & Company, 1894), 203–4.

53. Edmund James, "The Relation of the Modern Municipality to the Gas Supply," *Publications of the American Economic Association* 1 (1887): 53–122; Albert Shaw, "Cooperation in a Western City," *Publications of the American Economic Association* 1 (1887): 129–228; Edward Bemis, "Cooperation in New England," *Publications of the American Economic Association* 1 (1887): 335–464; Henry Carter Adams, "The Relation of the State to Industrial Action," *Publications of the American Economic Association* 1 (1887): 461–549.

54. Richard T. Ely, *Political Economy, Political Science and Sociology: A Practical and Scientific Presentation of Social and Economic Subjects* (Chicago: University Association, 1889), 255. See also Richard T. Ely, "Natural Monopolies and the Workingman: A Programme of Social Reform," *North American Review* 158, no. 448 (March 1894): 294–303.

55. Richard T. Ely, *Natural Monopolies and Local Taxation* (Boston: Robinson and Stephenson, 1889), 2.

56. Thomas McCraw, *Prophets of Regulation: Charles Francis Adams, Louis D. Brandeis, James M. Landis, Alfred E. Kahn* (Cambridge, MA: Belknap Press, 1984), 1–56. See also Maury Klein, "Competition and Regulation: The Railroad Model," *Business History Review* 64 no. 2 (July 1990): 311–25.

57. White, *Railroaded*, 5–7, 174–77. See also Herbert Hovenkamp, "Regulation History as Politics or Markets," review of *The Regulated Economy: A Historical Approach to Political Economy*, by Claudia Goldin and Gary D. Libecap, *Yale Journal on Regulation* 12 (Summer 1995): 549–63; McCraw, *Prophets of Regulation*, 1–79.

58. Adams, "The Relation of the State to Industrial Action," 513–14, 528. Italics in the original.

59. Charles D. Jacobson, *Ties that Bind: Economic and Political Dilemmas of Urban Utility Networks, 1800–1990* (Pittsburgh: University of Pittsburgh Press, 2000), 1–136; Mark Guglielmo and Werner Troesken, "The Gilded Age," in *Government and the American Economy*; Cutler and Miller, "Water, Water Everywhere."

60. The Boston University law professor Frank Parsons, for example, singled out public schools as one of the only institutions where the benefits of public ownership came without the establishment of monopoly. See *Report of the Industrial Commission on Transportation* 9 (Washington, DC: Government Printing Office, 1901), cxcvi.

61. Claudia Goldin and Lawrence Katz, *The Race Between Education and Technology* (Cambridge, MA: Belknap Press, 2008), 140–46; Kaestle, *Pillars of the Republic*, 148–51.

62. "True and False Socialism," *Public Policy* 9, no. 25 (December 17, 1904): 290.

63. "Editor of To-Day," *To-Day* 3, no. 76 (February 11, 1892): 811–12.

64. Clark, *The Philosophy of Wealth*, 217.

65. Richard T. Ely, *An Introduction to Political Economy* (New York: Hunt & Eaton, 1894), 242. The textbook that evolved from this work became the most widely adopted textbook on political economy in American colleges prior to World War II. Ross, *Origins of American Social Science*, 192.

66. Richard T. Ely, *Outlines of Economics* (New York: Chautauqua Century Press, 1893), 339.

67. Frank Parsons, *The City for the People: Or, the Municipalization of the City Government and of Local Franchises* (Philadelphia: C. F. Taylor, 1901), 18, 145. David Tyack has suggested that one of the reasons for the popularity of public schooling in the nineteenth century was the economic efficiency that came with large public school systems over many separate denominational institutions. See Tyack, *Seeking Common Ground*, 165.

68. Lester Frank Ward, "The Political Ethics of Herbert Spencer," *Annals of the American Academy of Political Science* 4, no. 4 (1894): 611–12.

69. Lester F. Ward, *Dynamic Sociology, or Applied Social Science, as Based upon Statical Sociology and the Less Complex Sciences* (New York: D. Appleton and Company, 1883), 2:584–92, 609.

70. James, "The Relation of the Modern Municipality to the Gas Supply," 79–80.

71. U.S. Bureau of Education, *Report of the Commissioner of Education for the Year 1887–88* (Washington, DC: Government Printing Office, 1889), 18–19.

72. *Eighth Annual Report of the Public Schools for the City of Savannah and County of Chatham for the Year 1872–73* (Savannah: Morning News Office, 1873), 11.

73. O. B. Wyman, "Compulsory Educational Law," *Wisconsin Journal of Education,* 9, no. 9 (September 1879): 366.

CHAPTER 2

1. *Reunion of the Old Scholars, Teachers and Directors of the First Ward School* (Pittsburgh, 1905), 7–8, Library & Archives Division, Senator John Heinz History Center, Pittsburgh, PA.

2. Prior to the 1834 Pennsylvania school law the state provided free education (in privately operated schools) only for the poor, as stipulated in its 1790 Constitution and authorized by an 1809 act of the legislature. On this history see Sarah H. Killikelly, *The History of Pittsburgh: Its Rise and Progress* (Pittsburgh: B. C. & Gordon Montgomery, 1906), 269–337. See also *Report of the Superintendent of Common Schools of the Commonwealth of Pennsylvania* (Harrisburg: Singerly and Myers, 1868), xxviii–xxxvii.

3. *Reunion of the Old Scholars*, 3–5. The range of schools are detailed in Killikelly, *The History of Pittsburgh*, 269–304, 323. Killikelly disputed the First Ward School's claim to being Pittsburgh's first public school.

4. Carl F. Kaestle, *Pillars of the Republic: Common Schools and American Society, 1780–1860* (New York: Hill and Wang, 1983), 51–53; William J. Reese, "Changing Conceptions of 'Public' and 'Private' in American Educational History," in *History, Education, and the Schools*, ed. William J. Reese (New York: Palgrave Macmillan, 2007), 99–100.

5. William J. Reese, "The Public Schools and the Great Gates of Hell," *Educational Theory* 32 (Winter 1982): 9–18; David Tyack and Elisabeth Hansot, *Managers of Virtue: Public School Leadership in America, 1820–1980* (New York: Basic Books, 1982), 15–43; David B. Tyack, "Onward Christian Soldiers: Religion in the Common School," in *History and Education: The Educational Uses of the Past*, ed. Paul Nash (New York: Random House, 1970), 215–55.

6. *Reunion of the Old Scholars*, 4.

7. Joel A. Tarr, "Transportation Innovation and Changing Spatial Patterns in Pittsburgh, 1850–1934," *Essays in Public Works History* no. 6 (April 1978): 3–4.

8. Tarr, "Transportation Innovation," 11–13. See also Francis G. Couvares, *The Remaking of Pittsburgh: Class and Culture in an Industrializing City, 1877–1919* (Albany: State University of New York University Press, 1984), 31–34; and S. J. Kleinberg, *The Shadow of the Mills: Working-Class Families in Pittsburgh, 1870–1907* (Pittsburgh: University of Pittsburgh Press, 1989), 41–99.

9. Joel A. Tarr, "Infrastructure and City-Building in the Nineteenth and Twentieth Century," in *City at the Point: Essays on the Social History of Pittsburgh*, ed. Samuel P. Hays (Pittsburgh: University of Pittsburgh Press, 1991), 228.

10. Department of the Interior, Census Office, *Report on Vital and Social Statistics in the United States at the Eleventh Census: 1890, Part II* (Washington, DC: Government Printing Office, 1896), 293.

11. "Report of the Pittsburgh Bureau of Health," *Pittsburgh Medical Review* 4 (August 1890): 253.

12. *Reunion of the Old Scholars*, 4–5.

13. Each of Pittsburgh's sub-district school boards had control over local taxes, school grounds and construction, and teacher appointments. For a description of the system see *Reports Concerning the Public Schools for 1909 and 1910, Volumes 41 and 42* (Pittsburgh: Shaw Brothers, 1910), Library & Archives Division, Senator John Heinz History Center, Pittsburgh, PA.

14. James T. McTighe, "The Pittsburgh Failure," *The Independent* 42 (September 4, 1890): 7–8.

15. "Pittsburgh Public Schools," *Chicago Tribune*, October 9, 1887.

16. "Parish School," *Pittsburgh Commercial Gazette*, August 25, 1888; "Trouble about Schools," *New York Times*, August 25, 1888.

17. "The Rev. Mr. Knox's Position," *Pittsburgh Commercial Gazette*, October 6, 1888.

18. "Parish School," *Pittsburgh Commercial Gazette*, August 25, 1888.

19. "The Local Resume," *Pittsburgh Dispatch*, January 1, 1889. See also "Pronounced Bigotry," *Pittsburgh Catholic*, September 15, 1888.

20. "Father Sheedy's School," *New York Times*, September 4, 1888.

21. "Editorial," *Pittsburgh Christian Advocate*, September 6, 1888.

22. "Trouble about Schools"; "The Local Resume." See also "Catholic Schools in Public School Buildings," *Pittsburgh Christian Advocate*, October 11, 1888; "Catholics and the Public Schools," *Chicago Tribune*, September 19, 1888.

23. Central Board of Education Minutes, 1882–1890, October 9, 1888, Pittsburgh School District Records, Pittsburgh, Minute Books, Box 28E, Archives Service Center, University of Pittsburgh.

24. "What Father Sheedy Says," *Pittsburgh Press*, October 2, 1888.

25. Morgan M. Sheedy, "The School Question: A Plea for Justice," *The Catholic World* 49 (August 1889): 653–54.

26. "The Parochial School Issue," *Journal of Education* 30, no. 7 (August 22, 1889): 121.

27. "Excitement among the Protestants of Pittsburgh, *New York Times*, September 4, 1888.

28. Sheedy, "The School Question," 654.

29. "Diocesan Statistics, 1880–1901," Associate General Secretariat (RG 4, 1 Chancellor), Historical Records Collection, Catholic Diocese of Pittsburgh; James H. Blodgett, *Report on Education in the United States at the Eleventh Census, 1890* (Washington, DC: Government Printing Office, 1893), 139.

30. "Public and Parochial Schools," *Pittsburgh Dispatch*, April 29, 1889.

31. "The Re-Opening of the Schools," *Pittsburgh Catholic*, September 1, 1888.

32. "A Talk to Parents," *Pittsburgh Dispatch*, August 26, 1889.

33. "A Preacher Replies," *Pittsburgh Dispatch*, August 26, 1889.

34. "A Large Increase," *Pittsburgh Dispatch*, September 9, 1889. The *Commercial Gazette* reported the previous year that roughly 300 pupils from the McGandless public school would leave for St. Kyran's. See "From the Public School," *Pittsburgh Commercial Gazette*, September 3, 1888.

35. "Catholics Want More Room," *Pittsburgh Dispatch*, November 4, 1889.

36. "The Opening Wedge," *Pittsburgh Press*, September 30, 1889; "First Ward Rivalry," *Pittsburgh Dispatch*, September 30, 1889.

37. "In His New School," *Pittsburgh Dispatch*, February 13, 1890; "Father Sheedy's School," *Pittsburgh Catholic*, February 22, 1890.

38. "Why Prof. Sullivan Resigned," *Pittsburgh Dispatch*, April 1, 1890.

39. *Reunion of the Old Scholars*, 4.

40. John T. McGreevy, *Catholicism and American Freedom: A History* (New York: W. W. Norton and Company, 2003), 7–42; Jay P. Dolan, *Catholic Revivalism: The American Experience, 1830–1900* (Notre Dame, IN: University of Notre Dame Press, 1978).

41. On Hughes, see Vincent Lannie, *Public Money and Parochial Education: Bishop Hughes, Governor Seward, and the New York School Controversy* (Cleveland, OH: Case Western Reserve University Press, 1968); on Purcell, see James A. Gutowski, "Politics and Parochial Schools in Archbishop John Purcell's Ohio" (PhD diss., Cleveland State University, 2009); on McQuaid, see Frederick James Zwierlein, *The Life and Letters of Bishop McQuaid: Prefaced with the History of Catholic Rochester Before His Episcopate* (Rochester: Art Print Shop, 1926), 2:119–53.

42. Jay P. Dolan, *The American Catholic Experience: A History from Colonial Times to the Present* (Garden City, NY: Doubleday & Company, 1985), 271–72.

43. "Decrees of the Council—Title VI," in *Catholic Education in America: A Documentary History*, ed. Neil G. McCluskey (New York: Bureau of Publications, Teachers College, 1964), 94. The text here is translated from the Latin. Parents could be exempted from enrolling their children in parochial schools if "a sufficient training in religion is given either in their own homes, or in other Catholic schools; or when because of a sufficient reason, approved by the bishop, with all due precautions and safeguards, it is licit to send them to other schools."

44. Philip Gleason, "Baltimore III and Education," *Catholic Historian* 4, no. 3/4 (1985): 273–313. See also *Memorial Volume: A History of the Third Plenary Council of Baltimore, November 9–December 7, 1884* (Baltimore: Baltimore Publishing Company, 1885), 17, 170.

45. Joel Perlmann, *Ethnic Differences: Schooling and Social Structure among the Irish, Italians, Jews, and Blacks in an American City, 1880–1935* (New York: Cambridge University Press, 1989), 74; Robert E. O'Brien, "The Cost of Parochial Education in Chicago," *Journal of Educational Sociology* 2, no. 6 (February 1929): 349–56.

46. John T. McGreevy, *Parish Boundaries: The Catholic Encounter with Race in the Twentieth-Century Urban North* (Chicago: University of Chicago Press, 1996), 12–13; Lizabeth Cohen, *Making a New Deal: Industrial Workers in Chicago, 1919–1939* (New York: Cambridge University Press, 1990), 84–94; Dolan, *The American Catholic Experience*, 279–83; Paula Fass, *Outside In: Minorities and the Transformation of American Education* (New York: Oxford University Press, 1993), 222–23.

47. John J. White, "Puritan City Catholicism: Catholic Education in Boston," in *Urban Catholic Education: Tales of Twelve American Cities*, ed. Thomas C. Hunt and Timothy Walch (Notre Dame, IN: Alliance for Catholic Education Press), 93–101; Joseph J. Casino, "From Sanctuary to Involvement: A History of the Catholic Parish in the Northeast," in *The American Catholic Parish: A History from 1850 to the Present*, ed. Jay P. Dolan (Mahwah, NJ: Paulist Press, 1987), 23–111; David W. Galenson, "Neighborhood Effects on the School Attendance of Irish Immigrants' Sons in Boston and Chicago in 1860," *American Journal of Education* 105, no. 3 (May 1997): 261–93; Dolan, *The American Catholic Experience*, 282–83.

48. Galenson, "Neighborhood Effects"; James W. Sanders, "Boston Catholics and the School Question, 1825–1907," in *From Common School to Magnet School: Selected Essays on the History of Boston Schools*, ed. James W. Fraser, Henry L. Allen, and Nancy Barnes (Boston: Boston Public Library, 1979), 43–75; Dolan, *The American Catholic Experience*, 264. Timothy Meagher found a similar dynamic in Worcester, MA, where Irish-American priests and congregations had neither the "will or even interest" to build schools. See Timothy Meagher, *Inventing Irish America: Generation, Class, and Ethnic Identity in a New England City, 1880–1928* (Notre Dame, IN: University of Notre Dame Press, 2001), 158–61.

49. Rev. David Sylvester, "Why Catholic Children Are Not Attending Catholic Schools: A Study of the Reasons Offered by Their Parents" (PhD diss., Catholic University of America, 1947), 30, 58.

50. Nathaniel H. R. Dawson, *Report of the Commissioner of Education for the Year 1887–88* (Washington, DC: Government Printing Office, 1889), 64–65.

51. Edwin D. Mead, "Has the Parochial School Proper Place in America?" *National Educational Association Journal of Proceedings and Addresses* (Topeka: Kansas Publishing House, 1889), 123–47.

52. J. B. Thayer, "Discussion," *National Educational Association Journal of Proceedings and Addresses* (Topeka: Kansas Publishing House, 1890), 199.

53. Ward McAfee, *Religion, Race, and Reconstruction: The Public School in the Politics of the 1870s* (Albany: State University of New York Press, 1998).

54. Thomas Nast, "Fort Sumter," *Harper's Weekly* (March 19, 1870), accessed June 28, 2014, http://pudl.princeton.edu/sheetreader.php?obj=og354f35p; Benjamin Justice, "Thomas Nast and the Public School of the 1870s," *History of Education Quarterly* 45, no. 2 (Spring 2005): 171–206.

55. For more on this transatlantic context see McGreevy, *Catholicism and American Freedom*, 7–42.

56. These themes are explored in McAfee, *Religion, Race, and Reconstruction*.

57. "Religion and Schools," in *Notes of Hearings before the Committee on Education and Labor, U.S. Senate, on Joint Resolution S.R. 86*, 50th Cong., 1st Sess. (February 15, 1889), 46, 53, 70, 103.

58. Joseph P. Viteritti, "Blaine's Wake: School Choice, the First Amendment, and State Constitutional Law," *Harvard Journal of Law and Public Policy* 21, no. 3 (Summer 1998): 657–718; Benjamin Justice, "The Blaine Game: Are Public Schools Inherently Anti-Catholic?" *Teachers College Record* 109, no. 9 (September 2007): 2171–206; Philip Hamburger, *Separation of Church and State* (Cambridge, MA: Harvard University Press, 2002), 287–334; and Steven K. Green, "Blaming Blaine: Understanding the Blaine Amendment and the No-Funding Principle," *First Amendment Law Review* 2 (Winter 2003): 107–51.

59. Rev. James Conway, "The Rights and Duties of Family and State in Regard to Education," *American Catholic Quarterly Review* 9 (January 1884): 106.

60. *Fifty-Ninth Annual Report of the Public Schools of Cincinnati for the School Year Ending August 31, 1888* (Cincinnati: Ohio River Valley Company, 1889), 32.

61. "The Catholic Agitation," *New York Times*, September 9, 1888.

62. "Waltham's Women Voters," *Boston Evening Transcript*, December 5, 1888. See also "Parochial Schools: How They Affect Waltham's Public Schools," *Boston Daily Advertiser*, September 10, 1888; "Boston's Fair Voters," *Pittsburgh Press*, October 7, 1888.

63. "Intimidation of Public School Children," *Boston Evening Transcript*, September 11, 1888; "Malden," *Boston Daily Globe*, September 11, 1881.

64. "Catholics and the Public Schools," *Chicago Tribune*, September 11, 1888.

65. "A House Divided," *Boston Daily Globe*, March 25, 1885. The *Boston Daily Globe* printed dozens of stories on the opening of new parochial schools around Boston, especially in the wake of the Third Plenary Council. See the following stories: "French Catholics Buy a Church Site," June 19, 1885; "New Parochial School in Cambridge," June 21, 1885; "New Parochial Schools," December 13, 1886; "Laying Corner-Stones," April 11, 1887; "A New Parochial School," June 22, 1887; "Watertown Parochial School," June 22, 1887; "Noble Structure," August 16, 1888; "New Parochial School," August 16, 1888; "New Parochial School," August 17, 1888; "The Mission Parish School, Roxbury District," February 3, 1888; "For Catholic Children," September 3, 1888; "Arlington Parochial School," September 5, 1888; "North Brookfield School," September 5, 1888; "Mission Church School," August 19, 1889; "St. Michael's R.C. Church, Hudson," August 26, 1889; "New Parochial School," September 4, 1889; "Malden's Parochial School," December 23, 1891; "Parochial School at Charlestown," December 23, 1891; "Parochial School Assured," April 20, 1891.

66. James W. Sanders, *The Education of an Urban Minority: Catholics in Chicago, 1833–1965* (New York: Oxford University Press, 1977), 40–55; Józef Miąso, *The History of the Education of Polish Immigrants in the United States* (New York: Kosciuszko Foundation, 1977), 126; Dolan, *The American Catholic Experience*, 162–63, 207–8; McGreevy, *Parish Boundaries*, 15.

67. "Our Polish Citizens," *Chicago Daily Tribune*, March 14, 1886.

68. Selwyn K. Troen, *The Public and the Schools: Shaping the St. Louis System, 1828–1920* (Columbia: University of Missouri Press, 1975), 53; *The Future of Foreign-Born Catholics; and Fears and Hopes for the Catholic Church and Schools in the United States: Two articles from the St. Louis Pastoral* (St. Louis: B. Herder, 1884), 76.

69. "German in the Public Schools," *Illinois Staats Zeitung*, December 31, 1879, Chicago Foreign Language Press Survey, accessed June 30, 2016, http://flps.newberry.org/article/5418474_1_0697/.

70. Milwaukee School Board, *Proceedings of the School Board* (1897): 37. See also William J. Galush, "What Should Janek Learn? Staffing and Curriculum in Polish-American Parochial Schools, 1870–1940," *History of Education Quarterly* 40, no. 4 (2000): 402; Jonathan Zimmerman, "Ethnics Against Ethnicity: European Immigrants and Foreign-Language Instruction, 1890–1940," *Journal of American History* 88, no. 4 (March 2002): 1400.

71. *Twenty-Seventh Report of the Board of Trustees of Public Schools of the City of Washington, 1873–74* (Washington, DC: M'Gill and Witherow, 1874), 151.

72. *Thirty-Ninth Annual Report of the Board of Education for the School Year Ending August 31, 1875* (Cleveland, OH: Robison, Savage, 1876), 77.

73. *Thirty-Seventh Annual Report of the Board of Education of the Cleveland Public Schools for the School Year Ending August 31, 1873* (Cleveland, OH: Robison, Savage, 1874), 52–53.

74. *Annual Report of the Cleveland Public Schools* (Cleveland, OH: Leader Printing Company, 1886), 25, 93; *Annual Report of the Cleveland Public Schools* (Cleveland, OH: Plain Dealer Publishing Company, 1887), 19. Also, *Annual Report of the Cleveland Public Schools* (Cleveland, OH: Wiseman and Harvey, 1879), 63.

75. Timothy Walch, *Parish School: American Catholic Parochial Education from Colonial Times to the Present* (New York: Crossroad Publishing Company, 1996), 68–71. On these arrangements in New York state, see Benjamin Justice, *The War that Wasn't: Religious Conflict and Compromise in the Common Schools of New York State, 1865–1900* (Albany: State University of New York Press, 2005), 189–218.

76. Justice, *The War that Wasn't*, 198, 209–11.

77. Walch, *Parish School*, 69–93.

78. See, for example, *Biennial Report of the State Superintendent of Public Education to the General Assembly, 1902–1903* (Baton Rouge: Advocate, 1904), 88, 91–92.

79. McGreevy, *Catholicism and American Freedom*, 120–22. For evidence of "Catholic district schools" see Folder 9, 10: Catholic District/Public Schools, 1923–1940, 1934, Box 7, Records of the United States Conference of Catholic Bishops Education Department, American Catholic History Research Center and University Archives, The Catholic University of America, Washington, DC. On post-1945 "Catholic-public" schools see Sarah Barringer Gordon, "'Free' Religion and 'Captive' Schools: Catholics, Protestants, and School Funding at Mid-Century," *DePaul Law Review* 56 (2007): 1177–220.

80. Jacqueline Jones, *Saving Savannah: The City and the Civil War* (New York: Vintage Books, 2009), 334; Michael J. McNally, "A Peculiar Institution: A History of Catholic Parish Life in the Southeast," in *The American Catholic Parish: A History from 1850 to the Present*, 171; Ralph Newton, "Catholic Schools as Public Schools in Georgia" (master's thesis, University of Georgia, 1941).

81. *Eighth Annual Report of the Public Schools for the City of Savannah and County of Chatham for the Year 1872–73* (Savannah: Morning News Office, 1873), 11.

82. John B. Alberts, "Black Catholic Schools: The Josephite Parishes of New Orleans during the Jim Crow Era," *U.S. Catholic Historian* 12, no. 1 (1994): 79–88; James B. Bennett, *Religion and the Rise of Jim Crow in New Orleans* (Princeton, NJ: Princeton University Press, 2005), 153–63.

83. Rev. John R. Slattery, "Facts and Suggestions about the Colored People," *Catholic World* 41 (April 1885): 38

84. James D. Anderson, *The Education of Blacks in the South, 1860–1935* (Chapel Hill: University of North Carolina Press, 1988), 9–12; Marcia E. Turner, "Black School Politics in Atlanta, Georgia, 1869–1943," in *Southern Cities, Southern Schools: Public Education in the New South*, ed. David Plank and Rick Ginsberg (Westport, CT: Greenwood Press, 1990), 179; Susie King Taylor, *Reminiscences of My Life in Camp with the 33d United States Colored Troops: Late 1st S. C. Volunteers* (Boston: Author, 1902), 54–55; Christopher M. Span, "Alternative Pedagogy: The Rise of the Private Black Academy in Early Postbellum Mississippi, 1862–1860," in *Chartered Schools: Two Hundred Years of Independent Academies in the United States, 1727–1925*, ed. Nancy Beadie and Kim Tolley (New York: RoutledgeFalmer, 2002), 211–27.

85. Anderson, *The Education of Blacks in the South*, 156.

86. Kathleen Holscher, *Religious Lessons: Catholic Sisters and the Captured Schools Crisis in New Mexico* (New York: Oxford University Press, 2012), Chapter 1.

87. U.S. Bureau of Education, *Report of the Commissioner of Education for the Year 1886–87* (Washington, DC: Government Printing Office, 1888), 90.

CHAPTER 3

1. William J. Novak, *The People's Welfare: Law and Regulation in Nineteenth-Century America* (Chapel Hill: University of North Carolina Press, 1996). See also Christopher Tomlins, "Necessities of State: Police, Sovereignty, and the Constitution," *Journal of Policy History* 20, no. 1 (2008): 47–63, and Charles W. McCurdy, "The Knight Sugar Decision of 1895 and The Modernization of American Corporation Law, 1869–1903," *Business History Review* 53 (1979): 305.

2. Morton J. Horwitz, "The History of the Public/Private Distinction," *University of Pennsylvania Law Review* 130, no. 6 (June 1982): 1425. Much has been written about *Dartmouth*'s implications for public and private higher education. For two contrasting accounts on the case's impact see John S. Whitehead, *The Separation of College and State: Columbia, Dartmouth, Harvard, and Yale, 1776–1876* (New Haven, CT: Yale University Press, 1973), and Jurgen Herbst, *From Crisis to Crisis: American College Government, 1636–1819* (Cambridge, MA: Harvard University Press, 1982). See also Herbst and Whitehead, "How to Think About the Dartmouth College Case," *History of Education Quarterly* 26, no. 3 (1986): 333–49.

3. *The Trustees of Dartmouth College v. William H. Woodward*, 65 N.H. 473, 631 (1817).

4. *Dartmouth*, 65 N.H. at 503, 642.

5. *The Trustees of Dartmouth College v. Woodward*, 17 U.S. 518, 634 (1819).

6. Herbert Hovenkamp, *Enterprise and American Law, 1836–1937* (Cambridge, MA: Harvard University Press, 1991), 17–35.

7. Albert Fishlow, "Levels of Nineteenth-Century American Investment in Education," *Journal of Economic History* 26, no. 4 (December 1966): 418–36; Carl F. Kaestle and Maris A. Vinovskis, *Education and Social Change in Nineteenth-Century Massachusetts* (New York: Cambridge University Press, 1980); Nancy Beadie, "Education, Social Capital, and State Formation in Comparative Historical Perspective: Preliminary Investigations," *Paedagogica Historica* 46, no. 1 (2010): 15–32.

8. Claudia Goldin and Lawrence Katz, *The Race Between Education and Technology* (Cambridge, MA: Belknap Press, 2008), 143.

9. Carl Kaestle, *Pillars of the Republic: Common Schools and American Society* (New York: Hill and Wang, 1983), 136–81.

10. *The School Manual: Containing the School Laws of Rhode Island; with Decisions, Remarks and Forms for the Use of School Officers* (Providence, RI: E. L. Freeman, 1882), 5–66. As evidence of the close link between Christianity and public schooling the manual also included suggested morning and afternoon prayers that spoke of "Jesus Christ Our Lord" and "our understandings by Thy Holy Spirit."

11. *School Manual*, 36–37.

12. See, for example, *Rules and Regulations of the Milwaukee Board of School Directors* (Milwaukee: Edward Keogh), 1898.

13. E. R. Potter, C.P.S., "Decision No. 58, Appeal from School Committee of North Kingstown" (1853), in *The School Manual* (1882), 128–29.

14. Potter, "Decision No. 58," 128. State laws granting children the right to a public school education were of course rarely treated with sanctity in practice in the North, where African-American children, children with disabilities, or simply boisterous children were excluded from public schools with tremendous frequency. On the tensions between state law and local practice see Davison M. Douglas, *Jim Crow Moves North: The Battles over Northern School Segregation, 1865–1954* (New York: Cambridge University Press, 2005); Joseph L. Tropea, "Bureaucratic Order and Special Children: Urban Schools, 1890s–1940s," *History of Education Quarterly* 27, no. 1 (Spring 1987): 29–53.

15. Potter, "Decision No. 58."

16. The minutes to these School Committee meetings were reproduced in *Report of the School Committee for the Year 1899–1900: Centennial Celebration of the Establishment of the Public Schools* (Providence, RI: Providence Press, 1901), 133. See also Charles Carroll, *Public Education in Rhode Island* (Providence, RI: E. L. Freeman, 1918), 155; David Gartner, "The Growth of a Catholic Educational System in Providence and the Protestant Reaction, 1848–1876," *Rhode Island History* 55 (1997): 136–37.

17. Barbara Tucker Cervone, "Rounding up the Children: Compulsory Education Enforcement in Providence, Rhode Island, 1883–1935" (PhD diss., Harvard Graduate School of Education, 1983), 39; Patrick T. Conley, *The Rhode Island State Constitution: A Reference Guide* (Westport, CT: Praeger, 2007), 257–58; Patrick T. Conley and Matthew J. Smith, *Catholicism in Rhode Island: The Formative Era* (Providence, RI: Diocese of Providence, 1976), 78–79. Ohio attempted to pass a similar law in 1853.

18. Provisions Respecting Corporations in General, R.I. Gen. Laws § 19-125-1 (1857). While non-parish-based Catholic academies and seminaries were incorporated individually, parochial schools were generally incorporated with their sponsoring parishes, dioceses, or, later, religious teaching orders. In 1869, the Rhode Island legislature passed an act to incorporate the entire Catholic diocese of Hartford (which at the time included Rhode Island), which granted the body power to receive and hold all property "for the support of the educational or charitable institutions of that church" within a specified dollar amount. See "An Act to Incorporate the Bishop and Vicar General of the Diocese of Hartford, Together with the Pastor and Two Laymen of Any Roman Catholic Church or Congregation in Rhode Island," 1869 R.I. Acts & Resolves 221–23.

19. On the history of tax exemptions see Stephen Diamond, "Efficiency and Benevolence: Philanthropic Tax Exemptions in 19th-Century America," in *Property Tax Exemptions for Charities*, ed. Evelyn Brody (Washington, DC: Urban Institute Press, 2002), 115–44; Carl Zollman, "Tax Exemptions of American Church Property," *Michigan Law Review* 14, no. 8 (1916): 646–57.

20. See, for example, "Of Property Liable to Taxation," R.I. Gen. Laws § 8-37-2 (1857). In New York, only incorporated parochial schools could claim property tax exemption. See *The Church of St. Monica v. The Mayor, Aldermen and Commonalty of the City of New York*, 119 N.Y. 91 (1890).

21. The Act read that "any school or asylum incorporated by or receiving aid from the state, either by direct grant or by exemption from taxation shall be liable to be examined or visited by the school committee of the town or city in which such institution is situated, whenever the committee shall see fit." See "An Act to enlarge the powers of the School Committee, passed January 1854," in E. R. Potter, *Report upon Public Schools and Education, in the State of Rhode Island* (Providence, RI: Sayles, Miller & Simons, 1854), 37. Two years earlier, the Assembly had limited the amount of tax-exempt property held by schools, academies, and colleges to three acres.

22. "General Assembly," *Providence Daily Post*, February 18, 1854.

23. Conley and Smith, *Catholicism in Rhode Island*, 78–79; Carroll, *Public Education in Rhode Island*, 179, 197–98.

24. Clifton K. Yearley, *The Money Machines: The Breakdown and Reform of Governmental and Party Finance in the North, 1860–1920* (Albany: State University of New York Press, 1970), 8–10, 15–17; R. Rudy Higgens-Evenson, *The Price of Progress: Public Services, Taxation, and the American Corporate State, 1877–1929* (Baltimore: Johns Hopkins University Press, 2003), 12–24.

25. Samuel T. Spear, "Taxation and Religious Corporations," *The Independent* 28, no. 1436 (June 8, 1876): 3; "The Taxation of Church Property," *Scribner's Monthly* 7, no. 6 (April 1874): 755.

26. Lyman H. Atwater, "Taxation of Churches, Colleges, and Charitable Institutions," *Presbyterian Quarterly and Princeton Review* no. 10 (April 1874): 343.

27. Ulysses S. Grant, "Seventh Annual Message," December 7, 1875, accessed June 28, 2014, http://www.presidency.ucsb.edu/ws/index.php?pid=29516.

28. "There Must Be Loans," *Boston Daily Globe*, March 8, 1890.

29. "Likely to Affect Catholics," *Pittsburgh Dispatch*, January 19, 1889.

30. Roger and Rodney Stark, *The Churching of America, 1776–2005: Winners and Losers in Our Religious Economy* (New Brunswick, NJ: Rutgers University Press, 1992), 113; Robert W. Hayman, *Catholicism in Rhode Island and the Diocese of Providence, 1780–1886* (Providence, RI: Diocese of Providence, 1982), 294.

31. Joel Perlmann, *Ethnic Differences: Schooling and Social Structure among the Irish, Italians, Jews, and Blacks in an American City, 1880–1935* (New York: Cambridge University Press, 1989), 66–67; Hayman, *Catholicism in Rhode Island*, 257.

32. Edwin M. Snow, *Report upon the Census of Rhode Island, 1875* (Providence, RI: Providence Press Company, 1877), 58–60. In 1872, the mayor of Providence even went so far as to veto the construction of a public school building because he feared the competition that the school would face from a nearby Catholic school. See Gartner, "Growth of a Catholic Educational System," 142.

33. *Message of Henry Howard, Governor of Rhode Island, to the General Assembly at Its January Session, 1874* (Providence, RI: Providence Press Company, 1874), 14.

34. "Of Property Liable to Taxation," R.I. Gen. Laws § 8-37-2 (1857).

35. Hayman, *Catholicism in Rhode Island*, 294.

36. *Report of the Joint Special Committee on the Subject of 'Property Liable to and Exempt from Taxation' Made to the General Assembly of the State of Rhode Island, at its January Session* (Providence, RI: Providence Press Company, 1875), 7–10.

37. Ibid., 12–13, 14–17.

38. "General Assembly," *Providence Evening Press*, March 17, 1876; "General Assembly," *Providence Evening Press*, March 31, 1876.

39. Board of Assessors, *List of Persons, Copartnerships, and Corporations Assessed in the City Tax Ordered by the City Council of the City of Providence* (Providence, RI: A. Crawford Greene, 1877), 216.

40. Calculated from the 1884 itemized property listings of Pawtucket's St. Mary's Church. Rhode Island Assessors, *A List of Persons, Corporations, Companies and Estates, Assessed in the Town Tax, Ordered By the Electors Qualified to Vote upon Any Proposition to Impose a Tax or Expend Money in the Town of Pawtucket, R.I. Assessors* (Pawtucket: Sibley and Lee, 1884), 21.

41. "Charles E. Gorman," *Encyclopedia of Biography* (American Historical Society, 1918), 287–89.

42. *Saint Joseph's Church v. The Assessors of Taxes of Providence*, 12 R.I. 19, 19-21 (1878); Hayman, *Catholicism in Rhode Island*, 196. On Durfee's views, see Thomas Durfee, *Some Thoughts on the Constitution of Rhode Island* (Providence, RI: Sidney S. Rider, 1884), 12–18. Durfee warned that if the state's large number of foreign-born voted the result would be wide-scale "corruption" and the rule of political bosses.

43. As the historian and Rhode Island public school official Charles Carroll wrote, "as [the 1875 law] abolished tax exemption, the new law took away from school committees the right, estab-lished by law in 1855, to visit and inspect private and parochial schools." Carroll, *Public Education in Rhode Island*, 198.

44. "Proposition No. 148," *Official Report of the Proceedings and Debates of the Third Constitutional Convention of Ohio, Volume I* (Cleveland, OH: W. S. Robison and Company, 1873), 1254.

45. Much has been written about these events. See, for example, Ward M. McAfee, *Religion, Race, and Reconstruction: The Public Schools in the Politics of the 1870s* (Albany: SUNY Press, 1998), 27–33.

46. *John Gerke and Walker Yeatman v. John B. Purcell*, 25 Ohio St. 229, 235 (1874, argument for plaintiff in error).

47. *Gerke*, 25 Ohio St. at 237.

48. *Bishop Gilmour v. Pelton*, 6 Am. L. Rec. 26, 31 (Ohio Ct. Comm. Pleas, 1887). The district court's decision was ultimately affirmed by the State Supreme Court, who found there to be "no material difference between the facts in this case and those in Gerke v. Purcell."

49. *Gilmour*, 6 Am. L. Rec. at 33.

50. Charles W. Eliot, "The Exemption from Taxation of Church Property, and the Property of Educational, Literary and Charitable Institutions," in *Report of the Commissioners Appointed to Inquire into the Expediency of Revising and Amending the Laws Relating to Taxation and Exemption Therefrom* (Boston: Wright and Potter, 1875), 384.

51. *Miller's Appeals*, 10 WNC 168 (1881).

52. "Legislative Hearings," *Manufacturers and Farmers Journal*, June 11, 1894.

53. *Munn v. Illinois*, 94 U.S. 113, 126 (1877). On the development and transformation of the "public purpose" doctrine in American law see Harry N. Scheiber, "The Road to *Munn*: Eminent Domain the Concept of Public Purpose in the State Courts," in *Perspectives in American History*, vol. 5, ed. Donald Fleming and Bernard Bailyn (Cambridge, MA: Charles Warren Center for Studies in American History, Harvard University, 1971), 329–404.

54. *Berea College v. Kentucky*, 211 U.S. 45, 48 (1908, argument for plaintiff in error).

55. *Berea*, 211 U.S. at 53. The state's lawyers argued explicitly that "to preserve race identity, the purity of blood, and prevent amalgamation, and such is the settled public policy of the State," and thus a reasonable extension of its police powers. *Berea,* 211 U.S. at 51 (1908, argument for defendant in error).

56. *Berea*, 211 U.S. at 60-70 (Harlan, J., dissenting).

57. "Editorial," *The Virginia Law Register* 14, no. 8 (December 1908): 643–44. David E. Bernstein explores the relationship between *Berea* and other early Fourteenth Amendment cases in "*Plessy* versus *Lochner*: The *Berea College* Case," *Journal of Supreme Court History* 25, no. 1 (March 2000): 93–111.

58. John O'Grady, "State Supervision of Catholic Institutions," *Ecclesiastical Review* 55 (July 1916): 12.

CHAPTER 4

1. On Brooks, see his obituary "Dr. Edward Brooks," *Journal of Education* 76, no. 2 (July 11, 1912): 66.

2. Archdiocese of Philadelphia, *Annual Report of the Superintendent of Parochial Schools of the Archdiocese of Philadelphia for the Year Ending June 30, 1898* (1898), 1, Philadelphia Archdiocesan Historical Research Center, Philadelphia, PA [hereafter PAHRC]; Board of Public Education, *Annual Report of the Superintendent of Public Schools of the City of Philadelphia for the Years 1898–9* (Philadelphia: Walther Printing House, 1899), 12.

3. Edward Brooks to Rev. John W. Shanahan, 18 January, 1898, Box 1, Superintendent of Schools Files (1998/01), PAHRC.

4. Harold A. Buetow, *Of Singular Benefit: The Story of Catholic Education in the United States* (New York: Macmillan, 1970), 179.

5. On the strong correlation between Catholicism (or religion, generally) and party affiliation, see Richard Jensen, *The Winning of the Midwest: Social and Political Conflict, 1888–1896* (Chicago: University of Chicago, 1971), xii, 58–88; Ballard Campbell, *Representative Democracy: Public Policy and Midwestern Legislatures in the Late Nineteenth Century* (Cambridge, MA: Harvard University Press, 1980), 4–17.

6. Stephen J. Provasnik, "Compulsory Schooling, from Idea to Institution: A Case Study of the Development of Compulsory Attendance in Illinois, 1857–1907" (PhD diss., University of Chicago, 1999), Appendix E, 332. Martin Jay Eisenberg also found strong correlations between Republican representatives and compulsory attendance laws. See Eisenberg, "Compulsory Attendance Legislation in America, 1870 to 1915" (PhD diss., University of Pennsylvania, 1988).

7. Ward M. McAfee, *Religion, Race, and Reconstruction: The Public Schools in the Politics of the 1870s* (Albany: State University of New York Press, 1998). Republicans conceived of economic policy in the late nineteenth century as accomplishing similar ends of national growth and partisan dominance. See Richard Bensel, *The Political Economy of American Industrialization, 1877–1900* (New York: Cambridge University Press, 2000).

8. Henry Wilson in "New Departure of the Republican Party," *Atlantic Monthly* 27 (January 1871): 104–20.

9. Stephen Provasnik has found that state courts throughout the nineteenth century gave school authorities broad discretion to regulate school policies surrounding student attendance, conduct, and discipline. In contrast, courts tended to side with parents over disputes concerning

curriculum, suggesting that judges still valued parental belief systems over those imposed by the state. See Stephen Provasnik, "Judicial Activism and the Origins of Parental Choice: The Court's Role in the Institutionalization of Compulsory Education in the United States, 1891–1925," *History of Education Quarterly* 46, no. 3 (Fall 2006): 321–28.

10. E. A. Higgens, "The American State and the Private School," *Catholic World* 53, no. 316 (July 1891): 522.

11. Carl F. Kaestle and Maris A. Vinovskis, *Education and Social Change in Nineteenth-Century Massachusetts* (New York: Cambridge University Press, 1980); Tracy Steffes, *School, Society, and State: A New Education to Govern Modern America, 1890–1940* (Chicago: University of Chicago Press, 2012), Chapter 4.

12. "Compulsory Education," *Providence Evening News*, April 9, 1883.

13. John William Perrin, "The History of Compulsory Education in New England" (PhD diss., University of Chicago, 1896), 69.

14. *Annual Report of the School Committee, of the City of Providence* (Providence, RI: Providence Press, 1887), 64–65.

15. *Fourteenth Annual Report of the Board of Education, Together with the Thirty-Ninth Annual Report of the Commissioner of Public Schools, of Rhode Island* (Providence, RI: E. L. Freeman, 1884), 80.

16. Perrin, "Compulsory Education in New England," 69.

17. *Eleventh Annual Report of the Board of Education, Together with the Thirty-Sixth Annual Report of the Commissioner of Public Schools, of Rhode Island* (Providence, RI: E. L. Freeman, 1881), 85–86.

18. *Twelfth Annual Report of the Board of Education, Together with the Thirty-Seventh Annual Report of the Commissioner of Public Schools, of Rhode Island* (Providence, RI: E. L. Freeman, 1882), 92.

19. See the "Canadian French in New England," in *Thirteenth Annual Report of the Bureau of Statistics of Labor* (Boston: Rand, Avery, 1882), 73–74.

20. *Annual Report of the School Committee, of the City of Providence* (1887): 64–65.

21. Peter H. Argersinger, "The Value of the Vote: Political Representation in the Gilded Age," *Journal of American History* 76, no. 1 (June 1989): 63. On the dominance of the Republican Party in Rhode Island see John D. Buenker, "The Politics of Resistance: The Rural-Based Yankee Republican Machines of Connecticut and Rhode Island," *New England Quarterly* 47, no. 2 (June 1974): 212–37.

22. In the 1870s, Rhode Island was the only state that set different voting rules for natives and foreign-born citizens. In 1885, only 15 percent of Providence's foreign-born met the property qualifications for voting. On the context surrounding these laws see Evelyn Savidge Sterne, *Ballots and Bibles: Ethnic Politics and the Catholic Church in Providence* (Ithaca, NY: Cornell University Press, 2003), 60–65.

23. "An Act to provide for the better Instruction of Youth employed in Manufacturing Establishments," 1836 Mass. Acts ch. 245, 950; "An Act in addition to an Act concerning the Employment of Children in Manufacturing Establishments," 1855 Mass. Acts ch. 379, 766–67; "An Act Relating to the Attendance of Children at School," 1873 Mass. Acts ch. 279, 708.

24. "An Act in Relation the Approval of Private Schools by School Committees," 1878 Mass. Acts ch. 171, 126.

25. "An Act in Relation to Truant Children, and of the Attendance of Children in the Public Schools," 1883 R.I. Acts & Resolves ch. 363, 146–50.

26. *Twenty-Seventh Annual Report of the State Board of Education, Together with the Fifty-Second Annual Report of the Commissioner of Public Schools of Rhode Island* (Providence, RI: E. L. Freeman, 1897), 28–29.

27. *Twenty-Eighth Annual Report of the State Board of Education, Together with the Fifty-Third Annual Report of the Commissioner of Public Schools of Rhode Island* (Providence, RI: E. L. Freeman, 1898), 25–26.

28. "Another Day's Work," *Providence Evening Press*, March 8, 1883; "At Work Again," *Providence Evening Press*, March 13, 1883; "The State Legislature," *Providence Evening Press*, March 20, 1883; "General Assembly," *Providence News*, March 5, 1884.

29. *Annual Report of the School Committee, of the City of Providence* (Providence, RI: Providence Press, 1891), 46.

30. *Eighteenth Annual Report of the Board of Education, Together with the Forty-Third Annual Report of the Commissioner of Public Schools, of Rhode Island* (Providence, RI: E. L. Freeman, 1888), Appendix, 53, 72.

31. *Twenty-Second Annual Report of the Board of Education, Together with the Forty-Seventh Annual Report of the Commissioner of Public Schools, of Rhode Island* (Providence, RI: E. L. Freeman, 1892), Appendix, 48.

32. *Twenty-Fourth Annual Report of the State Board of Education, Together with the Forty-Ninth Annual Report of the Commissioner of Public Schools of Rhode Island* (Providence, RI: E. L. Freeman, 1894), Appendix, 47–49.

33. *Annual Report of the Commissioner of Industrial Statistics, Made to the General Assembly* (Providence, RI: E. L. Freeman, 1889), 128. Bowditch's solution was to use the resources of the public treasury to provide public school students with free textbooks, which he believed parochial schools could not afford to offer.

34. "The Friends of Education," *Catholic World* 22, no. 132 (March 1876): 768.

35. On fears that compulsory attendance laws would increase overcrowding see David Tyack, *The One Best System: A History of American Urban Education* (Cambridge, MA: Harvard University Press, 1974), 70–71.

36. *Annual Report of the School Committee, of the City of Providence* (Providence, RI: Providence Press Company, 1888), 16.

37. *Annual Report of the School Committee, of the City of Providence* (Providence, RI: Providence Press Company, 1887), 24.

38. *Twenty-Third Annual Report of the State Board of Education, Together with the Forty-Eighth Annual Report of the Commissioner of Public Schools of Rhode Island* (January 1883), Appendix, 37.

39. *Providence School Committee* (1887), 24.

40. Calculations tabulated from *Annual Reports of the State Board of Education, Together with the Annual Report of the Commissioner of Public Schools of Rhode Island*, 1881–1899.

41. On the failure to enforce the "approval" of parochial schools by local school committees see Thomas Dwight, "The Attack on Freedom of Education in Massachusetts," *American Catholic Quarterly Review* 13, no. 51 (July 1888): 547.

42. "The Governor's Message," *Boston Evening Transcript*, January 5, 1888. See also "The School Question," *Boston Daily Advertiser*, January 11, 1888.

43. "Report of the Joint Special Committee of The General Court of 1887 on the Employment and Schooling of Children" (1888), Taylor Room, Wirtz Labor Library, U.S. Department of Labor, 26–28.

44. "The Protest against the Majority Report of the Joint Special Committee of the General Court of 1887, on the Employment and Schooling of Children (House Document No. 19) and Against any Legislative Interference with Private Schools, Being a Digest of the Remarks of the Remonstrants, at the Hearings of the Legislative Committee on Education in March, 1888" (1888), Catholic University Rare Books and Special Collections, 54–57.

45. "The Protest against the Majority Report," 54–57.

46. John T. McGreevy, *Catholicism and American Freedom: A History* (New York: W. W. Norton, 2003), 127–50.

47. "Current Events," *Catholic World*, 29, no. 171 (June 1879): 422.

48. Rev. James Conway, "The Rights and Duties of Family and State in Regard to Education," *American Catholic Quarterly Review* 9 (January 1884): 106.

49. Lorenzo J. Markoe, "Is There Any System of Public School That Would Satisfy Catholics?" *Catholic World* 75, no. 447 (June 1902): 333. See also "The Idea of a Parochial School," *American Catholic Quarterly Review* 16, no. 63 (July 1891): 461.

50. "The Protest against the Majority Report," 14–16.

51. Nathan Matthews Jr., *The Citizen and the State: An Argument by Nathan Matthews, Jr. in Defense of Private Schools, Before the Joint Committee on Education of the Massachusetts Legislature, April 25, 1889* (Boston: Geo H. Ellis, 1889), 6.

52. "The Protest against the Majority Report," 21.

53. "The Attack on Freedom of Education in Massachusetts," *American Catholic Quarterly Review*, 553.

54. "Our French Canadians," *Boston Daily Globe*, December 28, 1884.

55. "Private School Fight," *Boston Daily Globe*, April 4, 1889.

56. Lloyd Jorgenson, *The State and the Non-Public School, 1825–1925* (Columbia: University of Missouri Press, 1987), 176–78.

57. "The Decision," *Boston Evening Journal*, February 11, 1889. See also "The Haverhill School Case Again," *Boston Evening Transcript*, February 12, 1889. When several years later a town school committee charged another parent with violating the attendance law a Massachusetts court found, similarly, that the "great object of the provisions of the statutes has been that all the children shall be educated, not that they shall be educated in any particular way." See *Commonwealth v. Frank Roberts*, 159 Mass. 372, 373 (1893).

58. Jorgenson, *The State and the Non-Public School*, 179.

59. "The Parochial School Bill," *Journal of Education* 29, no. 24 (June 13, 1889): 377.

60. "Massachusetts Legislation," *Journal of Education* 29, no. 25 (June 29, 1889): 393.

61. "School Buildings: What Can Be Done to Improve Their Condition," *Boston Daily Advertiser*, February 1, 1889.

62. "Parochial Schools: Educational Situation in Massachusetts," *Boston Daily Advertiser*, November 12, 1889; see also "Parochial Schools: How They Affect Waltham's Public Schools," *Boston Daily Advertiser*, September 10, 1888.

63. "The Legislature," *Boston Morning Journal*, February 28, 1890.

64. "Mr. Matthews on City Finance," *Boston Daily Globe*, March 1, 1890. On Boston's tax burden see Charles Phillips Huse, *The Financial History of Boston from May 1, 1822, to January 31,*

1909 (Cambridge, MA: Harvard University Press, 1916); John B. Legler, Richard Sylla, and John J. Wallis, "U.S. City Finances and the Growth of Government, 1850–1902," *Journal of Economic History* 48, no. 2 (June 1988): 354.

65. "State and School," *Boston Daily Globe*, January 22, 1888.

66. "Public and Private Schools," *Boston Evening Transcript*, February 9, 1889.

67. "The Protest against the Majority Report," 14.

68. Lois Bannister Merk, "Boston's Historic Public School Crisis," *New England Quarterly* 31, no. 2 (June 1958): 180. The Republican ticket won the school board election and, according to Merk, Catholic women voters in Boston diminished thereafter.

69. "The Protest against the Majority Report," 7–9.

70. See "Massachusetts Legislation."

71. For other examples, see Sara Errington, "'The Language Question': Nativism, Politics, and Ethnicity in Rhode Island," in *New England's Disharmony: The Consequences of the Industrial Revolution*, ed. Douglas M. Reynolds and Katheryn Viens (Kingston: Rhode Island Labor History Society and Labor Research Center, 1993), 95. Benjamin Justice emphasizes this type of local compromise on issues of ethnic and religious strife in *The War that Wasn't: Religious Conflict and Compromise in the Common Schools of New York State, 1865–1900* (Albany: State University of New York Press, 2005).

72. The Illinois and Wisconsin laws were largely identical. For a side-by-side comparison, see *The Daily News Almanac and Political Register for 1891* (Chicago: Chicago Daily News, 1891), 66–67.

73. "Some Facts," *Milwaukee Journal*, March 29, 1890.

74. Paul Kleppner, *The Cross of Culture: A Social Analysis of Midwestern Politics, 1850–1900* (New York: Free Press, 1970), 162–68; Jensen, *The Winning of the Midwest*, 122–26.

75. "Notes," *Wisconsin Journal of Education* 13, no. 5 (May 1883): 217.

76. O. B. Wyman, "Compulsory Educational Law," *Wisconsin Journal of Education* 9, no. 9 (September 1879): 366.

77. "Official Department, Questions and Answers—The Compulsory Law," *Wisconsin Journal of Education* 9, no. 10 (October 1879): 442.

78. "Notes," *Wisconsin Journal of Education* 12, no. 6 (June 1882): 280–81.

79. "Editorial," *Wisconsin Journal of Education* 19, no. 9 (September 1889): 379.

80. "The Quintessence of a Slander," *The Catholic Citizen*, September 13, 1890.

81. Jensen, *The Winning of the Midwest*, 122–26. See also "The Bennett Law," *The Catholic Citizen*, July 26, 1890.

82. "Watch Words for Wisconsin Voters," *The Catholic Citizen*, November 1, 1890.

83. *Germania* (Milwaukee), March 25, 1890, quoted in Kleppner, *The Cross of Culture*, 160.

84. Jensen, *The Winning of the Midwest*, 127–44.

85. Robert C. Nesbit, *The History of Wisconsin: Urbanization and Industrialization, 1873–1893*, vol. 3 (Madison: State Historical Society of Wisconsin, 1985), 614.

86. Provasnik, "Compulsory Schooling, from Idea to Institution," 276–86. Provasnik found that school boards in at least eight counties sought to force parents to remove their children from local, unapproved parochial schools that instructed in foreign languages. In one case Provasnik found that a school board ordered parents to remove their child from a Lutheran school despite its compliance with state laws.

87. "Report of the Committee on State School Systems: Compulsory Education," *National Educational Association Journal of Proceedings and Addresses* (New York: J. J. Little, 1891), 295–96.

88. The National Educational Association featured a heated debate over Catholic education during its 1889 annual meeting. See *The Two Sides of the School Question* (Boston: Committee of One Hundred, 1890).

89. "Report of the Committee on State School Systems (Discussion)," 301–2.

CHAPTER 5

1. Bureau of the Census, *Religious Bodies, 1916* (Washington, DC: Government Printing Office, 1920), 30, 127.

2. David P. Baker, "Schooling All the Masses: Reconsidering the Origins of American Schooling in the Postbellum Era," *Sociology of Education* 72, no. 3 (1999): 197–215.

3. David Tyack, *The One Best System: A History of American Urban Education* (Cambridge, MA: Harvard University Press, 1974); Raymond E. Callahan, *Education and the Cult of Efficiency: A Study of the Social Forces That Have Shaped the Administration of the Public Schools* (Chicago: University of Chicago Press, 1962); Dorothy Shipps, *School Reform, Corporate Style: Chicago, 1880–2000* (Lawrence: Kansas University Press, 2006), 16–49; Tracy Steffes, *School, Society, and State: A New Education to Govern Modern America, 1890–1940* (Chicago: University of Chicago Press, 2012).

4. Timothy Walch, *Parish School: American Catholic Parochial Education from Colonial Times to the Present* (New York: Crossroad Publishing Company, 1996), 100–17; James W. Sanders, *The Education of an Urban Minority: Catholics in Chicago, 1833–1965* (New York: Oxford University Press, 1977), 141–60; James A. Burns, *The Growth and Development of the Catholic School System* (New York: Benziger Brothers, 1912), 197–216.

5. On how Catholic schools emulated public competitors see Marvin Lazerson, "Understanding American Catholic Educational History," *History of Education Quarterly* 17, no. 3 (1977): 297–317. See also Paula Fass, *Outside In: Minorities and the Transformation of American Education* (New York: Oxford University Press, 1993), 189–228.

6. Ernest L. Talbert, *Opportunities in School and Industry for Children of the Stockyards District* (Chicago: University of Chicago Press, 1912), 8.

7. The literature on these urban figures is extensive. Classic works include Richard Hofstadter, *The Age of Reform: From Bryan to FDR* (New York: Random House, 1955), 174–214. On padrones, see Gunther Peck, *Reinventing Free Labor: Padrones and Immigrant Workers in the North American West, 1880–1930* (New York: Cambridge University Press, 2000).

8. Morton Keller, *Regulating a New Society: Public Policy and Social Change in America, 1900–1933* (Cambridge, MA: Harvard University Press, 1994).

9. David Nasaw, *Going Out: The Rise and Fall of Public Amusements* (New York: Basic Books, 1993), 169–85.

10. Morton Keller, *America's Three Regimes: A New Political History* (New York: Oxford University Press, 2007), 166–68, 189.

11. Brian Balogh, *A Government Out of Sight: The Mystery of National Authority in Nineteenth-Century America* (New York: Cambridge University Press, 2009), 325.

12. William J. Novak, "Law and the Social Control of American Capitalism," *Emory Law Journal* 60, no. 2 (2010): 398.

13. These included regulative services other than public health. Tony A. Freyer, "Business Law and American Economic History," in *The Cambridge Economic History of the United States*, ed.

Stanley L. Engerman and Robert E. Gallman, vol. 2 (New York: Cambridge University Press, 2000), 462.

14. Richard Scylla, "Experimental Federalism: The Economics of American Government, 1789–1914," in *The Cambridge Economic History of the United States*, ed. Stanley L. Engerman and Robert E. Gallman, vol. 2 (New York: Cambridge University Press, 2000), 537–38.

15. Keller, *America's Three Regimes*, 181, 189. For an excellent summary of policy innovation in Massachusetts in the 1880s and 1890s, see Ballard C. Campbell, "Public Policy and State Government," in *The Gilded Age: Perspective on the Origins of Modern America*, ed. Charles William Calhoun (Lanham, MD: Rowan & Littlefield, 2007), 358.

16. Sophonisba P. Breckinridge, *Marriage and the Civic Rights of Women: Separate Domicil and Independent Citizenship* (Chicago: University of Chicago Press, 1931), 3; Sophonisba P. Breckinridge, *The Family and the State: Select Documents* (1934; repr., New York: Arno Press and New York Times, 1972), 231.

17. Steffes, *School, Society, and State*, 124. On compulsory attendance laws as a tool of state police power see "Constitutionality and Construction of Compulsory Education Laws," *Central Law Journal* 56, no. 19 (May 1903): 361–63.

18. New York City Department of Education, Bureau of Attendance, *First Annual Report of the Director of Attendance for the Year Ending July 31, 1915* (1916): 2–5.

19. New York City Department of Education, Bureau of Attendance, *Report of the Bureau of Attendance for the Period Between July 31, 1915 to July 31, 1918* (1919): 20, 271.

20. See also John Frederick Bender, *The Functions of Courts in Enforcing Compulsory Attendance Laws* (New York: Teachers College, 1927). On the explosion of judicial activity at the local level and its indebtedness to new social scientific ideas, see Michael Willrich, *City of Courts: Socializing Justice in Progressive Era Chicago* (New York: Cambridge University Press, 2003).

21. Ira Katznelson and Margaret Weir, *Schooling for All: Class, Race, and the Decline of the Democratic Ideal* (New York: Basic Books, 1985); Jeffrey Mirel, *The Rise and Fall of an Urban System: Detroit, 1907–1981*, 2nd ed. (Ann Arbor: University of Michigan Press, 1999); David Plank and Rick Ginsberg, eds., *Southern Cities, Southern Schools: Public Education in the New South* (Westport, CT: Greenwood Press, 1990); William J. Reese, *Power and the Politics of School Reform: Grassroots Movements during the Progressive Era* (1985; repr., New York: Teachers College Press, Columbia University, 2002); Julia Wrigley, *Class Politics and Public Schools* (New Brunswick, NJ: Rutgers University Press, 1982).

22. Stephen Provasnik, "Judicial Activism and the Origins of Parental Choice: The Court's Role in the Institutionalization of Compulsory Education in the United States, 1891–1925," *History of Education Quarterly* 46, no. 3 (2006): 311–47; Ethan Hutt, "Formalism over Function: Compulsion, Courts, and the Rise of Educational Formalism in America, 1870–1930," *Teachers College Record* 114, no. 1 (January 2012): 1–27; Joachim Frederick Weltzin, *The Legal Authority of the American Public School as Developed By a Study of Liabilities to Damages* (Grand Forks, ND: Mid-West Book Concern, 1931); Steffes, *School, Society, and State*, 135–43.

23. *Charles W. Hill v. City of Boston*, 122 Mass. 344 (1877). See also *Susie H. Wixon v. The City of Newport*, 13 R.I. 454 (1881); *Folk v. City of Milwaukee*, 108 Wis. 359 (1900); Weltzin, *The Legal Authority of the American Public School*.

24. Paul Blakeley, "Sociology: Are Parents Superfluous?" *America* 14, no. 5 (November 15, 1915): 118–19; William R. Brock, *Investigation and Responsibility: Public Responsibility in the United States* (Cambridge, UK: Cambridge University Press, 1985).

25. On this view see Lawrence A. Cremin, *The Transformation of the School: Progressivism in American Education, 1876–1957* (New York: Vintage Books, 1961).

26. Miriam Cohen, "Reconsidering Schools and the American Welfare State," *History of Education Quarterly* 45, no. 4 (Winter 2005): 512–37; Michael B. Katz, "Public Education as Welfare," *Dissent* 56, no. 3 (2010): 52–56.

27. Herbert Kliebard, *Schooled to Work: Vocationalism and the American Curriculum, 1876–1946* (New York: Teachers College Press, 1999); Reese, *Power and the Promise of School Reform*; William J. Reese, "After Bread, Education: Nutrition and Urban School Children, 1890–1920," *Teachers College Record* 81, no. 4 (1980): 496–525.

28. Ronald Cohen, *Children of the Mill: Schooling and Society in Gary, Indiana, 1906–1960* (New York: Routledge, 2002); Jeffrey Mirel, *Patriotic Pluralism: Americanization Education and European Immigrants* (Cambridge, MA: Harvard University Press, 2010); Michael Johanek and John L. Puckett, *Leonard Covello and the Making of Benjamin Franklin High School: Education as If Citizenship Mattered* (Philadelphia: Temple University Press, 2007).

29. See, e.g., Diocese of Pittsburgh, "De Jeventute Instituenda," Chapter IV, in *Statuta Dioeceos Pittsburgensis in Synodis Dioecesanis* (1906), 34–36, Historical Records Collection, Catholic Diocese of Pittsburgh; Diocese of La Crosse, "Rules and Regulations of the School Boards of the Diocese of La Crosse," Article VI, in *Second Annual Report of the Diocesan School Board of the Diocese of La Crosse*, 8, Wisconsin Historical Society Library and Archives Pamphlet Collection; Diocese of Fort Wayne, *Fifth Annual Report of the Diocesan School Board* (Fort Wayne, IN: Gazette, 1884), Georgetown University Special Collections.

30. On Cincinnati see Edward A. Connaughton, "A History of Educational Legislation and Administration in the Archdiocese of Cincinnati" (PhD diss., Catholic University of American, 1946), 91–106. On Cleveland and other cities see Thomas T. McAvoy, "Public Schools vs. Catholic Schools and James McMaster," *The Review of Politics* 28, no. 1 (1966): 24–25. For Detroit see JoEllen McNergney Vinyard, *For Faith and Fortune: The Education of Catholic Immigrants in Detroit, 1805–1925* (Urbana and Chicago: University of Illinois Press, 1998), 86–110.

31. Lizabeth Cohen, *Making a New Deal: Industrial Workers in Chicago, 1919–1939* (New York: Cambridge University Press, 1990), 83–84; Mirel, *Patriotic Pluralism*, 115–18; Ann Marie Ryan, "Negotiating Assimilation: Chicago Catholic High Schools' Pursuit of Accreditation in the Early Twentieth Century," *History of Education Quarterly* 46, no. 3 (2006): 354–55; Sanders, *The Education of an Urban Minority*, 105–20.

32. Józef Miąso, *The History of the Education of Polish Immigrants in the United States* (New York: Kosciuszko Foundation, 1977), 228–29.

33. Daniel Folkmar, "The Duration of School Attendance in Chicago and Milwaukee," *Transactions of the Wisconsin Academy of Sciences, Arts, and Letters* XII, no. 1 (1898): 279.

34. James T. Farrell, *Young Lonigan* (1932; repr., New York: Signet Classics, 2004), 61.

35. Fr. Walter, "Census-Taking and Its By-Products," *The Ecclesiastical Review* 71 (November 1924): 454.

36. See, e.g., John McNichols, "Education: School-Picking," *America* 15, no. 16 (July 29, 1916): 385; F. Heiermann, "Education: What School for Your Child," *America* 19, no. 20 (August 24, 1918): 485–86.

37. Joseph S. Hogan, "Education: The Parish School," *America* 23, no. 19 (August 28, 1920): 454; "Catholic Parents and the Catholic School," *America* 23, no. 23 (October 2, 1920): 567.

38. "The Selection of a School," *Dziennik Zjednoczenia*, August 19, 1926, Chicago Foreign Language Press Survey, accessed June 30, 2016, http://flps.newberry.org/article/5423968_1_0234.

39. Joseph S. J. Hogan, "Education: Can We Take a Chance," *America* 23, no. 19 (August 28, 1930): 454; "Catholic Parents and the Catholic School," *America* 23, no. 23 (October 2, 1920): 566–67.

40. Edwin D. Mead, "Has the Parochial School Proper Place in America?" in *National Educational Association Journal of Proceedings, and Addresses* (Topeka: Kansas Publishing House, 1889), 129, 142. For a similar sentiment on how Catholic schools were "under a compulsory system . . . from the clergyman" see "News and Notes," *Wisconsin Journal of Education* 20, no. 9 (September 1890): 389–90.

41. "Some Facts," *The Milwaukee Journal*, March 29, 1890; Lloyd Jorgenson, *The State and the Non-Public School, 1825–1925* (Columbia: University of Missouri Press, 1987), 179.

42. Burns, *Growth and Development of the Catholic School System*, 357–59.

43. Reverend David Anthony Sylvester, "Why Catholic Children Are Not Attending Catholic Schools: A Study of the Reasons Offered by Their Parents" (master's thesis, Catholic University of America, 1947), 57–60; Gerald J. Schnepp, "Leakage from a Catholic Parish" (PhD diss., Catholic University of America, 1942), 183, 187–88.

44. Schnepp, "Leakage from a Catholic Parish," 169–70, 174; Louise Montgomery, *The American Girl in the Stockyard District* (Chicago: University of Chicago Press, 1913), 11. See also Robert Enslow O'Brien, "A Study of the Roman Catholic Elementary Schools of Chicago" (PhD diss., Northwestern University, 1928), 44–45, 64; Jay P. Dolan, *The American Catholic Experience: A History from Colonial Times to the Present* (Garden City, NY: Doubleday & Company, 1985), 283.

45. Leonard V. Koos, *Private and Public Secondary Education: A Comparative Study* (Chicago: University of Chicago Press, 1931), 24. Koos's study found that 81.2 percent of students in Catholic high schools cited "religion" as their primary motive for attendance.

46. Robert E. Park, "The City: Suggestions for the Investigation of Human Behavior in the City Environment," *American Journal of Sociology* 20, no. 5 (March 1915): 577–612; Thomas J. Sugrue, *Sweet Land of Liberty: The Forgotten Struggle for Civil Rights in the North* (New York: Random House, 2008), 185–87; John T. McGreevy, *Parish Boundaries: The Catholic Encounter with Race in the Twentieth-Century Urban North* (Chicago: University of Chicago Press, 1996), Chapter 1; Gerald H. Gamm, *Urban Exodus: Why the Jews Left Boston and the Catholics Stayed* (Cambridge, MA: Harvard University Press, 1999), 14–15; Joshua M. Zeitz, *White Ethnic New York: Jews, Catholics, and the Shaping of Postwar Politics* (Chapel Hill: University of North Carolina Press, 2007); Johanek and Puckett, *Leonard Covello*, 48–76; Eileen M. McMahon, *What Parish Are You From?: A Chicago Irish Community and Race Relations* (Lexington: University Press of Kentucky, 1996); Dolan, *The American Catholic Experience*, 181.

47. Farrell, *Young Lonigan*, 16.

48. In many cities landlords contributed to this constant movement by offering new tenants one month's free rent. David Nasaw, *Children of the City: At Work and at Play* (New York: Oxford University Press, 1985), 32.

49. Stephen Thernstrom, *Poverty and Progress: Social Mobility in a Nineteenth-Century City* (Cambridge, MA: Harvard University Press, 1964), 31, 85.

50. Howard P. Chudacoff, Judith E. Smith, and Peter C. Baldwin: *The Evolution of American Urban Society*, 7th ed. (Upper Saddle River, NJ: Prentice Hall, 2010), 98–99. The pioneering

historical study of residential mobility is Howard P. Chudacoff, *Mobile Americans: Residential and Social Mobility in Omaha, 1880–1920* (New York: Oxford University Press, 1972). For studies of other cities see William Jenkins, "In Search of the Lace Curtain: Residential Mobility, Class Transformation, and Everyday Practice among Buffalo's Irish, 1880–1910," *Journal of Urban History* 35, no. 7 (2009): 970–97; Robert G. Barrows, "Hurryin' Hoosiers and the American 'Pattern': Geographic Mobility in Indianapolis and Urban North America," *Social Science History* 5, no. 2 (1981): 197–222.

51. S. J. Kleinberg, *The Shadow of the Mills: Working-Class Families in Pittsburgh, 1870–1907* (Pittsburgh: University of Pittsburgh Press, 1989), 53.

52. Chudacoff, Smith, and Baldwin, *Evolution of American Urban Society*, 113.

53. Le Roy E. Bowman, "Population Mobility and Community Organization," in *The Urban Community: Selected Papers from the Proceedings of the American Sociological Society, 1925*, ed. Ernest W. Burgess (Chicago: University of Chicago Press, 1926), 160.

54. Edith Abbott and Sophonisba P. Breckinridge, *Truancy and Non-Attendance in the Chicago Schools: A Study of the Social Aspects of the Compulsory Education and Child Labor Legislation of Illinois* (Chicago: University of Chicago Press, 1917), 102, 105.

55. Folkmar, "The Duration of School Attendance in Chicago and Milwaukee," 261. See also O'Brien, "A Study of the Roman Catholic Elementary Schools of Chicago," 60–62; Montgomery, *The American Girl in the Stockyard District*, 10.

56. *Twenty-Sixth Annual Report of the Board of Education, Together with the Fifty-First Annual Report of the Commissioner of Public Schools, of Rhode Island* (Providence, RI: E. L. Freeman, 1896), Appendix, 39.

57. Lila Ver Planck North, "Pittsburgh Schools," in *The Pittsburgh Survey*, ed. Paul Underwood Kellogg (New York: Russell Sage Foundation, 1914), 246.

58. *Annual Report of the New Orleans Public Schools of the Parish of New Orleans, 1913–1914* (New Orleans: Hauser, 1914), 75.

59. New York City Department of Education, Bureau of Attendance, *Report of the Bureau of Attendance*, 256, 265.

60. The Board of Public Education, School District of Philadelphia: Bureau of Compulsory Education, *Report for the Year Ending June 30, 1915* (1916): 12; *Report for the Year Ending June 30, 1919* (1920): 11; *Report for the Year Ending June 30, 1920* (1921): 16–17. For other examples of migrations between parochial and public schools see "Annual Report of the School Committee," in *Reports of the Town Officers of Southbridge* (Southbridge, MA: Journal Steam Book Print, 1887), 121; Providence School Committee, *Annual Report of the School Committee* (Providence, RI: Providence Press, 1892), 34. *Thirty-Second Annual Report of the Board of Education, Together with the Fifty-Seventh Annual Report of the Commissioner of Public Schools, of Rhode Island* (Providence, RI: E. L. Freeman, 1902), Appendix, 18; Edward Clinton Bixler, *An Investigation to Determine the Efficiency with which the Compulsory Attendance Law Is Enforced in Philadelphia* (Philadelphia: University of Pennsylvania, 1913), 52–53.

61. Robert E. Park and Ernest W. Burgess, *The City: Suggestions for Investigation of Human Behavior in the Urban Environment* (1925; repr., Chicago: University of Chicago Press, 1967), 153.

62. M. C. Elmer, "Maladjustment of Youth in Relation to Density of Population," in *The Urban Community*, 162.

63. *Twenty-Sixth Annual Report of the State Board of Education, Together with the Fifty-Second Annual Report of the Commissioner of Public Schools of Rhode Island* (Providence, RI: E. L. Freeman, 1896), Appendix, 38.

64. Leonard P. Ayres, *Laggards in Our Schools: A Study of Retardation and Elimination in City School Systems* (New York: Russell Sage Foundation, 1909), 198. See also Paul Klapper, "The Bureau of Attendance and Child Welfare of the New York City Public School System," *Educational Review* 50 (November 1915): 373–74.

65. The study found that "400 retarded children had 'done time' in 159 parochial schools and in 257 public schools other than the ones in which they were studied; or, each pupil averaged more than two schools." Caroline Hedges, "The Children of the Stockyards," *Transactions of the Fifteenth International Congress on Hygiene and Demography* 3, pt. I (Washington, DC: Government Printing Office, 1913), 180.

66. Frederick Earle Emmons, *City School Attendance Service* (New York: Teachers College, 1926), 71.

67. Sub-Commission on Causes and Effects of Crime, New York State Crime Commission, *From Truancy to Crime—A Study of 251 Adolescents* (Albany, NY: J. B. Lyon Company, 1928), 51–52. See also Jacob Riis's comments in "The Rights of Children," *Charities* 7, no. 2 (July 13, 1901): 48; Park, "The City," 594.

68. *Fifteenth Biennial Report of the Bureau of Labor and Industrial Statistics, Part II: Truancy in Wisconsin* (Madison: Democrat Printing Company, 1911), 54.

69. New York City Bureau of Attendance, *First Annual Report of the Director of Attendance*, 8–9.

70. Cleveland Public Schools, *Sixty-Fifth Annual Report of the Board of Education* (Cleveland, OH: W. M. Bayne Printing House, 1901), 44.

71. Gertrude Howe Britton, *An Intensive Study of the Causes of Truancy in Eight Chicago Public Schools including a Home Investigation of Eight Hundred Truant Children* (Chicago: Hollister, 1906), 23, 25–26, 30–31; Maryland State Board of Education, *Report Covering One Year of Compulsory School Attendance in the Counties of Maryland, Including an Account of Five Years of Compulsory School Attendance in Baltimore County* (1918), 19.

72. Maryland State Board of Education, *Report Covering One Year of Compulsory School Attendance*, 19.

73. H. C. Ginter, "Attendance Officer's Report," *Annual Report of the Public Schools of York, PA* (York: York Dispatch Print, 1913–14): 100. The idea might have come from licensed child laborers (selling newspapers, for example) wearing badges to certify their excuse from compulsory school attendance laws. Nasaw, *Children of the City*, 149.

74. Britton, *An Intensive Study of the Causes of Truancy*, 23–31.

75. Abbott and Breckinridge, *Truancy and Non-Attendance in the Chicago Schools*, 105. For Massachusetts see *Reports of the Town Officers of Southbridge* (1887), 121, "Public and Private Schools," *Boston Evening Transcript*, February 9, 1889. See also Harry Gustav Abraham, "A Study of Pupil Accounting in City School Systems as Revealed by School Surveys" (PhD diss., University of Chicago, 1929), 75–76.

76. *Biennial Report of the State Superintendent of the State of Wisconsin for the Two Years Ending June 30, 1884* (Madison: Democrat Printing, 1885), 13; *Biennial Report of the State Superintendent of the State of Wisconsin* (Madison: Democrat Printing, 1886), 19–20; *Biennial Report of the State Superintendent of the State of Wisconsin* (Madison: Democrat Printing, 1888), 1–2, 19.

77. William T. Harris, *Report of the Commissioner of Education for the Year 1888–89, Volume II* (Washington, DC: Government Printing Office, 1891), 611.

78. Patrick Francis Quigley, *Compulsory Education: The State of Ohio Versus The Rev. Patrick Francis Quigley, D.D.* (New York: Robert Drummond, 1894), iii, 94.

79. Charles N. Lischka, *Private Schools and State Laws: The Text as Well as a Classified Summary of All State Laws Governing Private Schools, in Force in 1924* (Washington, DC: National Catholic Welfare Conference, 1924), 107–8.

80. *Twenty-Sixth Annual Report of the State Board of Education of Rhode Island*, Appendix, 38.

81. Supt. Jas. L. Couglin, "Laws Necessary to Render the Compulsory Attendance Act Efficient," *Pennsylvania School Journal* 47 (Lancaster, PA: Wickersham Printing, 1899), 372.

82. John Mabry Mathews, *Principles of American State Administration* (New York: D. Appleton and Company, 1917), 334.

83. State of Wisconsin, *Fifteenth Biennial Report of the Bureau of Labor and Industrial Statistics*, 54. See *School Survey, Grand Rapids Michigan* (Grand Rapids: Board of Education, 1916), 16.

84. Hedges, "The Children of the Stockyards," 180.

85. Quigley, *Compulsory Education*, viii, 570–71. For other evidence of resistance to reporting see Abbott and Breckinridge, *Truancy and Non-Attendance in the Chicago Schools*, 105; State of Wisconsin, *Fifteenth Biennial Report*, 46.

86. David Tyack and Michael Berkowitz, "The Man Nobody Liked: Toward a Social History of the Truant Officer, 1890–1940," *American Quarterly* 29, no. 1 (Spring 1997): 31–54.

87. Paul Henry Neystrom, "The School Census" (master's thesis, University of Wisconsin, 1910).

88. The "efficiency" reformer David Snedden made the case for a continuous census in a book he co-wrote with William H. Allen, *School Reports and School Efficiency* (New York: Macmillan, 1908), 128–50. Forest Chester Ensign, *Compulsory School Attendance and Child Labor: A Study of the Historical Development of Regulations Compelling Attendance and Limiting the Labor of Children in a Selected Group of States* (Iowa City: Athens Press, 1921), 146–47; Lischka, *Private Schools and State Laws*, 107–8.

89. See, e.g., Arthur B. Moehlman, *Child Accounting: A Discussion of the General Principles Underlying Educational Child Accounting Together with the Development of a Uniform Procedure* (Detroit, MI: Friesema Bros. Press, 1924). On the culture of education administrators' expertise, generally, see Ellen Condliffe Lagemann, *An Elusive Science: The Troubling History of Education Research* (Chicago: University of Chicago Press, 2000); Raymond E. Callahan, *Education and the Cult of Efficiency: A Study of the Social Forces That Have Shaped the Administration of the Public Schools* (Chicago: University of Chicago Press, 1962); David Tyack, "Ways of Seeing: An Essay on the History of Compulsory Schooling," *Harvard Educational Review* 46, no. 3 (1976): 374.

90. Fernando V. Bermejo, *The School Attendance Service in American Cities* (Menasha, WI: George Banta, 1924), 35–36. For descriptions of the various methods used, see Ethel Hanks, "Administration of Child-Labor Laws, Part 4: Employment-Certificate System, Wisconsin," *U.S. Department of Labor Industrial Series* no. 2 (Washington, DC: Government Printing Office, 1921), 79; Klapper, "The Bureau of Attendance and Child Welfare," 360–74; School District of Philadelphia, *Report for the Year Ending June 30, 1922* (1923), 11–12; John Dearling Haney, *Registration of City School Children: A Consideration of the Subject of the City School Census* (New York: Teachers College, Columbia University, 1910), 60–112; Iowa State Teachers Association, *A Uniform Child Accounting System for the State of Iowa: Preliminary Report of the Committee on Child Accounting Submitted to the Educational Council of the Iowa State Teachers' Association, 1926* (Des Moines: Iowa Teachers Association, 1927).

91. Cleveland Public Schools, *Sixty-Fifth Annual Report of the Board of Education* (1901), 44. See also State of Wisconsin, *Fifteenth Biennial Report*, 46.

92. Ensign, *Compulsory School Attendance and Child Labor,* 147.

93. New York City Bureau of Attendance, *First Annual Report of the Director of Attendance,* 189.

94. New York City Department of Education, Bureau of Attendance, *Report of the Bureau of Attendance,* 265–67.

95. Joseph V. S. McClancy, "Discussion," in Brother Azarias, "The Accurate Keeping of School Records," *National Catholic Educational Association Bulletin* 13, no. 1 (November 1916): 275.

96. Rt. Rev. Joseph Schrembs, "Discussion," in Walter George Smith, "Educational Legislation as It Affects Catholic Interests," *NCEA Bulletin* 9 (November 1912): 133.

97. C. F. Hoban, "School Legislation in Relation to Non-State Schools," *The Catholic Educational Association of Pennsylvania Bulletin* 2, no. 1 (March 1922): 42.

98. Ellwood P. Cubberley, *State and County Educational Reorganization: The Revised Constitution and School Code of the State of Osceola* (New York: Macmillan, 1914), 194.

99. Sister M. de Sales to Philip R. McDevitt, 18 February 1910, Box 1, Folder: February 1910, Superintendent of Schools, Philadelphia Archdiocesan Historical Research Center [hereafter PAHRC], Philadelphia, PA; McDevitt to Captain William Thornton, 21 February 1910, Box 1, Folder: February 1910, Superintendent of Schools, PAHRC, Philadelphia, PA; Henry J. Gideon to McDevitt, 10 November 1911, Box 2, Folder: July–December 1911, Superintendent of Schools, PAHRC, Philadelphia, PA; McDevitt to Rev. M. A. Kopytkewicz, 11 November 1911, Box 2, Folder: July–December 1911, Superintendent of Schools, PAHRC, Philadelphia, PA; Gideon to McDevitt, 13 November 1912, Box 2, Folder: October–December 1912, Superintendent of Schools, PAHRC, Philadelphia, PA.

100. Callahan, *Education and the Cult of Efficiency*; Lagemann, *An Elusive Science.*

101. Reverend Paul E. Campbell, "School Records and Reports," in *National Catholic Educational Association Bulletin* 28, no. 1 (November 1931): 591.

102. Azarias, "The Accurate Keeping of School Records," 261–73; Reverend Charles F. M'Evoy, "The Superintendent's Report and Office Records," *National Catholic Educational Association Bulletin* 20 (November 1923): 390–98; Reverend George Johnson, "The Possible Value of a Survey to a Diocesan System," *National Catholic Educational Association Bulletin* 20 (November 1923): 414–20; Martin L. McNicholas, "Child Accounting in Catholic Elementary Schools" (PhD diss., Catholic University of America, 1931).

103. Philip R. McDevitt to the Principal, 1 September 1910, School Files, Office of the Superintendent, SF 2, PAHRC; McDevitt to the Principal, September 28, 1906, SF 2, PAHRC.

104. McClancy, "Discussion," 274.

105. William J. Reese, *America's Public Schools: From the Common School to "No Child Left Behind"* (Baltimore: Johns Hopkins University Press, 2005), 119; Claudia Goldin and Lawrence Katz, *The Race Between Education and Technology* (Cambridge, MA: Belknap Press, 2008); Edward Krug, *The Shaping of the American High School, 1880–1920* (Madison: University of Wisconsin Press, 1969), 170–71.

106. Joel Perlmann, *Ethnic Differences: Schooling and Social Structure among the Irish, Italians, Jews, and Blacks in an American City, 1880–1935* (New York: Cambridge University Press, 1989); Stephen Lassonde, *Learning to Forget: Schooling and Family Life in New Haven's Working Class, 1870–1940* (New Haven, CT: Yale University Press, 2007); Thomas Hine, *The Rise and Fall of the American Teenager* (New York: Perennial, 2000); Goldin and Katz, *The Race Between Education and Technology.*

107. William J. Reese, *The Origins of the American High School* (New Haven, CT: Yale University Press, 1999), 80–102

108. Edward Krug, *The Shaping of the American High School, Volume II, 1920–1940* (Madison: University of Wisconsin Press, 1972), 42–43; Krug, *The Shaping of the American High School, 1880–1920*, 440. Krug notes that even high schools in sparsely populated states like Idaho had many of these features.

109. Burns, *Growth and Development of the Catholic School System*, 293.

110. Rev. James A. Burns, "Catholic Secondary Schools," *American Catholic Quarterly Review* 26 (July 1901): 488–91. Burns assumed that many more parochial schools had one or more of the "higher grades," without having high schools.

111. Given this absence of Catholic high schools, prominent Catholic writers frequently encouraged parents to enroll their children in public institutions. See, e.g., John T. Murphy, "Catholic Secondary Education in the United States," *The American Catholic Quarterly Review* 22 (July 1897): 451–64.

112. "Promoting to the High School," *The School Journal* 64, no. 24 (June 14, 1902): 689. In the 1840s and 1850s urban high school typically required a year of prior public school attendance. See Reese, *Origins of the American High School*, 146–52, 157.

113. See, e.g., Boston Public Schools, *Rules of the School Committee and Regulations of the Public Schools of the City of Boston* (Boston: Rockwell and Churchill, 1888), 47.

114. I have not encountered any secondary sources discussing this process for private elementary schools. On the development of public high school accreditation see Marc VanOverbeke, *The Standardization of American Schooling: Linking Secondary and Higher Education* (New York: Palgrave Macmillan, 2008); for Catholic high school accreditation see Ryan, "Negotiating Assimilation"; Fayette Breaux Veverka, *"For God and Country:" Catholic Schooling in the 1920s* (New York: Garland Publishing, 1988), 127–52.

115. School Board of the City of Milwaukee, Wisc., *Rules and Regulations* (1885), 47; Milwaukee Board of School Directors, *Rules and Regulations* (1898), 43.

116. Milwaukee Board of School Directors, *Rules and Regulations* (1901), 56–57.

117. School Board of the City of Milwaukee, *Proceedings of the School Board from May, 1905 to May, 1906* (1906), 409.

118. For Chicago, see Robert E. O'Brien, "Relations Between the Public and Catholic Schools of Chicago," *Journal of Educational Sociology* 3, no. 2 (1929): 121–24. For Omaha, Nebraska's, accreditation system, see Transcript of Oral Argument of Arthur F. Mullen, in Behalf of Plaintiffs-in-Error at 5, *Meyer v. State of Nebraska*, 262 U.S. 390 (1923) (October Term, 1922, No. 325). For Parsons, Kansas, see *Patrick Creyhon et al. v. Board of Education of the City of Parsons, Kansas*, 99 Kan. 824 (1917).

119. O'Brien, "Relations Between the Public and Catholic Schools of Chicago," 124. O'Brien, a critic of parish education, reported that 162 out of Chicago's 214 Catholic elementary parochial schools were accredited, with "overcrowding" being the reason for those nonaccredited.

120. E. F. Gibbons, "School Supervision—Its Necessity, Aims and Methods," *Report of the Proceedings and Addresses of the Catholic Educational Association* (1905): 167.

121. Campbell, "School Records and Reports," 596.

122. Reverend Daniel Richard Sullivan, "Standardization in its Economic Aspects," *The Catholic Educational Association of Pennsylvania Bulletin* 3, no. 1 (March 1923): 53, 55.

123. George Johnson, "The Need of a Constructive Policy for Catholic Education in the United States," *National Catholic Educational Association Bulletin* 22 (1925): 59–60.

124. Helen C. Williams to America Press, January 20, 1928, Box 9, Folder 19, America Magazine Archives, Georgetown University Special Collections, Washington, DC.

125. Gibbons, "School Supervision," 164–75. Catholic high schools and academies that officially met these standards often did advertise their state approval. In bold letters, St. Mary's Academy in Indiana publicized its "Recognition by the Indiana State Board of Education" in the *New York Sun*. See "The Roman Catholic Schools of America," *New York Sun*, August 21, 1916, Box 16, Bishop Francis W. Howard Collection, American Catholic History Research Center and University Archives, The Catholic University of America, Washington, DC [hereafter ACUA].

126. For other Catholic praise of the Regents Exams, see Bishop McQuaid to Cardinal Leochowski, n.d. (likely 1895), in *The Life and Letters of Bishop McQuaid,* ed. Frederick J. Zwierlein (New York: Art Print Shop, 1927), 3:127; Rev. J. F. Mullaney, "Regents of the State of New York and the Catholic Schools," *American Catholic Quarterly Review* 17 (1892): 638–42; Rev. Joseph F. Smith, "Educational Legislation in New York in Relation to Catholic Interests," *National Catholic Educational Association Bulletin* 4 (1907): 87; J. B. Culemans, "A Plea for Diocesan Superintendents," *Catholic Educational Review* 11 (1916): 34.

127. E. F. Gibbons to Francis Howard, 23 January 1914, Folder: Gibbons, E.F, Box 9, Bishop Francis W. Howard Collection, ACUA.

128. Reverend F. A. Driscoll, "Teacher Preparation—The Present Problem," *The Catholic Educational Association of Pennsylvania Bulletin* 2, no. 1 (March 1922): 33–34.

129. Reverend Patrick J. McCormick, "Standards in Education," *The Catholic Educational Association Bulletin* 14 (1917): 81–82.

130. Rev. John J. Sullivan, "Educational Legislation of Pennsylvania in Relation to Catholic Interests," *National Catholic Educational Association Bulletin* 4 (1907): 82. On the competitive pressures placed on Catholic high schools to seek accreditation, see Ann Marie Ryan, "Negotiating Assimilation."

131. Mich. Comp. Laws §108-5840-20 (August 18, 1921); Leslie Woodcock Tentler, *Seasons of Grace: A History of the Catholic Archdiocese of Detroit* (Detroit, MI: Wayne State University Press, 1995), 449.

132. Vinyard, *For Faith and Fortune,* 244–66.

133. A. C. Monahan to Rev. Joseph J. Rice, June 23, 1921, Folder: Michigan School Bill, Box 21, Records of the U.S. Conference of Catholic Bishops [hereafter USCCB], Education Department, ACUA.

134. John Burke to Austin Dowling, June 24, 1921, Folder 1, Box 106, USCCB Office of the General Secretary, ACUA.

135. James Ryan to Burke, June 25, 1921, Folder 1, Box 106, USCCB Office of the General Secretary, ACUA.

136. Reverend William R. Kelly, "The Superintendent's Relations with Public Authorities and the Officials in the Public-School System," *The Catholic Educational Association Bulletin* 28 (1931): 639.

137. Jeremiah P. Shea, "The Extent of State Control over Catholic Elementary and Secondary Education in Pennsylvania" (PhD diss., Catholic University of America, 1948), 35–37.

138. Rev. James T. O'Dowd, "Standardization and Its Influence on Catholic Secondary Education in the United States" (PhD diss., Catholic University of America, 1935), 122.

139. Charles N. Lischka, *Private Schools and State Laws: The Text as Well as a Classified Summary of All State Laws Governing Private Schools, in Force in 1924* (Washington, DC: National Catholic Welfare Conference, 1924), 5. A summary of the laws appears on 102–8. For a later summary of these laws, refer to Sister Raymond McLaughlin, *A History of State Legislation Affecting Private Elementary and Secondary Schools in the United States: 1870–1945* (PhD diss., Catholic University of America Press, 1946).

140. Abbott and Breckinridge, *Truancy and Non-Attendance in the Chicago Schools*, 102.

CHAPTER 6

1. *Pierce v. Society of Sisters*, 268 U.S. 510, 535 (1925).

2. William G. Ross, *Forging New Freedoms: Nativism, Education, and the Constitution, 1917–1927* (Lincoln: University of Nebraska Press, 1994); Randall E. Vance, *Private Schools and Public Power: A Case for Pluralism* (New York: Teachers College Press, 1994); Ken I. Kersch, *Constructing Civil Liberties: Discontinuities in the Development of American Constitutional Law* (New York: Cambridge University Press, 2004); David E. Bernstein, *Rehabilitating Lochner: Defending Individual Rights Against Progressive Reform* (Chicago: University of Chicago Press, 2011); David M. Mayer, "The Myth of 'Laissez-Faire Constitutionalism': Liberty of Contract During the *Lochner* Era," *Hastings Constitutional Law Quarterly* 36, no. 2 (Winter 2009): 270–73; David B. Tyack, "The Perils of Pluralism: The Background of the Pierce Case," *American Historical Review* 74, no. 1 (October 1968): 74–98; Gary Gerstle, "The Resilient Power of the States Across the Long Nineteenth Century," in *The Unsustainable American State*, ed. Lawrence Jacobs and Desmond King (New York: Oxford University Press, 2009), 73.

3. *Pierce* was one of a handful of cases cited by Justice Harlan Stone in his fourth footnote to the 1938 case *United States v. Products Co.*, 304 U.S. 144, 155 (1938), where he suggested the Court would be turning away from careful scrutiny of economic legislation in favor of looking more closely at civil rights.

4. Dennis J. Hutchinson, "Unanimity and Desegregation: Decisionmaking in the Supreme Court, 1948–1958," *Georgetown Law Journal* 68 (1979–1980): 46–49.

5. *Griswold v. Connecticut*, 381 U.S. 479 (1965), citing *Pierce* as an example of the Court recognizing certain liberties ("penumbras") not explicitly mentioned in the U.S. Constitution; *Roe v. Wade*, 410 U.S. 113 (1973); Paula Abrams, *Cross Purposes: Pierce v. Society of Sisters and the Struggle over Compulsory Public Education* (Ann Arbor: University of Michigan Press, 2009), 217.

6. Hutchinson, "Unanimity and Desegregation," 46–49.

7. Barbara B. Woodhouse, "'Who Owns the Child?': *Meyer* and *Pierce* and the Child as Property," *William and Mary Law Review Quarterly* 995 (1992): 995–1122; James S. Liebman, "Voice Not Choice," *The Yale Law Journal* 101, no. 1 (October 1991): 259–314.

8. See, e.g., Ross, *Forging New Freedoms*; Bernstein, *Rehabilitating Lochner.*

9. Damon W. Root, "Top 10 Libertarian Supreme Court Decisions," *Reason*, August 2, 2012, accessed November 26, 2012, http://reason.com/archives/2012/08/02/top-10-libertarian-supreme-court-decisio. Accessed June 28, 2014.

10. Woodhouse, "'Who Owns the Child?'"; Liebman, "Voice Not Choice"; Robert C. Post, "Defending the Lifeworld: Substantive Due Process in the Taft Court Era," *Boston University Law Review* 78 (1998): 1536.

11. See, e.g., Abrams, *Cross Purposes*, 218; Kersch, *Constructing Civil Liberties*, 255–57.

12. *Pierce* 268 U.S. at 534.

13. John Burke to Judge P. Kavanaugh, June 10, 1925, Folder 11, Box 14, United States Conference of Catholic Bishops Office of the General Secretary [hereafter USCCB], American Catholic History Research Center and University Archives [hereafter ACUA], The Catholic University of America, Washington, DC.

14. Burke to Thomas O'Mara, June 10, 1925, Folder 11, Box 14, ACUA.

15. Brief on Behalf of Appellee, Society of the Sisters of the Holy Names of Jesus, in *Oregon Cases, Complete Record* (Baltimore: Belvedere Press, 1925), 259.

16. William D. Guthrie, "The Oregon School Law," *Columbia* (June 1924): 4.

17. *Pollock v. Farmers' Loan and Trust Company* 157 U.S. 429 (1895); *McCray v. United States* 195 U.S. 27 (1904); (1904); *The National Prohibition Cases* 253 U.S. 350 (1920).

18. Robert T. Swaine, *The Cravath Firm and its Predecessors, 1819–1947*, vol. 1 (New York: Cravath, 1946), 359–780. On the role of lawyers in facilitating corporate construction, see Robert W. Gordon, "'The Ideal and the Actual in the Law': Fantasies and Practices of New York City Lawyers, 1870–1910," in *The New High Priests: Lawyers in Post-Civil War America*, ed. Gerald W. Gawalt (Westport, CT: Greenwood Press, 1984), 52–74.

19. "To Aid French Catholics," *New York Times*, June 13, 1919.

20. Guthrie, "The Oregon School Law," 6.

21. Raymond E. Callahan, *Education and the Cult of Efficiency: A Study of the Social Forces That Have Shaped the Administration of the Public Schools* (Chicago: University of Chicago Press, 1962), 11–13; John Carson, *The Measure of Merit: Talents, Intelligence, and Inequality in the French and American Republics, 1750–1940*), 197–228.

22. John Dewey, "Our Educational Ideal in Wartime," in *John Dewey: The Middle Works, 1899–1924*, ed. Jo Ann Boydston (Carbondale: Southern Illinois University Press, 1979), 10:179; *Beloit Daily News*, "U.S. Education Needs Shakeup Says Authority," April 19, 1917; *Beloit College Round Table*, "Professor Dewey Has Large Audience," and "We are Fighting Ideas Declares Prof. Dewey," April 21, 1917.

23. Robert N. Gross, "'Lick a Stamp, Lick the Kaiser': Sensing the Federal Government in Children's Lives during World War One," *Journal of Social History* 46, no. 4 (July 2013): 971–88.

24. Douglas J. Slawson, *The Department of Education Battle, 1918–1932: Public Schools, Catholic Schools, and the Social Order* (Notre Dame, IN: University of Notre Dame Press, 2005), 19.

25. Charles N. Lischka, *Private Schools and State Laws: The Text as Well as a Classified Summary of All State Laws Governing Private Schools, in Force in 1924* (Washington, DC: National Catholic Welfare Conference, 1924), 105–7.

26. *The People of the State of New York v. American Socialist Society*, 196 N.Y.S. 943 (1922).

27. P. P. Claxton, "States Should Not Forbid Private Instruction," *School Life* 5, no. 9 (November 1, 1920): 8.

28. Slawson, *Department of Education Battle*, 19–23; Woodhouse, "'Who Owns the Child?'," 1004.

29. William D. Guthrie, "The Federal Government and Education," *The American Bar Association Journal* 7 (1921): 16; William D. Guthrie, "The Federal Government and Education," *Catholic Educational Association Bulletin* 16, no. 4 (August 1920): 53–63.

30. Slawson, *The Department of Education Battle*, 19–31. The Jesuit *America* magazine led the push to shape public opinion along these lines. See, e.g., "The Essentials of Liberty," *America* (July 3, 1920): 254–55; "Paternalism and the Smith Bill," *America* (October 9, 1920): 591.

31. JoEllen McNergney Vinyard, *For Faith and Fortune: The Education of Catholic Immigrants in Detroit, 1805–1925* (Urbana and Chicago: University of Illinois Press, 1998), 220–50; Timothy Mark Pies, "The Parochial School Campaigns in Michigan, 1920–1924: The Lutheran and Catholic Involvement," *Catholic Historical Review* 72, no. 2 (April 1986): 222–38; John Frederick Stach, *A History of the Lutheran Schools of the Missouri Synod in Michigan: 1845–1940* (Ann Arbor, MI: Edwards Brothers, 1943), 143–55.

32. Abrams, *Cross Purposes*, 89.

33. Abrams, *Cross Purposes*, 7–22; Robert D. Johnston, *The Radical Middle Class: Populist Democracy and the Question of Capitalism in Progressive Era Portland, Oregon* (Princeton, NJ: Princeton University Press, 2003), 227–33; Tyack, "Perils of Pluralism."

34. Vinyard, *For Faith and Fortune*, 235; Abrams, *Cross Purposes*, 36–88.

35. Rev. Phillip McDevitt, "The State and Education," *Columbia* (October 1922): 17, Box 12, Papers of Bishop Francis W. Howard, ACUA.

36. A. C. Monahan to Rev. Joseph J. Rice, June 23, 1921, Folder: Michigan School Bill, Box 21, USCCB, Education Department, ACUA.

37. Benjamin Twiss, *Lawyers and the Constitution: How Laissez Faire Came to the Supreme Court* (Princeton, NJ: Princeton University Press, 1942), 229.

38. See, e.g., Woodhouse, "'Who Owns the Child?,'" 1002; Liebman, "Voice Not Choice," 302, n. 209; Abrams, *Cross Purposes*, 115; Arnold M. Paul, *Conservative Crisis and the Rule of Law Attitudes of Bar and Bench, 1887–1895* (Ithaca, NY: Cornell University Press, 1960), 173. *Lochner* Era historiography is summarized in David Bernstein, "*Lochner* Era Revisionism, Revised: *Lochner* and the Origins of Fundamental Rights Constitutionalism," *Georgetown Law Journal* 92, no. 1 (2003): 1–13.

39. See, e.g., his attack on the Sherman Anti-Trust Act in "Unconstitutional," *The Sun* (New York), April 11, 1897.

40. Eric Foner, *Reconstruction: America's Unfinished Revolution* (New York: Harper and Row, 1988), 257. Women and minority groups, including freed slaves, rarely witnessed these ideals of color-blind voluntary exchange translated into law and policymaking.

41. The due process clause proved far more amenable to protecting citizens from state activity after the majority opinion in the *Slaughterhouse Cases*, 83 U.S. 36 (1873), significantly limited the scope of the Fourteenth Amendment's privilege and immunities clause. Bernstein, *Rehabilitating Lochner*, 12–13.

42. Thomas M. Cooley, *A Treatise on the Constitutional Limitations Which Rest upon the Legislative Power of the States of the American Union* (Boston: Little, Brown, and Company, 1871); Christopher G. Tiedeman, *A Treatise on the Limitations of Police Power in the United States* (St. Louis: F. H. Thomas Law Book, 1886); Ernst Freund, *Police Power: Public Policy and Constitutional Rights* (Chicago: University of Chicago Press, 1904).

43. Tony A. Freyer, *Forums of Order: The Federal Courts and Business in American History* (Greenwich, CT: Jai Press, 1979), xx, 99–120.

44. James Willard Hurst, *Law and the Conditions of Freedom in the Nineteenth-Century United States* (Madison: University of Wisconsin Press, 1956), 45–50; Charles W. McCurdy, "The Knight Sugar Decision of 1895 and The Modernization of American Corporation Law, 1869–1903," *Business History Review* 53 (1979): 309–11; Barry Cushman, "Formalism and Realism in Commerce Clause Jurisprudence," *University of Chicago Law Review* 67, no. 4 (2000): 1101–9. In two cases in front of the Supreme Court, *Champion v. Ames*, 188 U.S. 321 (1903) and *McCray*, 195

U.S., Guthrie himself argued on behalf of striking down federal laws that discriminated against particular goods (lottery tickets and oleomargarine) from being sold in interstate commerce.

45. See, for example, William D. Guthrie, "Criticism of the Courts," in *Magna Carta and Other Addresses* (New York: Columbia University Press, 1916), 130–58.

46. Swaine, *Cravath*, 363. Guthrie's former colleague at Columbia, Charles Beard, determined that his appointment was through "backstairs negotiations," as Guthrie was a business partner of one of the trustees. "Dr. Beard Attacks Columbia Trustees," *New York Times*, December 28, 1917.

47. William D. Guthrie, *Lectures on the Fourteenth Article of Amendment to the Constitution of the United States* (Boston: Little, Brown and Company, 1898), 30.

48. Guthrie, *Lectures*, 80–88.

49. The classic account of this jurisprudential view of neutrality is Howard Gillman, *The Constitution Besieged: The Rise and Demise of Lochner Era Police Powers Jurisprudence* (Durham, NC: Duke University Press, 1993).

50. Gillman argues that the majority in *Lochner* believed that the decision violated the principle of neutrality in another manner: that it singled out bakeries for regulation, leaving similar professions free from maximum hours legislation. Gillman, *Constitution Besieged*, 128–30.

51. William D. Guthrie, "Constitutional Morality," *The North American Review* 196, no. 681 (1912): 154–73.

52. See Guthrie, "Unconstitutional!," and Guthrie, *Lectures*, 80–81. The original quotation is from *Railroad Commission Cases*, 116 U.S. 307, 331 (1886). Waite evidently was playing on John Marshall's remarks on the taxing power in *McCulloch v. Maryland*, 17 U.S. 316, 431 (1819).

53. Guthrie, *Lectures*, 77–78. See *Lawton v. Steele*, 152 U.S. 133, 137 (1894).

54. Guthrie, *Lectures*, 80–83; *Chicago, Milwaukee and St. Paul Railway Company v. Minnesota*, 134 U.S. 418, 458 (1890).

55. Guthrie, *Lectures*, 74, 76.

56. Charles Warren, "The Progressiveness of the United States Supreme Court," *Columbia Law Review* 13, no. 4 (April 1913): 295.

57. William D. Guthrie, "Constitutional Morality," 165–67.

58. Julius Henry Cohen, *They Builded Better than They Knew* (New York: Julian Messner, 1947), 169.

59. Brief on Behalf of the Attorney-General and the Joint Legislative Committee on Housing of the State of New York, at 20, *Marcus Brown*, 256 U.S. 170.

60. Cohen, *They Builded Better than They Knew*, 169.

61. Father Francis Howard to William D. Guthrie, June 25, 1921, Box 25, Folder: Guthrie, W.D., Papers of Bishop Francis W. Howard, ACUA.

62. See the correspondence between them in Box 25, Folder: Guthrie, W.D., Papers of Bishop Francis W. Howard, ACUA.

63. Guthrie joined the Portland Catholic Archdiocese's attorney, Judge John P. Kavanaugh, in arguing the case, with the understanding that Kavanaugh would primarily be responsible for the district court arguments while Guthrie would take on the appellate court responsibilities.

64. Brief and Argument for Plaintiff in Error at 6, 14, *Meyer v. State of Nebraska*, 262 U.S. 390 (1923) (October Term, 1922, No. 325).

65. See *Bartels v. Iowa*, *Bohning v. Ohio*, *Pohl v. Ohio*, and *Nebraska District of Evangelical Lutheran Synod v. McKelvie*, 262 U.S. 404 (1923).

66. Brief for William D. Guthrie and Bernard Hershkopf as Amici Curiae at 6, *Meyer*, 262 U.S. 390.

67. Transcript of Oral Argument of Arthur F. Mullen, in Behalf of Plaintiffs-in-Error at 2, *Meyer*, 262 U.S. 390.

68. *Meyer*, 262 U.S. at 399, 401. McReynolds knew Guthrie well from their days as New York attorneys. When in 1907 Guthrie left the Cravath firm he had helped build, McReynolds took his place. See Abrams, *Cross Purposes*, 113.

69. Officially, the dissents were filed separately in the *Bartels* cases. *Bartels*, 262 U.S. at 412–13 (Holmes, J. dissenting).

70. Abrams, *Cross Purposes*, 124.

71. In addition to the Society of Sisters, the Hill Military Academy, a nonsectarian private school, also joined the lawsuit, though its legal funds derived from the Catholic Knights of Columbus.

72. William D. Guthrie to John Burke, January 5, 1923, Folder 7, Box 14, USCCB, ACUA.

73. See John Burke to William D. Guthrie, January 3, 1924, Folder 8, Box 14, USCCB, ACUA.

74. Guthrie to Burke, January 4, 1924, Folder 8, Box 14, USCCB, ACUA.

75. Ibid. Guthrie's partner in the case, John P. Kavanaugh, also distinguished *Berea* from *Pierce* in that the Kentucky statute incorporating *Berea* contained a provision reserving the power to alter corporate franchises, where none existed in Oregon. Kavanaugh to Guthrie, January 6, 1924, Folder 8, Box 14, USCCB, ACUA.

76. *Society of the Sisters of the Holy Names of Jesus and Mary v. Pierce*, 296 F. 928, 931, 936 (D. Oreg. 1924).

77. Brief on Behalf of Appellee, 257, 271.

78. Ibid., 232.

79. Ibid., 232.

80. Ibid., 259. John Kavanaugh added, "we conform to reasonable regulation . . . . We comply with all the regulations of the state. We are in favor of compulsory education. The state has a right to impose that."

81. *Pierce* 268 U.S. 510, at 535, 536.

82. Ibid., at 534.

83. *Farrington v. Tokushige*, 273 U.S. 287 (1927).

84. The concept of the Supreme Court acting as a "super board of education" stems from Robert Jackson's concurring opinion in *McCollum v. Board of Education of School District* 333 U.S. 203, 237 (1948).

85. James H. Ryan, "What the Oregon Decision Means for American Education," *NCWC Bulletin* 7 (July 1925): 9–10.

86. Charles N. Lischka, "The Appeal of the Oregon School Law," *NCWC Bulletin* (April 1925): 12, Folder 13: Oregon School Law, 1923–1924, Box 29, Records of the United States Conference of Catholic Bishops Education Department, ACUA. See also Ryan, "What the Oregon Decision Means for American Education," 9–10.

87. Guthrie to Burke, March 23, 1925, Folder 10, Box 14, USCCB, ACUA.

88. Burke to Kavanaugh, June 10, 1925.

89. Thomas F. O'Mara to John Burke, July 1, 1925, Folder 11, Box 14, USCCB, ACUA.

90. Ryan, "What the Oregon Decision Means for American Education," 10.

91. Calvin Kephart, "State Control and Regulation of Private and Parochial Schools of Primary and Secondary Grades" (PhD diss., American University, 1933), 176, 204.

92. William Jennings Bryan, "Text of Bryan's Proposed Address in Scopes Case," in *The World's Most Famous Court Trial: Tennessee Evolution Case* (Cincinnati, OH: National Book Company, 1925), 321–22.

93. *State v. Oscar Hoyt*, 84 N.H. 38, 40–41(1929).

94. *Stephens v. Bongart*, 15 N.J. Misc. 80, 83 (1937); *Rice v. Commonwealth of Virginia*, 188 Va. 224, 232 (1948); *People v. Donner*, 99 N.Y.S.2d 830, 834 (1950); *People v. Turner*, 121 Cal. App. 2d Supp. 861, 865 (1953).

95. "School, Church, and State," *New Republic*, June 24, 1925, 114–16.

96. Morris R. Cohen, "Social Policy and the Supreme Court," *New Republic*, July 15, 1925, 195.

97. Felix Frankfurter, "Can the Supreme Court Guarantee Toleration," in *Felix Frankfurter on the Supreme Court: Extrajudicial Essays on the Court and the Constitution*, ed. Philip B. Kurland (Cambridge, MA: Belknap Press of Harvard University Press, 1970), 174–78. The article was originally published as an unsigned editorial in the *New Republic*.

98. Felix Frankfurter to Justice Wiley Rutledge, January 22, 1944, General Correspondence, Rutledge, Wiley, Reel 61, Felix Frankfurter Papers, Microfilm Edition, Box 100, Reel 61, Manuscript Division, Library of Congress. The case was *Prince v. Massachusetts*, 321 U.S. 158 (1944).

99. *Lincoln Federal Labor Union v. Northwestern Iron & Metal Co.* 335 U.S. 525, 537 (1949).

100. Hutchinson, "Unanimity and Desegregation," 48.

101. Brief for Appellants, *Griswold*, at 23; Bernstein, *Rehabilitating* Lochner, 114.

102. *Griswold*, at 516 (Black, J. dissenting)

103. An advanced search of the JSTOR database reveals that in the thirty years between 1925 and 1956 there were seven articles that cited Pierce with "corporate," "corporation[s]," "private enterprise," or "private business" in the title, and twenty-four with "religion" or "religious." In the fifty years from 1956 to 2006 that number was two and sixty-seven, respectively.

104. Frederick Green, "Corporations as Persons, Citizens, and Possessors of Liberty," *University of Pennsylvania Law Review* 94, no. 2 (January 1946): 235–37; D. J. Farage, "Non-Natural Persons and the Guarantee of Liberty under the Due Process Clause," *Kentucky Law Journal* 28 (1939–1940): 273–75; and "Is a Corporation Always Entitled to Due Process of Law," *Georgetown Law Journal* 26 (1937–1938): 134–35.

105. Note, "Municipalities in Competition with Private Business: The Effect upon Governmental Powers," *Columbia Law Review* 34, no. 2 (February 1934): 328; Joseph Forer, "Power of the Federal Government to Compete with Private Enterprise," *University of Pennsylvania Law Review and American Law Review* 83, no. 5 (March 1935): 670; and Recent Decision, "Constitutional Law—Public Utilities—Standing of Public Utilities to Challenge the Constitutionality of the TVA," *Michigan Law Review* 37, no. 7 (May 1939): 1136.

EPILOGUE

1. Note, "The Judicial Role in Attacking Racial Discrimination in Tax-Exempt Private Schools," *Harvard Law Review* 93, no. 2 (December 1979): 388.

2. William J. Novak, "Common Regulation: Legal Origins of State Power in America," *Hastings Law Review* 45 (1993–1994): 1061–97; Gary Gerstle, "The Resilient Power of the States

Across the Long Nineteenth Century," in *The Unsustainable American State*, ed. Lawrence Jacobs and Desmond King (New York: Oxford University Press, 2009), 61–87; Daniel Carpenter, "Regulation," in *The Princeton Encyclopedia of Political History*, ed. Michael Kazin, Rebecca Edwards, and Adam Rothman (Princeton, NJ: Princeton University Press, 2009), 2:665; Charles W. McCurdy, "The Knight Sugar Decision of 1895 and The Modernization of American Corporation Law, 1869–1903," *Business History Review* 53 (1979): 309–11; Ira Katznelson, *Fear Itself: The New Deal and the Origins of Our Time* (New York: Liveright, 2013).

3. On the ways in which expanding the scope of education contributed to American political development see Tracy Steffes, *School, Society, and State: A New Education to Govern Modern America, 1890–1940* (Chicago: University of Chicago Press, 2012).

4. Jurgen Herbst, *School Choice and School Governance: A Historical Study of the United States and Germany* (New York: Palgrave Macmilan, 2006), 99–102; Jeffrey R. Henig, *Rethinking School Choice: Limits of the Market Metaphor* (Princeton, NJ: Princeton University Press, 1994), 64–66; James Forman Jr., "The Secret History of School Choice: How Progressives Got There First," *Georgetown Law Journal* 93 (2004–5): 1287–320; David K. Cohen and Eleanor Farrar, "Power to the Parents?—The Story of Education Vouchers," *Public Interest* 48 (Summer 1977): 72–97.

5. Virgil C. Blum, "Untitled Address," Subseries 3, Box 3, Folder: Untitled Address, 1955, Rev. Virgil C. Blum, S.J., Papers, Marquette Special Collections [hereafter Blum Papers]. On national battles over public aid to parochial schools in these years see Diane Ravitch, *The Troubled Crusade: American Education, 1945–1980* (New York: Basic Books, 1983), 27–42.

6. Reports of these arrangements are compiled in Folder 9: "Catholic District/Public Schools, 1923–1940," Box 7, Records of the United States Conference of Catholic Bishops Education Department, American Catholic History Research Center and University Archives, The Catholic University of America, Washington, DC. See also Martin Poluse, "Archbishop Joseph Schremb's Battle to Obtain Public Assistance for the Parochial Schools of Cleveland during the Great Depression," *Catholic Historical Review* 83, no. 3 (1997): 428–51; Ann Marie Ryan, "Keeping 'Every Catholic Child in a Catholic School' During the Great Depression, 1933–1939," *Catholic Education* 11, no. 2 (2007): 157–75. When President Lyndon Johnson lobbied for Catholic support for the Elementary and Secondary Education Act in 1964 he informed one influential Catholic congressmen that as Texas's director of the National Youth Administration during the Depression he had diverted federal funds to Catholic institutions. Gareth Davies, *See Government Grow: Education Politics from Johnson to Reagan* (Lawrence: University of Kansas Press, 2007), 27.

7. Poluse, "Archbishop Joseph Schremb's Battle to Obtain Public Assistance," 450; *Cochran v. Louisiana State Board of Education*, 281 U.S. 370 (1930); *Everson v. Board of Education*, 330 U.S. 1 (1947); *Board of Education v. Allen*, 392 U.S. 236 (1968).

8. Diane Ravitch, *The Troubled Crusade*, 27–41, 148; Davies, *See Government Grow*, Chapter 1.

9. Virgil C. Blum, "Freedom of Choice in Education," 3, Subseries 3, Box 3, Folder: Freedom of Choice in Education, Blum Papers.

10. See the correspondence in Subseries 3, Boxes 10 and 11, Folders: Correspondence—Freedom of Choice in Education, Blum Papers.

11. Jim Carl, *Freedom of Choice: Vouchers in American Education* (Santa Barbara, CA: Praeger, 2011), 88–122.

12. See Subseries 6, Box 9, Folder: Wabash College Conference on Economics and Freedom, Blum Papers.

13. Virgil C. Blum, *Freedom of Choice in Education* (New York: Macmillan Company, 1958), 18, 144.

14. Milton Friedman, "The Role of Government in Education," in *Economics and the Public Interest*, ed. Robert A. Solo (New Brunswick, NJ: Rutgers University Press, 1955), 124, 129, 130, 132.

15. Ibid., 124–26.

16. Teachers College professor George R. La Noue organized a 1972 edited volume that collected various voucher proposals into sections on "The Unregulated Voucher" (featuring essays by Blum and Friedman) and the "Regulated Voucher." George R. La Noue, "Vouchers: The End of Public Education?" in *Educational Vouchers: Concepts and Controversies*, ed. George R. La Noue (New York: Teachers College Press, 1972), ix, 136–37. See also Henig, *Rethinking School Choice*, 65, 234 n. 21.

17. Friedman, "The Role of Government in Education," 127–29. As Angus Burgin recently has pointed out, Friedman in the early 1950s was still in the process of becoming a free-market libertarian. In a 1951 essay, for example, Friedman had argued that government interventions such as welfare programs and the Sherman Antitrust Act were justified. See Angus Burgin, *The Great Persuasion: Reinventing Free Markets since the Depression* (Cambridge, MA: Harvard University Press, 2012), 170.

18. Friedman, "The Role of Government in Education," 132.

19. Forman Jr., "Secret History of School Choice: How Progressives Got There First."

20. Center for the Study of Public Policy, *A Report on Financing Elementary Education by Grants to Parents*, in *Education Vouchers: From Theory to Alum Rock*, ed. James A. Mecklenburger and Richard W. Hostrop (Homewood, IL: ETC Publications, 1972), 151–221. For a concise summary of the proposal see Christopher Jencks, "Giving Parents Money for Schooling: Education Vouchers," *Phi Delta Kappan* 52, no. 1 (September 1970): 49–52.

21. Coons, and his co-authors William H. Clune III and Stephen D. Sugarman, grounded their ideas about vouchers and school finance equalization in the Roman Catholic principle of "subsidiarity," which they defined, quoting Pope Pius XI, as "it is wrong to take from individuals what they can accomplish by their own initiative and industry and give it to the community. It is also an injustice . . . to assign to a greater and higher association what a lesser and subordinate organization can do." John E. Coons, William H. Clune III, and Stephen D. Sugarman, *Private Wealth and Public Education* (Cambridge, MA: Belknap Press of Harvard University Press, 1970), 14–15, 256–68. On Coons's support for Catholic education see John E. Coons, "Why the Catholic Inner City School Is Worth Saving," in *American Catholic Identity: Essays in an Age of* Change, ed. Francis J. Buther (Kansas City: Sheed & Ward), 178–84.

22. Theodore R. Sizer, "The Case for a Free Market," in *Education Vouchers*, ed. Mecklenburger and Hostrop, 24–43.

23. Friedman argued that private acts of persuasion, rather than public acts of compulsion, should guide delicate racial questions. See Friedman, "The Role of Government in Education," 131, n. 2. Jencks responded that "a voucher system which does not include these or equally effective safeguards would be worse than no voucher system at all. Indeed, an unregulated voucher system could be the most serious setback for the education of disadvantaged children in the history of the United States." See Judith Green and Christopher Jencks, "Education Vouchers: A Proposal for Diversity and Choice," in *Educational Vouchers*, ed. La Noue, 54.

24. Center for the Study of Public Policy, *A Report on Financing Elementary Education by Grants to Parents*, 164, 168–72.

25. Jencks, "Giving Parents Money for Schooling," 50.

26. Coons, Clune, and Sugarman, *Private Wealth*, 260–61.

27. James S. Coleman, "Foreword," in John E. Coons and Stephen D. Sugarman, *Education by Choice: The Case for Family Control* (Berkeley: University of California Press, 1978), xii.

28. Judith Green and Christopher Jencks, "Education Vouchers: A Proposal for Diversity and Choice," in *Educational Vouchers*, ed. La Noue, 53. Emphasis in original.

29. Charles T. Clotfelter, *After Brown: The Rise and Retreat of School Desegregation* (Princeton, NJ: Princeton University Press, 2004), 104.

30. James D. Anderson, *The Education of Blacks in the South, 1860–1935* (Chapel Hill: University of North Carolina Press, 1988), 156.

31. Gunnar Myrdal, *An American Dilemma, Volume 1: The Negro Problem and Modern Democracy* (1944; repr., New Brunswick, NJ: Transaction Publishers, 1996), 341.

32. Harry S. Ashmore, *The Negro and the Schools* (Chapel Hill: University of North Carolina Press, 1954), 91–92.

33. Thurgood Marshall, "Racial Integration in Education through Resort to the Courts and Summit Discussion," in *Supreme Justice: Speeches and Writings*, ed. J. Clay Smith, Jr. (Philadelphia: University of Pennsylvania Press, 2003), 47.

34. Bonastia, *Southern Stalemate: Five Years without Public Education in Prince Edward County, Virginia* (Chicago: University of Chicago Press, 2012), 72–73.

35. Joseph Crespino, "Civil Rights and the Religious Right," in *Rightward Bound: Making American Conservative in the 1970s*, ed. Bruce J. Schulman and Julian E. Zelizer (Cambridge, MA: Harvard University Press, 2008), 93; U.S. Commission on Civil Rights, "The Creation and Expansion of Segregated Schools for the Purpose of Evading School Desegregation," in *IRS Tax Exemptions and Segregated Private Schools: Hearing Before the Subcommittee on Civil and Constitutional Rights of the Committee on the Judiciary*, 97th Cong., 2d Sess. (1982), 65–76.

36. Walter Murphy, "Private Education with Public Funds?" *Journal of Politics* 20, no. 4 (November 1958): 636–37, 642; Carl, *Freedom of Choice*, 52–54. Bonastia, *Southern Stalemate*; Michael W. Fuquay, "Civil Rights and the Private School Movement in Mississippi, 1964–1971," *History of Education Quarterly* 42, no. 2 (Summer 2002): 159–80.

37. *Coffey v. State Educational Finance Commission*, 296 F.Supp. 1389, 1392 (1969).

38. *Poindexter v. Louisiana Financial Assistance Comm'n*, 296 F.Supp. 686; *Lee v. Macon County Board of Education*, 267 F.Supp. 458 (M.D. Ala.1967); *Griffin v. State Bd. of Educ.*, 239 F.Supp. 560 (E.D.Va.1965); *Hall v. St. Helena Parish School Bd.*, 197 F.Supp. 649 (E.D.La.1961).

39. Dennis J. Encarnation, "Public Finance and Regulation of Nonpublic Education: Retrospect and Prospect," in *Public Dollars for Private Schools: The Case of Tuition Tax Credits*, ed. Thomas James and Henry M. Levin (Philadelphia: Temple University Press, 1983), 178.

40. *Green v. Kennedy*, 309 F.Supp. 1127, 1135 (1970).

41. Ibid. See also Crespino, "Civil Rights and the Religious Right."

42. Crespino, "Civil Rights and the Religious Right," 90–105; U.S. Civil Rights Commission, "The Creation and Expansion of Segregated Schools for the Purpose of Evading School Desegregation," in *IRS Tax Exemptions and Segregated Private Schools: Hearing Before the Subcommittee on Civil and Constitutional Rights of the Committee on the Judiciary*, HR, 97th Cong., 2d Sess. (January 28, 1982), 65–76.

43. *Bob Jones University v. United States*, 461 U.S. 574, 582.

44. William J. Reese, "Soldiers for Christ in the Army of God: The Christian School Movement in America," *Educational Theory* 35, no. 2 (June 1985): 193–94.

45. Neal Devins, "State Regulation of Christian Schools," *Journal of Legislation* 10, no. 2 (1983): 351–53.

46. David J. Dent, "African-Americans Turning To Christian Academies," *New York Times*, August 4, 1996.

47. Andy Smarick, "Can Catholic Schools Be Saved," *National Affairs* (Spring 2011): 117–20. The percentage of the female religious in Catholic schools declined from around 90 percent in the 1950s to less than 5 percent by 2007. In roughly that same period the number of nuns fell from 180,000 in 1965 to 68,000. Peter Meyer, "Can Catholic Schools Be Saved," *Education Next* 7, no. 2 (Spring 2007): 14.

48. Commission on School Finance, The President's Panel on Nonpublic Education, *Nonpublic Education and the Public Good* (Washington, DC: Government Printing Office, 1972), 56–57.

49. James S. Coleman, Thomas Hoffer, and Sally Kilgore, *High School Achievement: Public, Catholic, and Private Schools Compared* (New York: Basic Books, 1982); James S. Coleman, "Quality and Equality in American Education: Public and Catholic Schools," *Phi Delta Kappan* 63, no. 3 (November 1981): 164. An earlier study financed by the Carnegie Corporation and the U.S. Office of Education found wide-ranging social benefits. See Andrew M. Greeley and Peter H. Rossie, *The Education of Catholic Americans* (Chicago: Aldine Publishing Company, 1966).

50. Richard Buddin, "The Impact of Charter Schools on Public and Private School Enrollments," *Cato Policy Analysis Series* no. 707 (August 28, 2012): 1–64; "Charter Schools Causing Collapse of Religious Schools," *CAPE Outlook*, no. 373 (March 2012): 3. See also Rajashri Chakrabarti and Joydeep Roy, "Do Charter Schools Crowd Out Private School Enrollment? Evidence from Michigan," *Federal Reserve Bank of New York Staff Reports*, no. 472 (September 2010): 1–31; Stephanie Ewert, "The Decline in Private School Enrollment," *U.S. Census Bureau SEHSD Working Paper*, no. FY12-117 (January 2013): 1–24.

51. Sean Kennedy, "Chartering a Future for Catholic Education," *City Journal* (October 15, 2012), http://www.city-journal.org/2012/eon1015sk.html

52. Julie F. Mead and Preston C. Green III, *Chartering Equity: Using Charter School Legislation and Policy to Advance Equal Educational Opportunity* (Boulder, CO: National Education Policy Center, February 2012), 1. See also Suzanne E. Eckes, "Charter School Legislation and the Potential to Influence Student Body Diversity," in *The Charter School Experiment: Expectations, Evidence, and Implications*, ed. Christopher A. Lubienski and Peter C. Weitzel (Cambridge, MA: Harvard Education Press, 2010), 51–72.

53. Sara Mead and Andrew J. Rotherham, "A Sum Greater than the Parts: What States Can Teach Each Other about Charter Schooling" (Washington, DC: Education Sector, 2007). http://www.educationsector.org/sites/default/files/publications/CharterSchoolSummary.pdf.

BIBLIOGRAPHY

ARCHIVAL COLLECTIONS

American Catholic History Research Center, Catholic University of America, Washington, DC
Archives Service Center, University of Pittsburgh, Pittsburgh, PA
Georgetown University Special Collections, Washington, DC
Historical Records Collection, Catholic Diocese of Pittsburgh, Pittsburgh, PA
Library & Archives Division, Senator John Heinz History Center, Pittsburgh, PA
Marquette Special Collections
Philadelphia Archdiocesan Historical Research Center, Philadelphia, PA

CODES

Mass. Acts
R.I. Acts & Resolves
R.I. Gen. Laws
Rules and Regulations for the Parochial Schools of the Diocese of Leavenworth Kansas
Rules and Regulations of the School Board of the City of Milwaukee
Rules and Regulations of the School Boards of the Diocese of La Crosse
Rules of the School Committee and Regulations of the Public Schools of the City of Boston
The School Laws of Rhode Island
Statuta Dioeceos Pittsburgensis in Synodis Dioecesanis

NEWSPAPERS

Boston Daily Advertiser
Boston Daily Globe
Boston Evening Transcript
Boston Morning Journal
Catholic Citizen
Chicago Tribune
Illinois Staats Zeitung
Manufacturers and Farmers Journal
Milwaukee Journal
New York Times
Pittsburgh Catholic
Pittsburgh Christian Advocate
Pittsburgh Commercial Gazette
Pittsburgh Dispatch
Pittsburgh Press
Providence Daily Post
Providence Evening News
Providence Evening Press
Providence News

JOURNALS

America
American Bar Association Journal
American Catholic Quarterly Review
American Journal of Sociology
Annals of the American Academy of Political Science
Catholic Educational Association of Pennsylvania Bulletin
Catholic Educational Review
Catholic World
Charities
Columbia
Contemporary Review
Dziennik Zjednoczenia
Ecclesiastical Review
Educational Review
Independent
Journal of Education
National Catholic Educational Association Bulletin
National Educational Association Journal of Proceedings, and Addresses
New Republic
North American Review
Pennsylvania School Journal

Political Science Quarterly
Popular Science Monthly
Presbyterian Quarterly and Princeton Review
Publications of the American Economic Association
Public Ownership
Public Policy
Report of the Proceedings and Addresses of the Catholic Educational Association
School Life
School Review
Scribner's Monthly
To-Day
Transactions of the Wisconsin Academy of Sciences, Arts, and Letters
Virginia Law Register
Wisconsin Journal of Education

COURT CASES

Bartels v. Iowa, 262 U.S. 404 (1923)
Berea College v. Kentucky, 211 U.S. 45 (1908)
Creyhon v. Board of Education of the City of Parsons, Kansas, 99 Kan. 824 (1917)
Farrington v. Tokushige, 273 U.S. 287 (1927)
Gerke v. Purcell, 25 Ohio St. 229 (1874)
Gilmour v. Pelton, 6 Am. L. Rec. 26, Ohio Ct. Comm. Pleas (1887)
Griswold v. Connecticut, 381 U.S. 479 (1965)
Marcus Brown Holding Co. v. Feldman, 256 U.S. 170 (1921)
Meyer v. State of Nebraska, 262 U.S. 390 (1923)
Miller's Appeals, 10 WNC 168 Penn. Ct. Comm. Pleas, (1881)
People of the State of New York v. American Socialist Society, 196 N.Y.S. 943 (1922)
Pierce v. Society of Sisters, 268 U.S. 510, 535 (1925)
Saint Joseph's Church v. The Assessors of Taxes of Providence, 12 R.I. 19 (1878)
State v. Oscar Hoyt, 84 N.H. 38 (1929)
The Trustees of Dartmouth College v. Woodward, 17 U.S. 518 (1819)

ANNUAL OR BIENNIAL REPORTS OF CITY, STATE, FEDERAL, AND
CATHOLIC AGENCIES

Archdiocese of Philadelphia Parochial Schools
Cincinnati, OH Public Schools
Cleveland, OH Public Schools
Diocese of La Crosse
Diocese of Pittsburgh Parish Schools
Fort Wayne Diocesan School Board
New York City Director of Attendance
Pennsylvania Superintendent of Common Schools
Philadelphia Bureau of Compulsory Education

Philadelphia, PA Public Schools

Pittsburgh, PA Public Schools

President's Panel on Nonpublic Education

Providence, RI Board of Assessors

Providence, RI Public Schools

Rhode Island Board of Education and State Commissioner

Rhode Island Census

Southbridge Town Officers

United States Commissioner of Education

York, PA Public Schools

PUBLISHED PRIMARY DOCUMENTS

Abbott, Edith, and Sophonisba P. Breckinridge. *Truancy and Non-Attendance in the Chicago Schools: A Study of the Social Aspects of the Compulsory Education and Child Labor Legislation of Illinois.* Chicago: University of Chicago Press, 1917.

Adams, Charles Francis. "Railway Commissions." *Journal of Social Science* 2 (1870): 233–36.

Adams, Henry Carter. "Relation of the State to Industrial Action." *Publications of the American Economic Association* 1 (1887): 461–549.

Ayres, Leonard Porter. *Laggards in Our Schools: A Study of Retardation and Elimination in City School Systems.* New York: Russell Sage Foundation, 1909.

Bender, John Frederick. *The Functions of Courts in Enforcing School Attendance Laws.* New York: Teachers College, Columbia University, 1927.

Bermejo, Fernando V. *The School Attendance Service in American Cities.* Menasha, WI: George Banta, 1924.

Blum, Virgil C. *Freedom of Choice in Education.* New York: Macmillan, 1958.

Bowman, Le Roy E. "Population Mobility and Community Organization." In *The Urban Community: Selected Papers from the Proceedings of the American Sociological Society, 1925,* edited by Ernest W. Burgess, 155–60. Chicago: University of Chicago Press, 1926.

Breckinridge, Sophonisba P. *Marriage and the Civic Rights of Women: Separate Domicil and Independent Citizenship.* Chicago: University of Chicago Press, 1931.

Britton, Gertrude Howe. *An Intensive Study of the Causes of Truancy in Eight Chicago Public Schools including a Home Investigation of Eight Hundred Truant Children.* Chicago: Hollister, 1906.

Bryce, James. *The American Commonwealth.* London and New York: Macmillan, 1888.

Clark, John Bates. "The Limits of Competition." *Political Science Quarterly* 2, no. 1 (1887): 45–61.

Clark, John Bates. *The Philosophy of Wealth: Economic Principles Newly Formulated.* Boston: Ginn & Company, 1894.

Cohen, Julius Henry. *They Builded Better than They Knew.* New York: Julian Messner, 1947.

Coleman, James S. "Quality and Equality in American Education: Public and Catholic Schools." *Phi Delta Kappan* 63, no. 3 (November 1981): 159–64.

Coleman, James S., Thomas Hoffer, and Sally Kilgore. *High School Achievement: Public, Catholic, and Private Schools Compared.* New York: Basic Books, 1982.

Cooley, Thomas M. *A Treatise on the Constitutional Limitations which Rest upon the Legislative Power of the States of the American Union.* Boston: Little, Brown, and Company, 1871.

Coons, John E., William H. Clune III, and Stephen D. Sugarman. *Private Wealth and Public Education*. Cambridge, MA: Belknap Press of Harvard University Press, 1970.

Cooper, Thomas. *Lectures on the Elements of Political Economy*. Columbia, SC: Telescope Press, 1826.

Curtin, James R. *Attitudes of Parents Toward Catholic Education*. Washington, DC: Catholic University of America Press, 1954.

Durfee, Thomas. *Some Thoughts on the Constitution of Rhode Island*. Providence, RI: Sidney S. Rider, 1884.

Ely, Richard T. *Ground Under Our Feet: An Autobiography*. New York: Macmillan, 1938.

Ely, Richard T. *An Introduction to Political Economy*. New York: Hunt & Eaton, 1894.

Ely, Richard T. *Natural Monopolies and Local Taxation*. Boston: Robinson & Stephenson, 1889.

Ely, Richard T. *Outlines of Economics*. New York: Chautauqua Century Press, 1893.

Ely, Richard T. *The Past and the Present of Political Economy*. Baltimore: N. Murray, 1884.

Ely, Richard T. *Political Economy, Political Science and Sociology: A Practical and Scientific Presentation of Social and Economic Subjects*. Chicago: University Association, 1889.

Ely, Richard T. *Problems of To-day: A Discussion of Protective Tariffs, Taxation, and Monopolies*. New York: Thomas Y. Crowell & Company, 1888.

Emmons, Frederick Earle. *City School Attendance Service*. New York: Teachers College, Columbia University, 1926.

Ensign, Forest Chester. *Compulsory School Attendance and Child Labor: a Study of the Historical Development of Regulations Compelling Attendance and Limiting the Labor of Children in a Selected Group of States*. Iowa City: Athens Press, 1921.

Farrell, James T. *Young Lonigan*. New York: Signet Classics, 2004. First published in 1932 by Vanguard Press.

Freund, Ernst. *Police Power: Public Policy and Constitutional Rights*. Chicago: University of Chicago Press, 1904.

Friedman, Milton. "The Role of Government in Education." In *Economics and the Public Interest*, edited by Robert A. Solo, 123–44. New Brunswick, NJ: Rutgers University Press, 1955.

Guthrie, William Dameron. "Constitutional Morality." *North American Review* 196, no. 681 (1912): 154–73.

Guthrie, William Dameron. "The Federal Government and Education." *American Bar Association Journal* 7 (1921): 14–16.

Guthrie, William Dameron. *Lectures on the Fourteenth Article of Amendment to the Constitution of the United States*. Boston: Little, Brown and Company, 1898.

Guthrie, William Dameron. "The Oregon School Law." *Columbia* (June 1924): 4–5, 18.

Haney, John Dearling. *Registration of City School Children: A Consideration of the Subject of the City School Census*. New York: Teachers College, Columbia University, 1910.

Jencks, Christopher. "Giving Parents Money for Schooling: Education Vouchers." *Phi Delta Kappan* 52, no. 1 (September 1970): 49–52.

Koos, Leonard V., and University of Minnesota. *Private and Public Secondary Education, a Comparative Study*. Chicago: University of Chicago Press, 1931.

La Noue, George R., ed. *Educational Vouchers: Concepts and Controversies*. New York: Teachers College Press, 1972.

Leggett, William. "Literary Corporations." In *A Collection of the Political Writings of William Leggett*, edited by Theodore Sedgwick Jr., 171–78. New York: Taylor & Dodd, 1840.

Lischka, Charles Nicholas. *Private Schools and State Laws*. Washington, DC: National Catholic Welfare Conference, Bureau of Education, 1926.

Mackenzie, James C. "The Supervision of Private Schools by the State or Municipal Authority." *School Review* 1, no. 7 (1893): 391–99.

Mathews, John Mabry. *Principles of American State Administration*. New York: D. Appleton and Company, 1917.

Matthews, Nathan Jr. *The Citizen and the State: An Argument by Nathan Matthews, Jr. in Defense of Private Schools, Before the Joint Committee on Education of the Massachusetts Legislature, April 25, 1889*. Boston: Geo. H. Ellis, 1889.

McVickar, John. *Outlines of Political Economy*. New York: Wilder & Campbell, 1825.

Mecklenburger, James A., and Richard W. Hostrop, eds. *Education Vouchers: From Theory to Alum Rock*. Homewood, IL: ETC Publications, 1972.

Moehlman, Arthur B. *Child Accounting: A Discussion of the General Principles Underlying Educational Child Accounting Together with the Development of a Uniform Procedure*. Detroit: Friesema Bros. Press, 1924.

Newman, Samuel P. *Elements of Political Economy*. New York: H. Griffin and Company, 1835.

O'Brien, Robert E. "Relations Between the Public and Catholic Schools of Chicago." *Journal of Educational Sociology* 3, no. 2 (1929): 121–29.

Park, Robert E. "The City: Suggestions for the Investigation of Human Behavior in the City Environment." *American Journal of Sociology* 20, no. 5 (March 1915): 577–612.

Parsons, Frank. *The City for the People: Or, The Municipalization of the City Government and of Local Franchises*. Philadelphia: C. F. Taylor, 1901.

Phillips, Willard. *A Manual of Political Economy: With Particular Reference to the Institutions, Resources, and Condition of the United States*. Boston: Hilliard, Gray, Little, and Wilkins, 1828.

Quigley, Patrick Francis. *Compulsory Education: The State of Ohio Versus The Rev. Patrick Francis Quigley, D.D.* New York: Robert Drummond, 1894.

Say, Jean Baptiste. *A Treatise on Political Economy; or, The Production, Distribution, and Consumption of Wealth*, trans. C. R. Prinsep. Boston: Wells and Lilly, 1824.

Shaw, Albert. "The American State and the American Man." *Contemporary Review* 51 (May 1887): 695–711.

Smith, Adam. *An Inquiry Into the Nature and Causes of the Wealth of Nations*. Dublin: Whitehead et al., 1776.

Spencer, Herbert. *Social Statics, or, The Conditions Essential to Human Happiness Specified, and the First of Them Developed*. London: John Chapman, 1851.

Sumner, William Graham. *What Social Classes Owe to Each Other*. New York: Harper & Brothers, 1883.

Thompson, Carl Dean. *Public Ownership, a Survey of Public Enterprises, Municipal, State, and Federal, in the United States and Elsewhere*. New York: Thomas Y. Crowell, 1925.

Tiedeman, Christopher G. *A Treatise on the Limitations of Police Power in the United States*. St. Louis: F. H. Thomas Law Book, 1886.

Vethake, Henry. *The Principles of Political Economy*. Philadelphia: P. H. Nicklin & T. Johnson, 1838.

Ward, Lester Frank. *Dynamic Sociology: Or Applied Social Science, as Based Upon Statical Sociology and the Less Complex Sciences*. New York: D. Appleton and Company, 1883.

Ward, Lester Frank. "The Political Ethics of Herbert Spencer." *Annals of the American Academy of Political Science* 4, no. 4 (1894): 90–127.

Warren, Charles. "The Progressiveness of the United States Supreme Court." *Columbia Law Review* 13, no. 4 (April 1913): 294–313.

Wayland, Francis. *The Elements of Political Economy*. New York: Leavitt, Lord & Company, 1837.

Wayland, Francis. *The Elements of Political Economy*. New York: Sheldon & Company, 1879.

Zollmann, Carl. *American Church Law*. St. Paul, MN: West Publishing, 1933.

DISSERTATIONS AND THESES

Abraham, Harry Gustav. "A Study of Pupil Accounting in City School Systems as Revealed by School Surveys." PhD diss., University of Chicago, 1929.

Connaughton, Edward A. "A History of Educational Legislation and Administration in the Archdiocese of Cincinnati." PhD diss., Catholic University of America, 1946.

Kephart, Calvin I. "State Control and Regulation of Private and Parochial Schools of Primary and Secondary Grades." PhD diss., American University, 1933.

McCaffrey, Augustine. "Youth in a Catholic Parish." PhD diss., Catholic University of America, 1941.

McNicholas, Martin L. "Child Accounting in Catholic Elementary Schools." PhD diss., Catholic University of America, 1931.

Neystrom, Paul Henry. "The School Census." Master's thesis, University of Wisconsin, 1910.

O'Brien, Robert Enslow. "A Study of the Roman Catholic Elementary Schools of Chicago." PhD diss., Northwestern University, 1928.

O'Dowd, Reverend James T. "Standardization and Its Influence on Catholic Secondary Education in the United States." PhD diss., Catholic University of America, 1935.

Perrin, John William. "The History of Compulsory Education in New England." PhD diss., University of Chicago, 1896.

Schnepp, Gerald J. "Leakage from a Catholic Parish." PhD diss., Catholic University of America, 1942.

Shea, Jeremiah P. "The Extent of State Control over Catholic Elementary and Secondary Education in Pennsylvania." Master's thesis, Catholic University of America, 1948.

Sylvester, Reverend David Anthony. "Why Catholic Children Are Not Attending Catholic Schools: A Study of the Reasons Offered by Their Parents." Master's thesis, Catholic University of America, 1947.

Voelker, Reverend John M. "The Diocesan Superintendent of Schools: A Study of the Historical Development and Functional Status of His Office." PhD diss., Catholic University of America, 1935.

Wozniak, Reverend B. L. "The Social and Religious Life of One Hundred Catholic Families." Master's thesis, Catholic University of America, 1938.

SECONDARY SOURCES

Anderson, James D. *The Education of Blacks in the South, 1860–1935*. Chapel Hill: University of North Carolina Press, 1988, 156.

Baker, David P. "Schooling All the Masses: Reconsidering the Origins of American Schooling in the Postbellum Era." *Sociology of Education* 72, no. 4 (October 1999): 197–215.

Balogh, Brian. *A Government Out of Sight: The Mystery of National Authority in Nineteenth-Century America*. New York: Cambridge University Press, 2009.

Beadie, Nancy. *Education and the Creation of Capital in the Early American Republic.* New York: Cambridge University Press, 2010.

Beadie, Nancy. "Market-Based Policies of School Funding: Lessons from the History of the New York Academy System." *Educational Policy* 13, no. 2 (May 1999): 296–317.

Beadie, Nancy. "Toward a History of Education Markets in the United States." *Social Science History* 32, no. 1 (2008): 47–73.

Beadie, Nancy. "Tuition Funding for Common Schools: Education Markets and Market Regulation in Rural New York, 1815–1850." *Social Science History* 32, no. 1 (2008): 107–33.

Bernstein, David E. *Rehabilitating Lochner: Defending Individual Rights Against Progressive Reform.* Chicago: University of Chicago Press, 2011.

Bickel, Alexander. *The Supreme Court and the Idea of Progress.* New York: Harper & Row, 1970.

Brock, William R. *Investigation and Responsibility: Public Responsibility in the United States.* Cambridge, UK: Cambridge University Press, 1985.

Buenker, John D. "The Politics of Resistance: The Rural-Based Yankee Republican Machines of Connecticut and Rhode Island." *New England Quarterly* 47, no. 2 (June 1, 1974): 212–37.

Buetow, Harold A. *Of Singular Benefit: The Story of Catholic Education in the United States.* New York: Macmillan, 1970.

Burns, James Aloysius. *The Growth and Development of the Catholic School System in the United States.* New York: Benziger Brothers, 1912.

Campbell, Ballard C. *Representative Democracy: Public Policy and Midwestern Legislatures in the Late Nineteenth Century.* Cambridge, MA: Harvard University Press, 1980.

Carl, Jim. *Freedom of Choice: Vouchers in American Education.* Santa Barbara, CA: Praeger, 2011.

Carpenter, Daniel. "Confidence Games: How Does Regulation Constitute Markets?" In *Government and Markets: Toward a New Theory of Regulation,* edited by Edward J. Balleisen and David A. Moss, 164–92. New York: Cambridge University Press, 2009.

Carper, James C., and Thomas C. Hunt. *The Dissenting Tradition in American Education.* New York: Peter Lang, 2007.

Carroll, Charles. *Public Education in Rhode Island.* Providence, RI: E. L. Freeman Company, 1918.

Casino, Joseph J. "From Sanctuary to Involvement: A History of the Catholic Parish in the Northeast." In *The American Catholic Parish: A History from 1850 to the Present, Volume I,* edited by Jay P. Dolan, 7–116. Mahwah, NJ: Paulist Press, 1987.

Cervone, Barbara Tucker. "Rounding up the Children: Compulsory Education Enforcement in Providence, Rhode Island, 1883–1935." PhD diss., Harvard Graduate School of Education, 1983.

Chudacoff, Howard P. *Mobile Americans: Residential and Social Mobility in Omaha, 1880–1920.* New York: Oxford University Press, 1972.

Cohen, David K., and Eleanor Farrar. "Power to the Parents?—The Story of Education Vouchers." *Public Interest* 48 (Summer 1977): 72–97.

Cohen, Lizabeth. *Making a New Deal: Industrial Workers in Chicago, 1919–1939.* New York: Cambridge University Press, 1990.

Cohen, Miriam. "Reconsidering Schools and the American Welfare State." *History of Education Quarterly* 45, no. 4 (Winter 2005): 512–37.

Cohen, Ronald D. *Children of the Mill: Schooling and Society in Gary, Indiana, 1906–1960.* New York: Routledge, 2002.

Conkin, Paul Keith. *Prophets of Prosperity: America's First Political Economists*. Bloomington: Indiana University Press, 1980.

Conley, Patrick T., and Matthew J. Smith. *Catholicism in Rhode Island: The Formative Era*. Providence, RI: Diocese of Providence, 1976.

Couvares, Francis G. *The Remaking of Pittsburgh: Class and Culture in an Industrializing City 1877–1919*. Albany: State University of New York Press, 1984.

Cutler, David, and Grant Miller. "Water, Water Everywhere: Municipal Finance and Water Supply in American Cities." In *Corruption and Reform: Lessons from America's Economic History*, edited by Edward L. Glaeser and Claudia Goldin, 153–86. Chicago: University of Chicago Press, 2006.

Davies, Gareth. *See Government Grow: Education Politics from Johnson to Reagan*. Lawrence: University of Kansas Press, 2007.

Diamond, Stephen. "Efficiency and Benevolence: Philanthropic Tax Exemptions in 19th-Century America." In *Property Tax Exemptions for Charities*, edited by Evelyn Brody, 115–44. Washington, DC: Urban Institute Press, 2002.

Dolan, Jay P. *The American Catholic Experience: A History from Colonial Times to the Present*. Garden City, NY: Doubleday & Company, 1985.

Dorfman, Joseph. *The Economic Mind in American Civilization, 1606–1865, Volume II*. New York: Viking Press, 1946.

Eisenberg, Martin Jay. "Compulsory Attendance Legislation in America, 1870 to 1915." PhD diss., University of Pennsylvania, 1988.

Errington, Sara. "'The Language Question': Nativism, Politics, and Ethnicity in Rhode Island." In *New England's Disharmony: The Consequences of the Industrial Revolution*, edited by Douglas M. Reynolds and Katheryn Viens, 92–111. Kingston: Rhode Island Labor History Society and Labor Research Center, 1993.

Everett, John Rutherford. *Religion in Economics: A Study of John Bates Clark, Richard T. Ely and Simon Patten*. New York: King Crown Press, 1946.

Fass, Paula. S. *Outside In: Minorities and the Transformation of American Education*. New York: Oxford University Press, 1991.

Fine, Sidney. *Laissez Faire and the General-Welfare State*. Ann Arbor: University of Michigan Press, 1969.

Fischel, William A. *Making the Grade: The Economic Evolution of American School Districts*. Chicago: University of Chicago Press, 2009.

Fishlow, Albert. "The American Common School Revival: Fact or Fancy?" In *Industrialization in Two Systems: Essays in Honor of Alexander Gerschenkron*, edited by Henry Rosovsky, 40–67. New York: John Wiley and Sons, 1966.

Fishlow, Albert. "Levels of Nineteenth-Century American Investment in Education." *Journal of Economic History* 26, no. 4 (December 1966): 418–36.

Forman, James Jr. "Secret History of School Choice: How Progressives Got There First." *Georgetown Law Journal* 93 (2004–5): 1287–320.

Freyer, Tony Allan. *Forums of Order: The Federal Courts and Business in American History*. Greenwich, CT: JAI Press, 1979.

Galenson, David W. "Ethnic Differences in Neighborhood Effects on the School Attendance of Boys in Early Chicago." *History of Education Quarterly* 38, no. 1 (1998): 17–35.

Galenson, David W. "Ethnicity, Neighborhood, and the School Attendance of Boys in Antebellum Boston." *Journal of Urban History* 24, no. 5 (July 1, 1998): 603–26.

Galenson, David W. "Neighborhood Effects on the School Attendance of Irish Immigrants' Sons in Boston and Chicago in 1860." *American Journal of Education* 105, no. 3 (1997): 261–93.

Galush, William. J. "What Should Janek Learn? Staffing and Curriculum in Polish-American Parochial Schools, 1870–1940." *History of Education Quarterly* 40, no. 4 (2000): 395–417.

Gamm, Gerald H. *Urban Exodus: Why the Jews Left Boston and the Catholics Stayed.* Cambridge, MA: Harvard University Press, 1999.

Gartner, David. "The Growth of a Catholic Educational System in Providence and the Protestant Reaction, 1848–1876." *Rhode Island History* 55 (1997): 133–45.

Gillman, Howard. *The Constitution Besieged: The Rise & Demise of Lochner Era Police Powers Jurisprudence.* Durham, NC: Duke University Press, 1992.

Gleason, Philip. "Baltimore III and Education." *Catholic Historian* 4, no. 3/4 (1985): 273–313.

Go, Sun, and Peter Lindert. "The Uneven Rise of American Public Schools to 1850." *Journal of Economic History* 70, no. 1 (2010): 1–26.

Goldin, Claudia Dale, and Lawrence F. Katz. *The Race Between Education and Technology.* Cambridge, MA: Harvard University Press, 2008.

Gordon, Robert W. "'The Ideal and the Actual in the Law': Fantasies and Practices of New York City Lawyers, 1870–1910." In *The New High Priests: Lawyers in Post-Civil War America*, edited by Gerald W. Gawalt, 52–74. Westport, CT: Greenwood Press, 1984.

Guglielmo, Mark, and Werner Troesken. "The Gilded Age." In *Government and the American Economy: A New History*, edited by Price Fishback and Douglass C. North, 255–77. Chicago: University of Chicago Press, 2007.

Gutowski, James A. "Politics and Parochial Schools in Archbishop John Purcell's Ohio." PhD diss., Cleveland State University, 2009.

Hayman, Robert W. *Catholicism in Rhode Island and the Diocese of Providence, 1780–1886.* Providence, RI: Diocese of Providence, 1982.

Henig, Jeffrey R. *Rethinking School Choice: Limits of the Market Metaphor.* Princeton, NJ: Princeton University Press, 1994.

Herbst, Jurgen. "Nineteenth-Century Schools Between Community and State: The Cases of Prussia and the United States." *History of Education Quarterly* 42, no. 3 (2002): 317–41.

Herbst, Jurgen. *School Choice and School Governance: A Historical Study of the United States and Germany.* New York: Palgrave Macmillan, 2006.

Higgens-Evenson, R. Rudy. *The Price of Progress: Public Services, Taxation, and the American Corporate State, 1877 to 1929.* Baltimore: Johns Hopkins University Press, 2002.

Horwitz, Morton J. *The Transformation of American Law, 1870–1960: The Crisis of Legal Orthodoxy.* New York: Oxford University Press, 1994.

Hovenkamp, Herbert. *Enterprise and American Law, 1836–1937.* Cambridge, MA: Harvard University Press, 1991.

Hovenkamp, Herbert. "Regulation History as Politics or Markets," review of *The Regulated Economy: A Historical Approach to Political Economy*, by Claudia Goldin and Gary D. Libecap. *Yale Journal on Regulation* 12 (Summer 1995): 549–63.

Hunt, Thomas C., and Timothy Walch. *Urban Catholic Education: Tales of Twelve American Cities.* Notre Dame, IN: Alliance for Catholic Education Press, 2010.

Hutchinson, Dennis J. "Unanimity and Desegregation: Decisionmaking in the Supreme Court, 1948–1958." *Georgetown Law Journal* 68 (1979–1980): 1–96.

Jacobson, C. *Ties That Bind: Economic and Political Dilemmas of Urban Utility Networks, 1800–1990*. Pittsburgh: University of Pittsburgh Press, 2000.

Jensen, Richard J. *The Winning of the Midwest: Social and Political Conflict, 1888–1896*. Chicago: University of Chicago Press, 1971.

Johanek, Michael, and John L. Puckett. *Leonard Covello and the Making of Benjamin Franklin High School: Education as If Citizenship Mattered*. Philadelphia: Temple University Press, 2007.

Jones, Alan. "Thomas M. Cooley and 'Laissez-Faire Constitutionalism': A Reconsideration." *Journal of American History* 53, no. 4 (March 1, 1967): 751–71.

Jorgenson, Lloyd P. *The State and the Non-public School, 1825–1925*. Columbia: University of Missouri Press, 1987.

Justice, Benjamin. "The Blaine Game: Are Public Schools Inherently Anti-Catholic?" *Teachers College Record* 109, no. 9 (September 2007): 2171–206.

Justice, Benjamin. "The Originalist Case Against Vouchers: The First Amendment, Religion, and American Public Education." *Stanford Law and Policy Review* 26, no. 2 (2015): 437–84.

Justice, Benjamin. *The War That Wasn't: Religious Conflict and Compromise in the Common Schools of New York State, 1865–1900*. Albany: State University of New York Press, 2009.

Kaestle, Carl F. "Common Schools Before the 'Common School Revival': New York Schooling in the 1790's." *History of Education Quarterly* 12, no. 4 (1972): 465–500.

Kaestle, Carl F. *Pillars of the Republic: Common Schools and American Society, 1780–1860*. New York: Hill & Wang, 1983.

Keller, Morton. *Affairs of State: Public Life in Late Nineteenth Century America*. Cambridge, MA: Belknap Press of Harvard University Press, 1977.

Keller, Morton. *Regulating a New Society: Public Policy and Social Change in America, 1900–1933*. Cambridge, MA: Harvard University Press, 1994.

Kersch, Ken I. *Constructing Civil Liberties: Discontinuities in the Development of American Constitutional Law*. New York: Cambridge University Press, 2004.

Killikelly, Sarah H. *The History of Pittsburgh: Its Rise and Progress*. Pittsburgh: B. C. & Gordon Montgomery, 1906.

Kleinberg, S. J. *The Shadow of the Mills: Working-Class Families in Pittsburgh, 1870–1907*. Pittsburgh: University of Pittsburgh Press, 1991.

Kleppner, Paul. *The Cross of Culture: A Social Analysis of Midwestern Politics, 1850–1900*. New York: Free Press, 1970.

Kristufek, Richard. "The Immigrant and the Pittsburgh Public Schools: 1870–1940." PhD diss., University of Pittsburgh, 1975.

Lannie, Vincent. *Public Money and Parochial Education Bishop Hughes, Governor Seward, and the New York School Controversy*. Cleveland, OH: Press of Case Western Reserve University, 1968.

Lassonde, Stephen. *Learning to Forget: Schooling and Family Life in New Haven's Working Class, 1870–1940*. New Haven, CT: Yale University Press, 2007.

Lazerson, M. "Understanding American Catholic Educational History." *History of Education Quarterly* 17, no. 3 (1977): 297–317.

Liebman, James S. "Voice, Not Choice." *Yale Law Journal* 101, no. 1 (October 1, 1991): 259–314.

McAfee, Ward. *Religion, Race, and Reconstruction: The Public School in the Politics of the 1870s*. Albany: State University of New York Press, 1998.

McAvoy, Thomas. T. "Public Schools Vs. Catholic Schools and James McMaster." *Review of Politics* 28, no. 1 (1966): 19–46.

McCraw, Thomas K. *Prophets of Regulation: Charles Francis Adams, Louis D. Brandeis, James M. Landis, Alfred E. Kahn*. Cambridge, MA: Belknap Press of Harvard University Press, 1984.

McCurdy, Charles W. "American Law and the Marketing Structure of the Large Corporation, 1875–1890." *Journal of Economic History* 38, no. 3 (September 1978): 631–49.

McGreevy, John T. *Catholicism and American Freedom: A History*. New York: W. W. Norton & Company, 2004.

McGreevy, John T. *Parish Boundaries: The Catholic Encounter with Race in the Twentieth-Century Urban North*. Chicago: University of Chicago Press, 1998.

McLaughlin, Sister Raymond. *A History of State Legislation Affecting Private Elementary and Secondary Schools in the United States: 1870–1945*. Washington, DC: Catholic University of America Press, 1946.

Merk, Lois Bannister. "Boston's Historic Public School Crisis." *New England Quarterly* 31, no. 2 (June 1958): 172–99.

Meyer, Peter. "Can Catholic Schools Be Saved." *Education Next* 7, no. 2 (Spring 2007): 13–20.

Miąso, Józef. *The History of the Education of Polish Immigrants in the United States*. New York: Kosciuszko Foundation, 1977.

Mirel, Jeffrey. E. *Patriotic Pluralism: Americanization Education and European Immigrants*. Cambridge, MA: Harvard University Press, 2010.

Nesbit, Robert C. *The History of Wisconsin, Volume III: Urbanization and Industrialization, 1873–1893*. Madison: State Historical Society of Wisconsin, 1985.

Novak, William J. "Law and the Social Control of American Capitalism." *Emory Law Journal* 60, no. 2 (2010): 377–405.

Novak, William J. "The Myth of the 'Weak' American State." *American Historical Review* 113, no. 3 (2008): 752–72.

Novak, William J. *The People's Welfare: Law and Regulation in Nineteenth-Century America*. Chapel Hill: University of North Carolina Press, 1996.

O'Donnell, Margaret G. *The Educational Thought of the Classical Political Economists*. Boston: University Press of America, 1985.

Opal, J. M. "Exciting Emulation: Academies and the Transformation of the Rural North, 1780s–1820s." *Journal of American History* 91, no. 2 (2004): 445–70.

Paul, Arnold M. *Conservative Crisis and the Rule of Law Attitudes of Bar and Bench, 1887–1895*. Ithaca, NY: Cornell University Press, 1960.

Perlmann, J. *Ethnic Differences: Schooling and Social Structure Among the Irish, Italians, Jews, and Blacks in an American City, 1880–1935*. New York: Cambridge University Press, 1989.

Pies, Timothy Mark. "The Parochial School Campaigns in Michigan, 1920–1924: The Lutheran and Catholic Involvement." *Catholic Historical Review* 72, no. 2 (April 1, 1986): 222–38.

Poluse, Martin. "Archbishop Joseph Schremb's Battle to Obtain Public Assistance for the Parochial Schools of Cleveland during the Great Depression." *Catholic Historical Review* 83, no. 3 (1997): 428–51.

Praszalowicz, Dorota. "The Cultural Changes of Polish-American Parochial Schools in Milwaukee, 1866–1988." *Journal of American Ethnic History* 13, no. 4 (1994): 23–45.

Prindle, David F. *The Paradox of Democratic Capitalism: Politics and Economics in American Thought*. Baltimore: Johns Hopkins University Press, 2006.

Provasnik, Stephen. "Compulsory Schooling, from Idea to Institution: A Case Study of the Development of Compulsory Attendance in Illinois, 1857–1907." PhD diss., University of Chicago, 1999.

Provasnik, Stephen. "Judicial Activism and the Origins of Parental Choice: The Court's Role in the Institutionalization of Compulsory Education in the United States, 1891–1925." *History of Education Quarterly* 46, no. 3 (2006): 311–47.

Radford, Gail. *The Rise of the Public Authority: Statebuilding and Economic Development in Twentieth-Century America*. Chicago: University of Chicago Press, 2013.

Rafferty, Edward C. *Apostle of Human Progress: Lester Frank Ward and American Political Thought, 1841–1913*. Lanham, MD: Rowman & Littlefield, 2003.

Ravitch, Diane. *The Troubled Crusade: American Education, 1945–1980*. New York: Basic Books, 1983.

Reese, William J. *America's Public Schools: From the Common School to "No Child Left Behind."* Baltimore: Johns Hopkins University Press, 2005.

Reese, William J. "Changing Conceptions of 'Public' and 'Private' in American Educational History." In *History, Education, and the Schools*, edited by William J. Reese, 95–112. New York: Palgrave Macmillan, 2007.

Reese, William J. *The Origins of the American High School*. New Haven, CT: Yale University Press, 1999.

Reese, William J. *Power and the Promise of School Reform: Grassroots Movements during the Progressive Era*. New York: Teachers College Press, Columbia University, 2002. First published in 1986 by Routledge & Kegan Paul.

Rodgers, Daniel T. *Atlantic Crossings: Social Politics in a Progressive Age*. Cambridge, MA: Belknap Press of Harvard University Press, 1998.

Ross, Dorothy. *The Origins of American Social Science*. New York: Cambridge University Press, 1991.

Ross, William G. *Forging New Freedoms: Nativism, Education, and the Constitution, 1917–1927*. Lincoln: University of Nebraska Press, 1994.

Ryan, Ann Marie. "Negotiating Assimilation: Chicago Catholic High Schools' Pursuit of Accreditation in the Early Twentieth Century." *History of Education Quarterly* 46, no. 3 (2006): 348–81.

Sanders, James. W. *The Education of an Urban Minority: Catholics in Chicago, 1833–1965*. New York: Oxford University Press, 1977.

Scheiber, Harry N. "Private Rights and Public Power: American Law, Capitalism, and the Republican Polity in Nineteenth-Century America." *Yale Law Journal* 107, no. 3 (December 1, 1997): 823–61.

Scheiber, Harry N. "State Law and 'Industrial Policy' in American Development, 1790–1987." *California Law Review* 75, no. 1 (January 1987): 415–44.

Schumacher, Carolyn Sutcher. "School Attendance in Nineteenth Century Pittsburgh: Wealth, Ethnicity and Occupational Mobility of School Age Children, 1855–1865." PhD diss., University of Pittsburgh, 1977.

Slawson, Douglas. J. *The Department of Education Battle, 1918–1932: Public Schools, Catholic Schools, and the Social Order*. Notre Dame, IN: University of Notre Dame Press, 2005.

Smarick, Andy. "Can Catholic Schools Be Saved." *National Affairs* (Spring 2011): 113–30.

Stach, John Frederick. *A History of the Lutheran Schools of the Missouri Synod in Michigan: 1845–1940*. Ann Arbor, MI: Edwards Brothers, 1943.

Steffes, Tracy L. *School, Society, and State: A New Education to Govern Modern America, 1890–1940*. Chicago: University of Chicago Press, 2012.

Sterne, Evelyn Savidge. *Ballots and Bibles: Ethnic Politics and the Catholic Church in Providence*. Ithaca, NY: Cornell University Press, 2003.

Swaine, Robert T. *The Cravath Firm and its Predecessors, 1819–1947*. New York: Cravath, 1946.

Tarr, Joel. "Infrastructure and City-Building in the Nineteenth and Twentieth Century." In *City at the Point: Essays on the Social History of Pittsburgh*, edited by Samuel P. Hays, 213–64. Pittsburgh: University of Pittsburgh Press, 1991.

Tarr, Joel. "Transportation Innovation and Changing Spatial Patterns in Pittsburgh, 1850–1934." *Essays in Public Work History* Essay Number 6 (April 1978).

Teaford, Jon C. *The Unheralded Triumph, City Government in America, 1870–1900*. Baltimore: Johns Hopkins University Press, 1984.

Tentler, Leslie Woodcock. *Seasons of Grace: A History of the Catholic Archdiocese of Detroit*. Detroit, MI: Wayne State University Press, 1995.

Twiss, Benjamin. *Lawyers and the Constitution: How Laissez Faire Came to the Supreme Court*. Princeton, NJ: Princeton University Press, 1942.

Tyack, David B. *The One Best System: A History of American Urban Education*. Cambridge, MA: Harvard University Press, 1974.

Tyack, David B. "Onward Christian Soldiers: Religion in the Common School." In *History and Education: The Educational Uses of the Past*, edited by Paul Nash, 215–55. New York: Random House, 1970.

Tyack, David B. "The Perils of Pluralism: The Background of the Pierce Case." *American Historical Review* 74, no. 1 (October 1, 1968): 74–98.

Tyack, David B. "Ways of Seeing: An Essay on the History of Compulsory Schooling." *Harvard Educational Review* 46, no. 3 (1976): 355–89.

Tyack, David, and Michael Berkowitz. "The Man Nobody Liked: Toward a Social History of the Truant Officer, 1840–1940." *American Quarterly* 29, no. 1 (April 1, 1977): 31–54.

Tyack, David, Thomas James, and Aaron Benavot. *Law and the Shaping of Public Education, 1785–1954*. Madison: University of Wisconsin Press, 1991.

Vance, Randall E. *Private Schools and Public Power: A Case for Pluralism*. New York: Teachers College Press, 1994.

Veverka, Fayette Breaux. *For God and Country: Catholic Schooling in the 1920s*. New York: Garland Publishing, 1988.

Vinyard, McNergney JoEllen. *For Faith and Fortune: The Education of Catholic Immigrants in Detroit, 1805–1925*. Urbana and Chicago: University of Illinois Press, 1998.

Viteritti, Joseph. P. "Blaine's Wake: School Choice, the First Amendment, and State Constitutional Law." *Harvard Journal of Law & Public Policy* 21 (1997): 657–718.

Walch, Timothy. *Parish School: American Catholic Parochial Education from Colonial Times to the Present*. New York: Crossroad Publishing Company, 1996.

West, E. G. "The Political Economy of American Public School Legislation." *Journal of Law and Economics* 10 (October 1, 1967): 101–28.

West, E. G. "Private Versus Public Education: A Classical Economic Dispute." *Journal of Political Economy* 72, no. 5 (October 1, 1964): 465–75.

White, Richard. *Railroaded: The Transcontinentals and the Making of Modern America*. New York: W. W. Norton & Company, 2011.

Wiebe, Robert. *The Search for Order: 1877–1920*. New York: Hill and Wang, 1967.

Wiecek, William M. *The Lost World of Classical Legal Thought: Law and Ideology in America, 1886–1937*. New York: Oxford University Press, 1998.

Woodhouse, Barbara B. "'Who Owns the Child?': *Meyer* and *Pierce* and the Child as Property." *William and Mary Law Review Quarterly* 995 (1992): 995–1122.

Yearley, Clifton K. *The Money Machines: The Breakdown and Reform of Governmental and Party Finance in the North, 1860–1920*. Albany: State University of New York Press, 1970.

Zimmerman, Jonathan. "Ethnics Against Ethnicity: European Immigrants and Foreign-Language Instruction, 1890–1940." *Journal of American History* 88, no. 4 (2002): 1383–404.

INDEX

Abbott, Edith, 36, 91

abolition: of parochial schools, 52, 110–11; of private education, 105–8; Protestant groups and, 5; regulation and, 110–11, 117, 118, 125. See also *Pierce v. Society of Sisters* (1925)

academies: African Americans and, 11; competition with, 10; denominational, 17; government aid to, 11; post-Revolutionary War era, 10, 14; private source funding, 17; segregation academies, 132–3

access to education market, 11

accountability, 126, 136

accreditation: Catholic compliance with, 102–3; Catholic parochial schools, 84, 85, 100, 166n119, 167n125; policies of, 103; standards, 99–100

Adams, Henry Carter, 19, 20, 21, 142n47

administrative professionals: anti-Catholicism and, 81; Catholic school administrators, 4, 83, 96–7, 98, 100, 101–2; Progressive Era, 87; state education administrators, 6; urban school administrators, 82, 103; urban school reformers and, 86

administrative structures: bureaucratic attendance mechanisms, 96–7; Catholic school administrators, 96–7;

decentralization, 29; Jefferson's tiered system, 14; Progressive Era, 129; public school alternatives and, 8

African Americans: assimilationism and, 65; Catholic communities of, 44; double taxation of, 44; educational access for, 11, 43–4; excluded from public schools, 150n14; Fourteenth Amendment and, 113; Manumission Society schools, 17

American Catholicism: Americanization efforts, 7; Catholic revival effects, 34; church law, 7; diversity of, 35; Hispano-Catholicism, 43; Poughkeepsie Plan, 43; state education and, 34; Third Plenary Council of Baltimore (1884), 34, 39

American Economic Association (AEA), 19, 20. See also economists

Americanization: Catholic church and, 67; of foreign-born, 67; post-WWI, 105, 110

American Philosophical Society, 14

American regulatory state: incomplete histories of, 7; public officials/private education alliance and, 6, 126; rise of, 85; urban school reform and, 86. See also regulations

Ames, Oliver, 73–4

ROBERT N. GROSS is a history
teacher and the Assistant Academic Dean
at Sidwell Friends School in Washington,
DC. He holds a PhD from the University of
Wisconsin-Madison and writes about
the social and educational history of the
United States.